Love you to bits and pieces

To my children, Sue and Scott, for their wisdom,

guidance and love

contents

Love you to bits and pieces

LIFE WITH DAVID HELFGOTT

GILLIAN HELFGOTT

WITH ALISSA TANSKAYA

PENGUIN BOOKS

Permission to reproduce extracts from Perth's *Sunday Times* is
gratefully acknowledged.

Some names in the text have been changed to protect the identity
of individuals.

Penguin Books Australia Ltd
487 Maroondah Highway, PO Box 257
Ringwood, Victoria 3134, Australia
Penguin Books Ltd
Harmondsworth, Middlesex, England
Viking Penguin, A Division of Penguin Books USA Inc.
375 Hudson Street, New York, New York 10014, USA
Penguin Books Canada Limited
10 Alcorn Avenue, Toronto, Ontario, Canada M4V 3B2
Penguin Books (N.Z.) Ltd
Cnr Rosedale and Airborne Roads, Albany, Auckland, New Zealand

First published by Penguin Books Australia Ltd 1996

10 9 8 7 6 5 4 3 2 1

Typeset in Garamond by Midland Typesetters, Maryborough, Victoria
Printed in Australia by Australian Print Group, Maryborough, Victoria

National Library of Australia
Cataloguing-in-Publication data

Helfgott, Gillian.
    Love you to bits and pieces: life with David Helfgott.

    Includes index.
    ISBN 0 14 026546 5.

    1. Helfgott, David, 1947– . 2. Pianists – Australia – Biography.
    I. Tanskaya, Alissa. II. Title. III. Title: Shine (Motion picture).

786.2092

part 1

The Dommage

"Oh David, where on earth did I find you?"

"In a Weeties box, Gillian darling, in a Weeties box."

A Proposition

"I am about to introduce you to the most unforgettable person", announced Dr Chris Reynolds as he carried my bags into his house.

I had just arrived in Perth on business and was feeling slightly frazzled from the long plane journey and the scorching November heat. As I entered the living room and my eyes adjusted to the light, I was suddenly faced with an extraordinary creature. Having just emerged from the pool, and dripping wet, he gently took my hand and would not let go. Bouncing up and down and smiling, occasionally pressing his wet face to mine, he launched into a verbal hurricane: "Hello Gillian darling.

Great to meet you, Gillian darling. Chris told me you were coming, didn't he, and well now you're here. Isn't that wonderful? Ha-ha! Hoo-hoo! Are you coming to Riccardo's tonight, Gillian darling? Come to hear me play, to Riccardo's. You will come tonight, won't you . . . to Riccardo's, Gillian darling?"

These words and phrases were frantically repeated as I found myself whisked into the lounge room towards the Yamaha grand, embraced, kissed all over my face, and somewhere, in the haze of chatter, I heard Chris say, "Gillian, I'd like you to meet David Helfgott."

I was completely disorientated, which was unusual for me. The man was a flurry of agitated babbling and bouncing, head bent forward, arms aimlessly dangling in front, now gently stroking my arm, now patting the Yamaha. His partially closed eyes peered up at me now and then through thick glasses reminiscent of the bottom of Coke bottles. David's body was tanned, but his face did not reflect the same healthy glow. The cigarette clenched between his teeth was only removed for kissing.

Another cuddle, more funny, open-mouthed pecks on my forehead, my cheek, my ear: "Gillian darling, you came especially for me, all the way from Sydney, just for me. Imagine that! All that way! Just to hear me play, today, stay, anyway, anyhow. How amazing! Amazing grace, graceful, grateful, gotta be grateful. Well, that's nice, that's nice, darling. So you will come to Riccardo's tonight, Gillian darling? You will come?" The monologue continued, interrupted only by little gasps for air.

As I tried to decipher some meaning out of the continuous stream of words, I found myself mysteriously drawn to this

eccentric, exhausting, but extremely friendly man. It was as if
Peter Pan had come and was enticing me to a magical world.

A little while later, Chris had to return to his surgery, and
on the way there dropped David off at the house where he was
boarding. Left alone in Chris's house, I was able to draw breath
and endeavoured to reorientate myself, "Gillian darling, come
to Riccardo's" still echoing in my head. How could I refuse?

That evening, as I prepared to go out, I felt a great sense
of anticipation and excitement. I dressed with care, thinking that
David might respond to something very feminine. So, gold and
white lace it was. But why was I seeking a response from him?
What had this strange person done to me?

Still in this rather disconnected state, I drove with Chris to
pick up David. On the way, Chris told me that in the '60s David
was a famous child prodigy and that the Perth musical community had held great hopes for his future. But David had suffered a nervous breakdown and been away from the professional
concert platform for more than a decade, living in virtual obscu-
rity. Like everyone else who knew of David in the '60s, Chris
hadn't given him much thought as he knew that David had gone
to study in London and simply assumed he was still overseas.
That is, until David's brother phoned one day to see if there was
any work at Riccardo's, a wine bar Chris part-owned.

A few weeks later, by chance, the regular classical pianist
at Riccardo's became unavailable. After ringing a few other pianists, who declined to play in a wine bar, Chris tried David's
number. David's immediate response was, "Yes Chris, would love
to play, would love to play." When Chris started to discuss
money, David interrupted: "I will play for nothing, for nothing."

After some convincing from Chris, David agreed to a fee.

That night, Chris watched in horror as a nervous, chain-smoking apparition snuck his way through the bar-crowd to the piano, pulled out tattered and stained copies of Christmas carols and sing-along charts, and with his two index fingers prodded a few keys. But just as the crowd began to get out of control, and a mortified Chris was making his way towards the piano to rectify the situation, a technically perfect volley of notes resounded through the room, as David attacked the keyboard with *The Flight of the Bumble Bee*. The awe-struck crowd was hushed, and David had been a regular Riccardo's act ever since.

As we pulled up at his lodgings, David appeared with a briefcase tucked under his arm, still-tattered music fighting for space in it. His trousers looked sadly neglected and a little too short, but he was wearing a clean white shirt and a black bow tie. His curly blond hair, thinning on top, was slicked back with water and the inevitable cigarette was gripped in his teeth. He was raring to go.

Riccardo's was by no means situated in a trendy part of town. Above the wine bar was a backpackers' hostel, and the bar itself had a '50s look with dark walls, chrome chairs and no windows, but lots of indoor plants. As we entered, one could feel the audience's anticipation, 'Hello's, 'Hi's, 'How are you?'s all bringing a grin to David's face. Patrons from all walks of life and of all ages were lining the bar, the walls, all seats taken, awaiting the 'genius'. Many had been attending two or three times a week – almost a fan club. There was a glow on David's face, as if to say, "This is all too good to be true."

The focus of the room was the piano, elevated on a small

stage, and, like a child running to his mother, David immediately rushed to it. His love of the instrument, even before he played it, was apparent. When he sat down – a cigarette dangling from his mouth – a cup of coffee was immediately handed to him and he swallowed it in one huge gulp. Most of the audience was now settling down, the regulars waiting, the newcomers curious.

David's fingers gently touched the keys and from the first sounds I could sense the crowd being drawn towards him. A change had come over David. The gangling, maniacally noisy creature, seemingly so insecure, became another person, completely absorbed and confident in his craft. There was a wicked, all-knowing little grin on his face, and a joy emanated from him as he played many of the great classical works: the Chopin *Ballade* in G minor, Liszt's *Hungarian Rhapsody* No. 2, Beethoven's *Appassionata* Sonata.

Throughout the performance, women sitting on the edge of the stage were lighting new cigarettes and putting them in David's mouth. Cups of coffee appeared and the contents were soon demolished, yet the music continued without pause. The fans and bar-patrons clutching their glasses, the music lovers and those experiencing live classical music for the first time all seemed enthralled by the spell he cast.

David's energy seemed to be inexhaustible. When a break was suggested, he said, "Golly, can't I keep playing?", and just carried on.

Finally, when David did take a minute's rest, I asked him what his favourite work was. "Rak 3, Serge's Rak 3", he replied. He then went straight back to the piano and proceeded to play the whole of Sergei Rakhmaninov's Piano Concerto No. 3, filling in the *tutti* for the orchestra. This monumental work, considered by many concert pianists as the most difficult of all piano concertos, seemed to pour out from his soul. He was surrendering to the music. The keys appeared to be an extension of his self, as the man, the music and the piano became one.

I was spellbound. My tears were unconfinable. I had attended many recitals by great musicians, but this had a majesty and passion which I found unique.

At the end of the performance, Chris came up to David and told him he'd never heard him play like that during the three months he had been at Riccardo's. Pleased, David turned to me and smiled. Eagerly but firmly he replied, "It is because of Gillian."

After we dropped David back at his boarding house, Chris noticed the incredible impact David had made on me. Chris told me that, at the time he started playing at Riccardo's, David was living at a church-run institution called Guildercliffe Lodge. Part-hospital, part-halfway house, the Lodge was nothing like a 'home away from home', and communication with other inmates was almost impossible.

Having given David a job, Chris decided that David could cope with taking another step towards living in a 'normal' society, so he arranged for David to live in the boarding house, where he was allowed to play the piano at any time of the day or night. Chris hoped that by doing all this David would finally break the pattern of psychiatric institutions which had had such a traumatic effect on him for the past twelve years.

The next morning, David came around to Chris's home

to use the swimming pool. He was his usual hyperactive, babbling but irresistible self. As he stood by the pool, mumbling to himself, I observed his figure. He was stooping terribly, shoulders hunched over, arms dangling low, chin down on his chest. He was almost trying to hide his head, a posture indicating deep insecurity, nervous tension and complete lack of self-esteem. I was longing to see him straighten up, pull his shoulders back and stand tall. But what could I do about it?

David threw away his cigarette butt and dived in. As I watched him swim, I could sense his love of water. In the even way he stroked up and down the pool, one could detect a gentle rhythm taking control of him and see his agitation dissolve. He swam for a considerable time, keeping the same rhythm. It was beautiful to watch. However, when he came out of the water, he immediately attempted to shrivel up, head bowed, arms dangling. David was again clothed in the garment of his insecurities.

We stood by the pool and chatted about music and history in the now-familiar fragmented way. David was a flurry of restless movements and gestures. But suddenly his demeanour changed and a stillness came over him. He put his arms around me, and in a calm, quiet voice asked, "Gillian, will you marry me?"

My surprise was followed by joy, followed by an irresistible urge to say, "YES." But common sense decreed otherwise. I told him we had just met, but that I would love to be his friend. From that moment, a special connection was established between us which would never be broken.

Dreamlike days passed. With David's help, my usual concentration and efficiency went 'walkabout', and I was all off-balance. The feeling was new to me and it was rather disconcerting. I had to force myself to concentrate on my reason for being in Perth. I had come to convene a meeting to form a branch of the Astrologers' Federation, and it was successfully launched, but the rest of the time had a Helfgott glaze over it.

Soon it was time to return to Sydney, time to farewell David. I mentioned to Chris that I intended to keep in touch with David. "That's good", Chris replied, "because David needs all the friendship he can get." Thus, our regular correspondence began. Sometimes I would also phone David, and he would be so terribly excited that I couldn't help but feel quite thrilled myself.

David wrote in the same way as he spoke and played: prolifically, passionately and rapturously. His letters always began in a similar manner: "I received your letter, sweetheart, thanks a million, Darling!!!", or "Thanks for your letter, sweetheart, it cheered me up a lot. You are an angel, darling!!"

David would then express deep gratitude: "Thanks for ringing up, darling Gillian, it gave me a thrill ... Thanks for looking after me ... Thanks for the Chaik tape, darling Gillian – I listened to it yesterday, it inspired me, darling Gillian, you inspire me too, sweetheart! ... Also, Gillian darling, thanks for the Shakespeare sonnets. I read them this morning, they are inspiring. I love you darling."

In almost every letter, David would remind me of our meeting: "I remember hugging and kissing you by the swimming pool, Gillian sweetheart! Do you remember, darling? You made me very happy and relaxed, sweetheart. I couldn't have played well, if you hadn't been there, Gillian darling! and now when I play, I think of you, and I play better."

David would also often add: "Chris has been an angel too, darling. I'm very lucky to have found him and even luckier to have found you! ... <u>Gillian Darling</u> ... I hope to see you soon, Gillian Darling – and we'll have lots of Hugs and kisses etc!! Hurray!!"

My letters to David were warm and loving, but cautious. David's was a kind of wild and boundless love that I had never experienced before. But how could I contemplate a relationship with a man Chris had described as "an acute psychotic", who was fifteen years younger than me, with no financial resources and a huge question mark looming over any future career possibilities? And, while he was Jewish, I was a gentile. Not exactly the perfect match! And yet, he continued to haunt me.

Discoveries

By 1983, the year I met David, I felt as if I had already led a rich and eventful life. I was married at sixteen and spent the next twenty-two years as a working mother and wife. When my children finished school, I decided I needed a long holiday and set off alone around the world, visiting such countries as India, France and Portugal, as well as achieving my long-held dream of going to Russia. I delighted in my new-found sense of self-reliance, and a year later divorced my husband.

At the age of thirty-eight, I suddenly found the need to catch up on all those things I'd missed out on as a teenager. Ironically, this did not last long, as I formed a relationship with an older man and spent the next decade leading a pleasant life in the peaceful atmosphere of Noosa Heads on the Queensland coast.

It was during this time that I discovered an interest in consultative astrology. Fascinated by the scientific aspects of this ancient discipline, especially those advanced by Reinhold Ebertin, I set about gaining my diploma. I achieved this after three years' study under the caring guidance of Doris Greaves, whom many people consider to be the 'mother of astrology' in Australia. I then branched out into teaching others. I enjoyed sharing my knowledge with students and found it stimulating to have them challenge it.

As my relationship in Noosa came to an end, I began to realise that, for the first time in my life, I had complete independence. I had no financial burdens, house payments or other commitments to worry about. My children were now adults with developing careers and living in different states. After thirty-three years of family life, there were no more houses to clean, meals to prepare or others' needs to meet, and I could now truly appreciate my freedom.

I moved to Sydney and astrology became a full-time occupation. Life was busy and satisfying as I travelled overseas and around Australia for conferences and workshops. I lectured on the P&O cruise ships in the Pacific, and had a totally carefree and fun-filled time sailing from island to island, and meeting interesting people.

It was on one of these cruises that I became acquainted with Chris Reynolds, who was travelling with a friend. Chris was a general practitioner with an interest in psychology. We would often chat after dinner about his life in Perth, his two sons and his medical practice. A Gemini, with wide interests and the capacity to do many things at once, Chris told me then about his partnership in Riccardo's. At the conclusion of the cruise, he said, "If you ever come to Perth, you are welcome to stay with me." Little did I realise what a catalyst this meeting would prove to be . . . but a catalyst to what? David had asked me to marry him, and I was unable to stop thinking about him. But what was I getting myself into?

When I returned to Sydney, Eleanor, a friend with strong psychic abilities, phoned and asked to come for an astrological consultation. After we finished, she offered to do a reading for me. She knew nothing of my contact with David, but described "an extraordinary man with a childlike character, and very special hands".

"You know", she said, "I feel that this man has a gentleness about him. But there is something else: he has great needs . . . It is his hands, his hands!", she exclaimed. "He works with his hands and has this special ability." Finally, she said that I would marry him.

I have had many psychic readings before and always kept an open mind about the predictions, but, considering the recent events, her comment made me sit up with a jolt.

Some weeks later, I was reading in the lounge, hardly paying attention to the television on in the background. Suddenly I heard a familiar voice and had to look up. There was David being profiled on the 'Nationwide' program. Emotion overwhelmed me as I watched the man who had filled much of my thoughts since my visit to Perth. His warmth and charm, and his odd little ways, seemed to leap out of the television and embrace me. I knew then that I was deeply in love with him. I sat there rather stupefied and wondered what on earth to do. It was glorious but strange to feel this incredible bond with another person, and a love that seemed bigger than self.

I rang my daughter, Sue, and told her of my feelings. "But Gills, I knew you were in love with him when you came back from Perth in December. I am glad you now realise it", she said. When she asked me why I loved him, I spoke of David's guilelessness and trust, of his warmth, kindness and humour. The music was an added bonus.

I also rang my son, Scott, whose reaction was simple: "If you love him, go for it!" When I got off the phone, I was overcome with gratitude for my children's ready acceptance of my feelings for a person some considered to be 'psychotic', and obviously an enormous handful.

But circumstances began to change in Perth. With each phone call, David seemed to be increasingly sad and lonely, unhappy even with his playing. He kept asking me, "Couldn't you come and see me, Gillian darling? Could I come and see you? When can I see you? When can we be together?"

David's disjointed handwriting also reflected a far greater agitation. He wrote: "How was the voyage, sweetheart? Isn't that lovely going off on another cruise to do your lecturing! It must be a wonderful life! I hope I can come with you on a voyage soon; that would be grand too!! . . . I wish I could hug and kiss you again, Darling – in the very near future I hope!!"

A month earlier, Chris had become dissatisfied with David's lodgings and taken him to live at his own home. David had been comfortable at the boarding house, however, and had enjoyed the company of the other boarders. I was concerned by his change of residence, as I had seen what a handful David could be. Each day, he would make himself fifteen to twenty cups of coffee, with five sugars in each, spilling the coffee and the sugar all over the floor. He took innumerable showers, leaving up to ten wet towels lying around the house, smoked 125 cigarettes a day, was extremely untidy with his clothes, books and sheet music, and his constant talking made peace and quiet virtually unattainable.

One of David's greatest vulnerabilities was that he agreed with everyone, and, when Chris told him he was moving, David did not object, even though he knew he would prove to be a trial to live with. At the end of January, David wrote to me, "I am moving in with Chris this weekend – so that's really lovely!! – if Chris can put up with me somehow – I'm a bit difficult!!"

A particularly unfortunate aspect of David's condition was that, even though he understood his behaviour could be intolerable, he was unable to control himself. But he did feel enormously grateful to Chris and was determined to do his best: "I won't let you and Chris down, darling Gillian! I have very good food, a very good room; a very good piano – so no worries."

But "worries" there were aplenty when Chris soon discovered the reality of living with David, who raided the fridge, drank all the coffee, used up all the hot water, littered music books and possessions around the house, and even managed to burn a hole in the piano stool. Chris was under enormous stress, often at the end of his tether and losing his patience with David.

Coping with a medical practice, running Riccardo's and looking after David was an impossible ask.

David was acutely aware of all this, but was meanwhile experiencing a difficulty of his own. Being left completely alone during the day while Chris went to work was a big change for David after years of institutional and communal living. He was missing the companionship of other boarders, and he was missing me.

The phone rang at 11 pm one night. It was Eleanor, my psychic friend, and I wondered what could be so urgent that she should ring so late. She said she'd just had an 'awareness' that David was experiencing "a great anguish". "Oh, Gillian," she said, "I fear that he is greatly distressed and I am not sure how to put it any other way, but I feel he is regressing." Eleanor also told me that she had had a vision of David curling up into a foetal position. "I know it's not my place to say so, but I feel you should go to him at once." As David had been sounding progressively worse on the phone during the week, it was easy to understand Eleanor's concern.

I rang Sue to tell her of David's difficulties and that I was planning to go to Perth. She offered me whatever support I needed. But unsure of Chris's reaction, and anxious, I drew a tarot card. It was the painfully sad Ten of Swords, depicting a male figure lying face down on the ground with ten swords in his back and the fingers of one hand in the form of a blessing. I interpreted this as indicating that Chris may not agree with my intentions immediately.

When I rang Chris, I could tell he was very stressed. I offered to come over, but he said that there did not seem to be much point in my coming as he was thinking of returning David to an institution. I did not press the matter; the image of the tarot card was with me. I knew Chris wanted to do what was best for David, but, after thinking it over, I realised that my feelings for David were such that I would never let him be institutionalised again.

I could not get David's agony out of my mind and two days later I drew another card. This time it was the Chariot, a far more positive card. Now I felt sure I would get a different response from Chris, and I did. I told him I would come over for ten days, during which time he could go and have a break. He agreed. The next day, having organised my flight, I rang David, who sounded totally despondent. I told him I would be there in three days' time. "I hope I can last till you get here" was his reply.

As I flew to Perth, queries about how David was coping with his fears and pain were constantly in my thoughts. I wondered how we would react to seeing each other again. What would it be like to be face to face with this man who had touched me so deeply in the past few months, and whom I now loved?

When I arrived at Chris's, all my questions were answered by David's embrace. Chris went off on his break, and a testing time was now upon me.

Left together on our own for the first time, David's excitement was infectious, his delight in seeing me total. His health seemed to improve instantly. However, when it came time to go to bed, David started searching for his medication and was having great trouble finding it. "Hurry, hurry, Chris left in a hurry, a dash, a real dash, a rash decision", he kept repeating as he anxiously ran around the house. "He forgot my tablets, he forgot. It's a worry, a real worry, Gillian darling. Where are they? Where? Why? ... No tablets, no tablets, no sleep."

David had been on the anti-psychotic drug Serenace for many years, but at this time was only taking four Serepax a night. He was becoming increasingly panic-stricken at not having any tablets. After years of being on medication, his fear was justifiable. I went and sat on the bed with him and held him in my arms. We made love and eventually he went to sleep.

In the morning, when he awoke, David looked at me and said, "You sure beat Serepax!" It was my greatest compliment ever and David has never taken a sleeping tablet since.

Those ten days that David and I spent in Perth changed both our lives. We walked and swam together, relishing our union. However, having only seen David in public at Riccardo's, where he was recognised and appreciated for his talent, I was not prepared for the different picture that was soon presented to me.

One day, I suggested to David that we go on a ferry trip down the Swan River to Fremantle, and then come back by bus. He seemed somewhat hesitant, but agreed. It was a glorious sunny day, the view was wonderful and I had packed an afternoon tea for us.

We walked onto the ferry and found seats right at the back. David clung to me tightly. When the boat started to move and other people came to the back, I could feel David's discomfort. Surrounded by a group of strangers, without a piano for security, instead of showing his usual over-friendly enthusiasm, David began retreating. Here, there was no adulation, and his body language showed fear of rejection. He wrapped his arms around himself and huddled closer to me. He was chattering and bab-bling, and I could see people backing away from him. I got the impression they were all thinking, "Who the hell's that? What's wrong with him? Is he contagious? Is he dangerous?"

I held David tightly and my heart ached for him. He had so much to give the world, but, hampered by his nervous dis-ability, there was a wall of acceptance still to be climbed. Watch-ing him cowering under this overwhelming fear of rejection, of not belonging, I realised how much he must have been suffering. Riccardo's was helping with the healing, but there was still the world to be faced, where people who did not know of his extraordinary talent made no concessions.

After the ferry trip, I was more aware of David's great needs – his almost compulsive desire to be liked and accepted – and the barriers that were facing him. My feelings for him now gained an added dimension and strength. He desperately needed twenty-four-hour care and a constant source of affection.

We sat in the little sleep-out at the back of Chris's house and talked about our love. David really wanted to get married and again asked me. Though still unsure about marriage, I knew that, in my heart, I had made a commitment.

When Chris returned after his few days away and saw us walking down the street arm in arm, he said, partly joking, "Why don't you two get married?" We replied we just might do that, which rather floored Chris. But it did offer him a solution.

That afternoon, I had a quiet chat to Chris about my

relationship with David and our decision to be together. He was very frank about his perception of David's condition and said that, because of his fear of rejection and other insecurities, David always had to tell everyone they were the best. He wondered if David's attachment to me was sincere, and what I would be getting out of the relationship. Chris was caring but cautious, obviously not wanting either of us to do the wrong thing.

I greatly appreciated his honesty, but felt that David genuinely wanted to be with me, that our destinies were intertwined and that I was to be part of his life. Just how intimate that part would be, I was not sure. It did not seem to be the vital point at that stage whether I would be carer, lover, wife, friend, or a combination. I knew, however, that once I made a commitment to David there would be no turning back and there would be no trial runs with this relationship. As I was to discover later, many people went in and out of David's life, showing care but not being ready or able to make a complete commitment. Chris suggested that we not rush into marriage and offered for me to come and stay with David in his home. I agreed.

Many people have since questioned me as to how I could make this commitment to David when I had only spent about two weeks with him. If I had analysed the situation, I guess I would have run a mile, but I had a conviction and faith that it was right. And I was in love. I told David that I would return as soon as I could and went back to Sydney to rearrange my life.

Surprises

Impulsive? Foolhardy? Maybe. Sagittarians are considered to be the 'Pollyannas' of the zodiac. They often rely on their intuition and react spontaneously, bravely rushing into situations without giving much thought to the consequences. A common Sagittarian trait is their optimism; the glass is always half-full, never half-empty. They also end up doing things rather than talking about them.

Being a triple Sagittarian, it took me ten days to wrap up my life in Sydney. I cancelled my astrology classes, moved out of the beautiful house I was living in and said goodbye to all my friends.

On the plane to Perth, doubts briefly clouded my mind. What was I doing? Could I really fulfil David's needs? Was I really going to be able to cope with someone who had severely tested Chris's patience and that of many others who had attempted to care for him? But then I remembered some wise words I had once heard from a woman called Grace.

A minister of the Unity Church, Grace had survived a near-death experience, had conquered alcoholism and was helping others to overcome their addictions. She told me that the most futile words one could use when taking on a challenge were 'try', 'should' and 'impossible'. 'Try' meant doubting the success of your endeavours before you even began. 'Should' meant that you were possibly doing it out of a sense of guilt and not because you genuinely felt free to do it. And the word 'impossible' to Grace was synonymous with restricting the power of the divine and a refusal to believe in the miraculous. For years I had approached life with these thoughts in mind, and I decided that now, as the plane was about to land in Perth, was the wrong time to change.

David was overjoyed to see me, and it was so wonderful to be with him again that I did not mind my new abode. The small sleep-out at the back of Chris's house had a single bed, a wardrobe and a chair. The walls were bare and David had no personal effects, apart from an old and battered radio-cassette player. Neither did I mind the fact that, apart from Chris and David, I had few real friends in Perth. The whole thing was clearly going to be a major test of adaptability, but there was one definite bonus: David! Consequently, I was completely taken aback when the bonus announced the next day that he was going to spend the weekend with another woman.

"Going to Dotty-Scotty, to Dotty-Scotty, darling. It's all been planned, all been planned, all weekend, all weekend", said David, without a hint of regret in his tone. I felt terribly empty and lost. "Dotty-Scotty" was David's nickname for Dorothy, a woman some years older than him, who was separated from her husband and had several children. David had told me about her soon after I'd met him. "In a way," he said, "when everything was very little for me, in a sense that I wasn't getting much help from the world, I had Dotty-Scotty and so more or less she kept me alive. Dotty-Scotty fed me and fed me and said I played the piano very nicely."

Dorothy had met David during the darkest and most difficult time of his life. During a three-month period in 1976, when David was between institutions, a Christian couple, Fred and Evelyn Price, invited him to live in their home as a matter of charity. One day, when attending a church function with the Prices, David timidly walked over to the piano and started turning the pages for the pianist, who was Dorothy. Though surprised that this scruffy, stumbling figure could read music, she appreciated his help and inquired about his musical knowledge and his name. When he told her, she was shocked. Like most musicians in Perth, she knew of David, but not of his period of mental turmoil.

Dorothy was a music teacher and, being a committed Christian, she immediately wanted to help David. She invited him to visit her home and play the piano. This David did most weekends. However, David's health deteriorated once again and he moved from the Prices' to Graylands Mental Hospital.

Though Dorothy was convinced that David would be worse off in Graylands, she was unable to take on the responsibility of looking after him full-time because of commitments to her own family. So she arranged for him to go to Guildercliffe Lodge, which was only semi-institutional.

David continued to visit Dorothy on weekends. They shared their love of music, and went to many recitals and other outings. For a few years, she was the only true friend he had. At that time, David's playing was affected by the chaos in his mind, and tape recordings from that period reveal the depths of his despair. But with Dorothy's help over the next five years, his playing gradually improved.

Several months before I met David, however, he and Dorothy had begun to grow apart. David had been doing some small recitals with the local Karrinyup Orchestra, an activity in which Dorothy did not seem to take much interest. "I was really doing my own thing, wasn't I? I was sort of looking after myself in a way" is how David explained the waning of their friendship.

Before flying back to Sydney to pack up, I had rung Dorothy on Chris's advice to introduce myself. I let her know that I cared deeply for David and was coming back to Perth to be with him. She gave no hint that she perceived him to be her 'boyfriend'. On the contrary, she said that, as she was unable to make a commitment to David because of her family situation, she was glad I was coming over to take on that role. She did, however, say that Chris should never have taken David out of Guildercliffe Lodge, and that he was working David too hard at Riccardo's. She added that Chris was trying to separate her from

David and, consequently, she and David were no longer seeing much of each other.

Apparently, this was not going to be the case on the upcoming weekend. Chris confirmed that David had arranged the visit to Dorothy's some time ago, and now I had to deal with a mass of confused feelings and loneliness.

I realised that David did not fully understand that I had come to Perth to be with him forever, that I had left all my friends and my job, and was starting a new life. I knew that, caught up in his own foggy world of pain, and over-appreciative of any kindness shown towards him, David totally lacked the capacity to differentiate between those who were even vaguely pleasant to him and those who truly loved him. He wanted to please every human being he encountered, and was unable to say no to anything that was asked of him. I knew that these were some of the realities of living with David before I came, but could not believe how quickly I was being confronted with them.

I could have asked David to change his plans and not go, and he would have immediately agreed, but this would have placed him in the sort of dilemma which usually stressed his already fragile mind. Besides, I felt that it would not be morally right to tell him what to do in this situation. He had to work it out for himself.

For the next twenty-four hours, I struggled with my emotions and, during the night, I remembered some more wise advice from my friend Grace. She had spoken to me about the freedom of love and of not trying to possess the 'loved one'. She said that the love we feel for one another does not really belong to us, but is a part of the one great, whole, divine Love which embraces us all and knows no bounds. Everyone is capable of giving and receiving unlimited amounts of Love. But when we desire to appropriate and confine a little chunk of this great Love just for ourselves, we are restricting it from reaching its full potential.

I applied these ideas to the situation at hand and, by morning, was able to let my disappointment and hurt dissolve. I arrived at a state of mind in which I could genuinely wish David a happy weekend.

The phone rang during breakfast. It was Dorothy's daughter, who said to tell David not to come. It was a rather abrupt phone call, and a few weeks later, when David was again about to leave for another prearranged visit, he received another call, with the same message. According to her daughter, Dorothy was feeling unwell. I was somewhat disappointed at this, and feared that David might be losing a special friend because of his relationship with me – the last thing I wanted to happen. David really did need all the friends he could get.

But more surprises were in store when, on the fourth day after my arrival, David mumbled something about a concert recital. I double-checked with Chris and found out that David was indeed going to be giving a recital; not just any concert recital, but the 'comeback concert' of his career. It had been organised for 8 June 1984 at the Octagon Theatre of the University of Western Australia as part of a series called "Michael Parry's Classical Concerts". Mike, a musical entrepreneur, had approached Chris about this some weeks earlier, and Chris had agreed. When I realised that there were only seven weeks to go to the big day, I felt extremely concerned. The truth of the situation was that David was in no condition to carry off any such performance successfully.

The first time I saw David at Riccardo's, I was too overwhelmed to clearly assess all aspects of his performance. Now I had to be honest with myself, otherwise David was really going to hurt himself and jeopardise his chance to re-establish a career as a serious concert pianist.

Riccardo's provided David with the wonderful opportunity to perform to very responsive audiences for three nights a week under fairly casual conditions, and it was certainly building his confidence. Chris guarded David's classical reputation with much dedication and would not allow him to play the pop music requested from time to time.

One evening when a patron asked for Chaikovsky's *1812 Overture*, I explained that it was written for a large orchestra and cannons, and, even if we substituted banging the oven doors in the kitchen for the cannons, it would be a poor imitation. So the creed was: classical and written for piano only. Occasionally, David would slip into Beethoven's Fifth Symphony, but this was a Liszt transcription!

Overall, though, David's playing at Riccardo's had no dignity about it. He would play for hours, starting at about 8 pm and going on past midnight. He played continuously without breaking his performance into brackets.

I also had to admit there was the rather unusual picture of the chain-smoking artist himself. The ashtrays at either end of the piano were overflowing, butts lined the ledge above the keyboard and the upper part of David's body was shrouded in thick cigarette smoke. "It was a shield, smoke-shield, Brooke-shield, a screen, a smokescreen" was one of his recent explanations. The chain-smoking also resulted in less-than-perfect playing, because every now and then he would need to use one hand to remove the butt from his mouth so it would not burn his lips. Also, he would often need one of his hands to gulp down one of the endless mugs of coffee.

David would chew gum as well – a necessary "prop", according to him. And, to top it all off, he would natter nonstop to the nearby audience, explaining the technical merits of the passages as he played them, or else he would just sing the melody a bar or so ahead of his hands.

The combination of nicotine, caffeine and enormous amounts of sugar resulted in extreme hyperactivity and over-stimulation. The music became fragmented; some pieces would be curtailed midstream and others started. David's fans were delighted by the sight of this overcharged 'genius' and did not mind the eccentricities, but this was a suburban wine bar. How could any artist be taken seriously in a prestigious concert hall if he behaved like this?

I talked to David about my concerns and he agreed that something had to be done. He certainly did not want to appear undignified at the piano. In some ways, because we had the seven-week time frame, it was easier to obtain his co-operation.

Reducing the smoking at the piano was our primary goal. It was also the hardest. The only time David did not have a cigarette in his mouth or in his hand was when he was swim-ming. The moment he was out of the water, he had to have a cigarette. Chris told me the story of how one day, when David emerged from the pool and found he was out of cigarettes, he immediately phoned for a taxi. When it arrived, he hopped in, still wearing only his bathers, but holding onto his briefcase. He instructed the driver to take him to the shopping centre, only about one kilometre away, and to wait while he went into the tobacconist. David then got back into the cab and, feeling more protected from the world behind his "smokescreen", asked to be driven home.

Nonstop swimming seemed to be the key here, but that was of course impossible. Nevertheless, I encouraged David to swim in Chris's pool for many hours a day. I asked him to time his swims by the length of various pieces. "Darling, swim the *Appassionata*", I'd say, and then recommend some Chopin preludes. David would 'play' through the pieces in his mind as he did the laps.

Controlling the smoking at Riccardo's, however, was not as easy a task. The first step was to break David's playing into brackets, so that he would have definite breaks, which would eventually become the only times for his smoking and coffee-drinking. Then I said, "David, let's try playing one short piece without a cigarette, like *Flight of the Bumble Bee.*" David replied, "All right, darling." He got through the piece well, and I gave him a tremendous amount of praise, making it sound like an exciting journey.

David's adoring fans did not welcome my intervention, however. The women who sat around the piano, lighting cigarettes for David, were convinced they were helping him. When I asked them not to do it, they said, "Oh, leave him alone! Why are you trying to stop us from making him happy?" I knew that they perceived me as some sort of dragon. I was a newcomer at

Riccardo's and the regulars were not pleased about my telling them what to do with "their friend" David.

David, however, has always had the capacity to be willing when he knows it's for his own good, and he never once criticised me or made me feel bad for trying to take his "props" away from him.

Step by step, I let him consolidate. In the first week, during his performances, all I asked him to do was to get through one short piece at a time without a cigarette; in the second week, through two short pieces. In the third, we increased the number of cigarette-free pieces to three. Clearly, it was going to be a long, slow battle. Everything had to be judged by the mood David seemed to be in; everything had to happen gradually. It would have been quite inhuman for me to have taken away all his "props" in one go.

However, I had no doubts that our goal would be achieved eventually, because I was completely naive about the nature of addictions, and David was willing. Had I known more, I probably would not have tried. It was easy for me to keep saying to him, "That's all right, darling. You can do it, you can do it", because I totally meant what I said.

After three weeks, David could play for fifteen minutes without a cigarette; in the fourth week, a whole twenty-five-minute sonata. After five weeks, he could do forty-five minutes.

The coffee was also gradually reduced. At first, he could have a cup after three short pieces, and then one after a sonata, and only during a break. Of course, with his chewing, talking and singing, he was still far from being the model concert pianist, but every step counted, no matter how small.

chapter 4

Taurus

While it was most generous of Chris to let David and me stay in the sleep-out, it was obvious that we needed our own place. I felt it would increase David's sense of belonging and improve his self-esteem.

Being at Chris's on weekends, when his two sons, his girl-friend and her young son would also be there, prevented anyone from getting any peace and quiet. Though everyone was friendly and I found it heartening to watch the boys' ready acceptance of David, these weekends usually broke out into total chaos. Perhaps the three active young boys on their own would not have been as much of a distraction to the three adults, but with the addition of David – who incessantly jabbered to himself, played his radio continuously and, when he had an opportunity, dashed in and switched on the television before proceeding to play the piano – the cacophony was a test of anyone's sanity.

I was quickly to learn that I had to put up with David's noise and try to block it out, or end up in a state of nervous collapse. As all of this usually happened while I was trying to prepare notes for an astrology client, I felt that I might as well have set up shop on the tarmac of Sydney airport.

Our need to move was also necessitated by financial circumstances. I had to start teaching astrology again, and we couldn't possibly invade Chris's house with my classes. Luckily, by the first week of May I found a clean but rather uninspiring cottage in Lathlain, a suburb adjacent to Chris's. A quick dash around second-hand shops, new curtains and plenty of indoor plants transformed this rented house into a home – David's first home in thirteen years.

The next concern was getting our own piano. This was solved when Chris made a wonderful gift of a deposit on an upright.

The importance of having his own space soon manifested. David was able to wander around the house naked – his preferred state of being. "Less, less, less! You feel free!", he would say. He could play whenever he felt like it, which was most of the time, including the early hours of the morning, and have a cat, his favourite animal, which he not surprisingly named Rakhmaninov.

It was crucial for David to have the freedom to play whenever he wished and, concerned about how the neighbours would react to the constant sound of the piano, I made sure the windows were always tightly closed. One day, a neighbour appeared at the door and my heart sank. She told me she could hear David's playing, and my heart sank even further. She then asked, "Could you possibly leave the windows open so I can hear him better?"

Living in a house with David made me more aware of his Taurean qualities. I had studied his astrological chart before I came to live with him, and that had helped me understand his motivations, creativity and emotional make-up. But what I was to learn in the first couple of months of living with him was the exact manner in which he would personify some of the stock Taurean characteristics.

Most Taureans have great determination, which can be a close ally of stubbornness. Without this characteristic, David could never have perfected his craft at the piano. However, in everyday life it had a rather different effect. The very demanding side of David soon became apparent. Chris had warned me that David had an incredible ability to keep asking and asking until he got what he wanted, and I soon realised that he was a master of this technique. When he requested that something be given to him, or done for him, if it was not done immediately he became a verbal battering ram, going over and over the same request with complete disregard for the needs of others and without any understanding of why his request could not be met. If it was still not met after a short time, he would start to whine: a three-year-old in a body of a thirty-six-year-old. David could not handle any disturbance of his small routines, nor would he ever attempt to rectify a situation himself. It had to be done for him, and done quickly, or his agitation and his incredible ability to distract and disturb others increased to the point where one simply had to give in and do whatever was asked. It was at those times that one could no longer be near him, unless one kept in mind his other, gentle, charming and loving side.

David also had the appetite of a Taurean, but in him it revealed itself in regular and total raids on the fridge and the pantry, consumption of loaves and loaves of bread, and kilos of fruit and raw vegetables. At dinner time, he had to have at least six lamb chops, which had to be charred to a crisp, covered with HP Sauce and accompanied by a bowlful of chips – or else the verbal battering ram would appear. I could not stop him from the fridge-and-pantry raids, short of placing a lock on both, which would hardly have been beneficial for his sense of security. We could never invite guests and be completely sure that what was bought or prepared for dinner would still be in the fridge by the time the meal was to be served. All I could do was shop and re-stock the shelves.

However, it was not only the amount or type of food he ate, but also how he ate it. When I first came to stay with David for those ten days in March, he would always ask to have his meals alone. One day when I gave him his lunch, he took it, thanked me very much and, after I left, closed the door of the sleep-out behind me. Then, having forgotten something, I went back into the sleep-out. David was sitting on the bed. The plate was on his lap, a sauce-covered lamb chop was in his sauce-covered hands and his startled face was smeared with sauce. For a moment, he looked terribly embarrassed and confused. He put the chop back on the plate and, with a sigh of deep regret, said,

"I have no table manners." I then realised that the only reason he ate alone was because he was ashamed.

I sat down on the bed, hugged him and assured him it did not matter to me, and that if he wanted to learn to eat properly we would be able to work on it together. At the time, he mumbled, "Not very civilised, not civilised. Helfgotts were a wild bunch. Grateful to Mrs Luber, got me ready for London." As he did not explain much in the early days, I was not to find out the meaning of those words till some months later. I simply decided that he'd forgotten some of his table manners during his institutional life. In the meantime, David was willing to give cutlery a try, but it was not going to be easy. Even today, when everyone at the table is using their knife and fork, he often asks for a spoon.

Another common trait of Taureans is that they are very tactile, and in David that quality manifested to an extreme. His great desire to hold, touch and nestle into one's arms was quite irresistible to me. After a month or so of being with me, he began to feel somewhat safer in certain public gatherings and, instead of withdrawing, developed a habit of reaching out to complete strangers, trying to shake their hand, hug and kiss them, much like a cat would nuzzle another cat to communicate that it did not wish to be threatening. But in human beings not schooled in the language of cats, this often produced undesirable reactions. The sight of David, who was still stooping, chattering like an agitated magpie, and slightly dribbling – a side effect of Cogentin, which he was now taking with Serenace in order to counteract some of its side effects – was very threatening to some and they would quickly back away. My initial reaction was one of great hurt for David, but he had experienced rejection for years and was usually able to cope with it.

One night at Riccardo's, a slightly inebriated woman approached me and pointed to the dribbling, muttering pianist, who was but four feet away, playing with one hand and using the other to transfer chewing gum from his mouth to the under-side of the piano stool. "Why would a woman like you want be with *him*?", she asked. "I love him", I replied quietly, before walking over to David and putting my arms around him.

In the years following, I was to watch many incidents of people backing away or verbally abusing David. I had to do my best to block these out or the pain would have been unbearable.

These incidents often happened when we had to use public transport, my car having still to be transported from Sydney. David and I would get on the bus, and immediately I could see that people did not want us to sit next to them. The sight of people retreating in their wariness of David necessitated the speedy pur-chase of an old bomb, which I thought would make life easier. In some ways it did, but I was soon to learn how David felt about cars. The ten-minute drive to Riccardo's was fine, but any journey longer than that and out would come the whining and the nagging: "When are we going to get there, darling? Why aren't we there yet, darling?", repeated in an anxious drone. The sense of pro-longed confinement in a small vehicle, over which he had no control – David has never driven – caused great agitation, and then sheer panic. He had a similar fear of planes, which had developed after his breakdown.

David also hated going shopping with me, because crowds in supermarkets would bring on the panic attacks. I had to accept that this was one of the many routine activities which we would not be able to do together often.

In order to keep my wits about me through all this, I needed occasional space and time out, and to be with people other than David. When I had first arrived in Perth, Barbara Brackley, a fellow astrologer, was the only person I knew there apart from Chris. Previously, I had only run into her at various astrological conferences, but now our friendship strengthened.

When I told Barbara I was going to live with David, she was deeply concerned. I said to her, "You think I am mad, don't you?", but, though she sighed and disapprovingly shook her head, she offered me her unconditional support.

After we settled into the Lathlain house, Barbara and I agreed to start the Perth Academy of Astrology, offering classes for beginners and advanced students. We started the classes with a dozen or so eager women, sitting in my back garden on Saturday afternoons. The courses went for ten weeks at a time, and there was a lot of preparation to be done, but it was a great contrast and counterbalance to the demands of my life with David.

Barbara's husband, Peter, was also a great friend, and would come over and do handyman chores. David is utterly useless in that area, having never held a wrench or hammer in his life. "Gotta protect my hands, darling, my hands!", he would say, and it would have been foolish of me to disagree.

Life settled into as much of a routine as it was possible to establish, considering all of David's eccentric behaviour. As there was no pool at the Lathlain house and David still needed to swim, I took him to the local public pool in the mornings and afternoons. This took up four hours a day, and I would often go over my work notes while waiting for him to finish swimming. Though time-consuming, the swimming, with the addition of jogging, was starting to show some results, and David's nicotine consumption decreased.

Swimming, and water in general, had other therapeutic effects on David: it calmed and settled him. His obsessive showering at least four, and often ten, times a day seemed to have a cleansing effect on his psyche; fear dissolved and harmony took over. Fortunately, as the weeks went by, David took fewer showers, which meant that his mind did not need to be as frequently soothed.

David's sleep also gradually improved. He could sleep quite soundly through the night without running to the piano for a quick nocturnal performance. As his trust in me grew, there was less and less nervous agitation in his speech, and he was becoming more coherent. Weekly deep-breathing and relaxation exercises with a professional yoga teacher were also enormously beneficial.

Better health led to longer practice periods, until David was averaging around six hours a day. Usually, the television and radios would be going full blast at the same time. When I asked David how he could concentrate with such a racket, he replied, "Well, it's a miracle, darling. I seem to be able to listen, to hear every note, every note . . . My brain is brilliant, it's brilliant!"

Not all his time at the piano was practice; many hours were spent in just sheer enjoyment of the music. Listening to him at the piano was the ideal way to gain knowledge of the pieces, and soon I was able to pick up when he left out notes, added horrible extra octaves or repeated sections unnecessarily.

I had always been a great lover of music, but had never played an instrument myself. With David, my life immediately became something of a crash course in musical appreciation, and my knowledge of the piano repertoire, particularly the Romantic works, expanded.

The radio was permanently tuned to the ABC Classic FM station and I was being introduced to many exciting new pieces. The radio announcers' comments about the music were usually followed by David's own observations, and I was acquiring a better understanding of great musicianship.

This musical-appreciation course continued through the night, as David needed the radio to be on twenty-four hours. But by that time I was an inattentive student: I was so exhausted, nothing could have kept me awake.

As well as the radio in the house, David's old radio-cassette player was also permanently switched on. David and his cassette player were inseparable. He never left the house without it, except when he was going to Riccardo's. Along with cigarettes and chewing gum, it was his main security blanket, and he listened to it as he carried it with him everywhere. Jokingly I would say, "Don't your legs work, David, unless you've got that thing in your hand?" As I very rarely left his side, I always listened to it also. Some of the time it too was tuned into ABC Classic FM, but often David would play one of his numerous cassette tapes, and what a motley lot they were: some had torn labels, some were home recordings, some had ink which had run over the covers, and some even looked as if they had been immersed in water. Amazingly, most of them played.

One of these worn tapes was to introduce me to a piece of music that became one of the most important in David's repertoire: Liszt's B minor Sonata. When I first heard the sonata, performed by Terence Judd, it was one of those rare musical experiences which verged on the transcendental. I felt as if the soul playing it was breaking free and could not stay on this earth for much longer.

I made inquiries about Judd, and found that he had won a section of the Chaikovsky Piano Competition in 1978, but had committed suicide before he turned twenty-one. Judd's playing conveyed his vulnerability; it was very much on edge, that edge between sanity and madness, between life and death. I could truly relate to this: there was a man in my lounge room whose playing was also often on edge.

Magic Time

"It's all daddy's fault. It's all daddy's fault." A new refrain had appeared in David's mumble, whenever he felt he was in the wrong or somehow inadequate.

"What is daddy's fault?", I would have to ask.

"The damage, the damage", he'd reply, pointing to the outer corner of his left eye, as if there really was something wrong with his eyelid.

At the Lathlain house, the growing trust and coherence were opening doors to the ghosts of David's past. To begin with, the reminiscences were fragmented and mysterious. David would come out with a statement like "Djadja smashed the violin" and expect me to know exactly what he was referring to. "Who is Djadja?", I'd ask for clarification, and he would sigh, rather incredulous at my ignorance about something that was obvious to him. "The grandfather! Father's father, of course. Smashed the violin, just like that! And poor father slaved and slaved for that violin, but Djadja said, 'You be a rabbi', and smashed the violin into bits and pieces, into bits and pieces, anyhow."

David acted out the scene of the angry "Djadja" as he spoke, but it took some months for the whole story to emerge, and many more years for it to fit into my understanding of the Helfgott family history.

Apparently, David's father, Elias Peter Helfgott, was the son of a Chassidic rabbi in the Jewish settlement of Kamyk, near Czestochowa, Poland. Born in 1903, he was raised in a region which was then under Russian occupation.

As Peter grew up, the socialist-communist doctrine was spreading like wildfire through Eastern Europe, capturing the imagination of many a young Jewish boy. For Peter, the holy word of the Torah, unquestioningly accepted and strictly followed by his family, was soon replaced by the words of Marx and Engels. Fierce arguments ensued between the rabbi and his son. David remembers hearing the story of how "Father tried to cut off his father's beard. He chased his father around the table with the scissors, because my father wasn't scared of his father, you see. He stood up for himself in the world." To attempt to cut the hair of a Chassidic rabbi was indeed a daring and subversive gesture and, at the time, Peter was only twelve or thirteen years old.

Peter's arguments with his father were also fuelled by his

desire to become a musician. Though for the Chassidim song, dance and pure self-abandonment were proper expressions of religious impulse – considered to be faith through pure emotion – they were not the sort of artistic expression that the young Peter yearned for.

There was a violin in the shop window in the village and, in order to buy it, Peter worked and surreptitiously saved enough money. He brought the violin home but, when his father saw it, the precious instrument was ripped from his hands and smashed into "bits and pieces". For Rabbi David Helfgott, it was inconceivable that his son would defy tradition, and tradition decreed that a rabbi's son had to follow in his father's footsteps. He had to become a teacher of the Lord's word, always striving to preserve his people's religious heritage.

However, David has often claimed that, "My father never went to Hebrew school and he didn't have his education." Indeed, there would have been little time for study, as young Peter, according to family lore, kept running away from home. He was caught and returned to his family several times before he finally succeeded in escaping, in 1917 – a tumultuous time for a boy of fourteen to be wandering around Eastern Europe alone.

Myths and stories abound about Peter's activities over the next twenty-one years; however, only three things are really known for certain. The first is that at some stage in his travels he worked for a circus, and had a scar on his arm from a lion's bite and a host of acrobatic skills to prove it. The second is that during 1926 Peter Helfgott lived in Palestine. The third is that he worked in the merchant navy, which in 1934 brought him to Melbourne, Australia.

Among the migrant Jews of that period, the main thing in life was getting out of the 'ghetto', so to speak. The three methods by which most Jews believed this could be achieved were, in order of preference: to become wealthy and successful in business; to become a professional, such as a doctor or lawyer; or to be musically gifted, or have a child who was. And, like everyone else, Peter set out to escape the 'ghetto'.

Upon his arrival he busied himself with study of the English language, and consequently not only learnt how to read and write, but also developed a grasp of various sciences, going so far as to invent a labour- and cost-saving type of industrial iron which he patented and distributed to clothing factories in Australia. He kept up his interest in communism and, most significantly, taught himself how to read music and play the piano and violin.

In Melbourne, Peter stayed close to the Jewish community, both in his work and social activities. Though initially he seemed to be 'earning' on a par with the rest of the migrants who had come to Australia at roughly the same time, after a while he began to fall behind. At social gatherings, his friends began to notice twinges of bitterness and resentment towards them and their more successful financial situations.

In 1944, he married twenty-four-year-old Rachel Granek, a Jewish girl from Czestochowa, whom he had met through business dealings with her father, Mordecai, and her brother, Morry.

David, the second of Peter and Rachel's five children, was born in 1947. His childhood, and his relationship with his father, have haunted him all his life.

Once the floodgates of David's memories opened for me at Lathlain, they never closed again. For the first two years we were together, the topic of David's father and the multitude of misfortunes which had happened to David throughout his life – which David was convinced were all somehow connected to his father – bordered on the obsessional. Apart from the accounts of his various musical achievements, the stories about his father were the only conversations which inspired David to speak with true passion and involvement, and with a coherence unequalled at other times.

Peter Helfgott was "daddy" if the event David remembered was positive, or one which David still experienced in the state of a young child. However, "daddy" would become "father" if the memory was being shared by a David who remained in the consciousness of his real age, or referred to events that had pained him. The recounting of these memories evolved into a strange and inexplicable ritual, during which I came to know the bulk of David's past life.

Most nights, after driving home from Riccardo's, we would pull up in our driveway, switch off the ignition and stay in the car talking for a few hours. It somehow never occurred to either of us to continue our discussions in the comfort of our lounge room or bed. All I can say is "This is how it happened and I don't know why", which could easily be something that David might say about his entire life.

The early years of David's life were relatively happy and peaceful, even if not exactly luxurious. Living in a flat in the predominantly Jewish suburb of Elwood in Melbourne, David seems to have been much like any other child. Rachel, whom

David called "Marmena", stayed home and took care of him, his older sister, Margaret, and his baby brother, Les, while Peter went to work in Mordecai and Morry's clothing business.

"We had magic time most of the time. When it was all working with dad, it was all just magic", David has often said of his early childhood days. There was a piano in the house, and David remembers that he started to play sometime around the age of four, following after Margaret. "Father thought you have to get to that piano early, because you can't teach an old dog new tricks. It's hard when you get older, you get more set in your ways" is how David explained his father's philosophy. "From the first night I played on the piano, my father said every note was like a journey or something, like a miraculous discovery", he recalled.

It was an easy and rewarding beginning, because David performed even the first little ditties he learnt from *John Thompson's First Grade Book*: "I was playing for all my neighbours, very nice! The neighbours always enjoyed my playing and they took me out to shops and bought me blocks of chocolate and everything, and they were very pleasant."

The rewards did not just come in the form of gifts from the neighbours, but also in the form of special affection from Peter. David's great musical potential was apparent to Peter as soon as his son touched the keyboard, and nothing in life could have been more satisfying to this man whose own dreams of becoming a professional musician had been thwarted by fate and for whom other methods of escaping the 'ghetto' seemed untenable. To add to his musical talent, David also happened to be the eldest son in a Jewish household, thus making him Peter's absolute favourite. Peter called him "my little prince", lavished extra attention on him, spent every spare pound on David's needs, and generally invested as much of himself in his son's development as was humanly possible.

But neither time nor money were easy to come by for Peter, for, after a falling out with Rachel's family, the Helfgott finances went from bad to worse. Peter tried to go out on his own and start a coffee lounge, but was not successful. He was becoming stressed and another child was on the way. At home, Rachel was not coping by herself and often required Peter's assistance during work hours. She had no choice but to ask for his help, as the traditional routine of having one's mother help with the children was denied her, because Peter had barred all the Graneks from the Helfgott household after the disagreement with his in-laws.

In 1953, when David started school and his sister, Suzie, was born, the Helfgott family entered the financially dark times from which they would not emerge for years. David began to show signs of slight nervousness, which manifested in his inability to get to the school lavatory in time. Panic, embarrassment and fear of being discovered would send him scurrying into the long grass behind the school, where Margaret would find him and dutifully take him home so that Rachel could bath him.

However, the schooling was soon interrupted as Peter, having lost all hope of ever making a go of things in Melbourne, decided to relocate his family to Perth.

"It was very rough, very rough and we were all sick. All

the family got sick" is how David remembered that journey by ship. "And I was the *scarydiest* cat in the world, and I wouldn't eat my soup 'cause cats are the most *finickety* eaters in the world and father belted me to the daylights, he did. He was worried to death, because he had no money, no job, no prospects and he had to throw himself on the mercy of all those rich Jews."

As the Perth-bound ship sailed into rough waters, Peter was indeed anxious. Prior to leaving Melbourne, he had not established any secure means of providing for his young brood at the other end, nor had he arranged any dwelling for the family. Consequently, upon arrival the Helfgotts had to take shelter in a warehouse, where they had one mattress to sleep on, a radiator for both their heating and cooking needs, and walls made up of row upon row of brand-new shiny fridges. Peter had no choice but to ask for charity from Perth's Jewish community, in particular the Breckler family, who owned a chain of footwear stores. "We had no money, no food. I think father did go to see the rich Jews, he did go to see Alec Breckler and he did ask them for things. He wanted them to help him", said David, also recalling how his Marmena tried to toast a piece of bread on the side of the electric heater.

Apparently, the wealthy members of the Jewish community agreed to help, but they were quite unprepared for what they found when they came to visit Mr Helfgott and his needy family in the warehouse. Bizarrely, Peter had used up what little savings he had left for a deposit on a piano, which had promptly been delivered to the warehouse so that David could practise. "We were so poor – I'm a man from nowhere – and the father had no money and he still bought me a piano! Father bought me a piano!", recalled David, with a mixture of incredulity at his father's foolhardiness and grateful appreciation of Peter's priorities. But it seems that the "rich Jews" were not entirely impressed by Mr Helfgott's personal brand of martyrdom.

David vividly recalled the visit by the well-meaning Jews and he passionately acted out with gestures the whole scene as he spoke: "Yes, we had a piano and the Jews, the rich Jews, oh God, they were so upset by father! The rich Jews said to father, 'And what do you come to us for? You haven't got no money, you haven't got a job and you come to Perth and we gotta look after you!' And Alec Breckler, he felt sorry for us kids and he says, 'You should come away from your father. You don't stay with your father, 'cause your father's quite dangerous.'"

Mindful of David's ability to exaggerate, I tried to clarify the story: "Surely he didn't say that your father was dangerous, did he?"

"Well, the father did scream and shout a lot", David said firmly. "The point was that Mr Breckler, Smart Alec, said that the father had no money for food and we were all very poor and we should go. And the poor father was crying, father was weeping, and he said, 'Ahh, you'll never make me cry again! You'll never make me weep again!' So there we are. And those rich Jews – we all know – did support us. And the father was very proud, father was too proud and too poor. And father accepted the help but then he criticised them behind their backs, which wasn't very nice. That's a bit snitchy-bitchy, isn't it?"

When I thought about this story, I felt I could understand why Peter Helfgott, all of whose family, except for a sister, was swallowed up in the horror of the Holocaust, was not exactly enamoured of strangers advising him to split up his family, no matter how well-meaning. This, mixed with feelings of pride and inadequacy, would have been hard on any man.

However, what I did not know at the time was how this one incident, so early in David's youth, was to become the first in a chain of events that would take on qualities of great pathos and tragedy and, in David's comprehension of his life, become one of many things which, over a long time, would lead to his breakdown.

In 1953, however, Peter Helfgott's criticism and resentment of the "rich Jews" did not, as yet, prevent him from sensibly accepting their help, and soon the family was installed in a house, at the front of which Peter again attempted to run a coffee shop, again unsuccessfully.

For the next five years the family moved house several times, always in the poorer areas of Perth's working-class suburbs. Finally, in 1958, they settled into a cosy but basic house in Bulwer Avenue, Highgate, which was conveniently located across the road from the children's primary school.

No matter what basic comforts the Helfgotts lacked during these years, "Father always made sure I wasn't deprived of pianos", said David. And no matter what odd jobs Peter took on to earn money, he never relinquished his task as David's piano teacher and general educator. He taught his son chess and, as soon as the "little prince" could read, a special night-time routine evolved. "I always read to dad every night", David would proudly recall. "Bittersweet William, Byron, Shelley. Yes, lots of Shakespeare, lots of sonnets and lots of poetry, plays, *Hamlet*, *Macbeth* and *King Lear*."

Peter also taught all his children, and David in particular, the principles of socialist ideology. David was also the one Peter took with him to local meetings of the Communist Party. David remembered these little outings as being quite adventurous: "Father was never a card-carrying member and of course we didn't go to all the communist meetings, 'cause it was dangerous, it was being monitored all the time. It took a great deal of courage. You were being monitored every time you went into one of those meetings in the middle of Perth. There were all these security police, all from Menzies, monitoring everyone who came in. It was very dangerous."

David was also the only member of his family whom Peter took along to the synagogue. Talking about it, David would become somewhat wistful: "Father used to take me to the synagogue all the time. Every Friday night and every Saturday morning. Every Kaddish and every Sabbath. We always went to the synagogue. 'Course those were the happy times. I was proud. I used to walk to the synagogue with my father, very chutzpah-like, and we used to enjoy that wonderful, glorious music."

But whereas many of Peter's discussions with his son were devoted to politics, no mention, it seems, was ever made of Jewish religion, history or culture. David would often refer to the precise nature of Peter's attitude to these things with disdain: "It was a bad upbringing, a bad upbringing. I didn't have a Jewish atmosphere at home. We never lit the *candillas*, I didn't even know what it was all about. We went to the synagogue and I had no idea what was going on. Father never told me much about Jews or anything. Father's just a hypocrite, he's Janus, he's two-faced. Father never liked going to the synagogue, 'cause he didn't believe in all that ritual. He thought it was all hocus-pocus and mumbo-jumbo, 'cause he was a communist. Father'd go to synagogue to try and please the rich Jews, please Smart Alec and Meyer Breckler and things like that."

Members of the Jewish community would often come to visit the Helfgott family to see how they were coping. David tried hard to explain the relationship: "Dad would never go to see them. When we first came to Perth, father went to see them, but after that they always came to us. They came all that way, miles and miles especially, in the very wealthy car, and they always gave us presents and money and things like that. So father went to the synagogue to please them."

"Didn't he ever tell you what being Jewish meant?"

"Never, never, never. We used to talk about communism. Russian and Chinese communism, and not Jewish, never Jewish."

Not all of David's time with his father was devoted to music and political matters, though, as Peter encouraged all his children to do physical exercise. "Push-ups, pull-ups, father insisted. Father insisted on all the exercise in the world!", David recalled. "'Cause he said, 'You have to be fit, you have to be fit.' It makes your thoughts a bit more positive, a bit more wholesome, a bit more gentle, a bit more concentrated. You get a better quality of thought."

David would often boast that he could walk on his hands all the way down the street to meet his father on his way home from work: "I used to always run to him. It was great exercise, of all exercises. No one else could do it. It was unusual! It was rare! It was unique! ... Well, we think so, anyhow."

Despite such moments, the more details David revealed about his childhood, the darker the image of his father became. By the late 1950s, the hardships of Peter Helfgott's life were starting to take their toll on his health and his nerves. He was having frequent heart attacks and often became extremely frustrated about the smallest thing. Even the special time of sitting at the piano with his "little prince" was becoming a hardship.

One day, when talking about those piano lessons, David said, "I'm grateful to father for teaching me in a way, but he was a bit stern with his lessons." I asked him to elaborate, but was quite unprepared for what he said.

"Well, all I remember is that I had no option at all, because father was so stern and he said, 'You bloody well do what you're told!'" David sadly shook his head. "Father was a very stern taskmaster and he expected a very high standard. I did my best to try to understand, but father was not a very good teacher, 'cause father was self-taught, so what do you expect? Father taught me in a very brusque, in a very Russky, Russky way. He'd put you on the piano and, if you don't play well, he'd shout and sternly throw you off the piano."

Using both hands and the upper part of his body, David demonstrated the impatient and forceful dislocation from the piano stool of his nine-year-old self by Peter: "Like that. Very firmly push you away, very fiercely. Push you away from the piano, always rough, and I'd just run to Marmena in tears, always run to Marmena in tears. It always ended in tears anyhow. The same as when the cat sticks out its claws, dad throws it across the room, very rough and very stern. And that's how father taught me, see? 'Cause father was self-taught and he'd learnt in the school of hard knocks." David chuckled sadly at his own pun and continued. "And that's all he knew, that's the only thing he knew how to do." After a moment, he added, "But he could be nice too."

"And what did your Marmena do when the father did that?"

"Poor little Marmena had absolutely no say in the house at all. She was absolutely just . . . just crushed completely. Completely crushed", replied David as his eyes filled with tears. But then he smiled and, puckering up, said, "*Potchnagoola, potchnagoola.*" I kissed him and the tears vanished.

It would seem, though, at least as far as David's skill at the piano was concerned, that Peter's "brusque", "Russky" ways were paying off. At the age of ten, David performed Chopin's *Polonaise* in A flat at a country music festival competition. It was one of his first major public performances and, though the piano started moving away from him while he played, he did not stop. A born performer, with an awesome power of concentration and a natural sense of professionalism, David stood up and, without missing a beat, continued to play, following the piano across the stage as it moved.

Peter was furious. Thinking that David had no hope of winning, through no fault of his own, Peter told his son that he was in a great rush for a meeting and took the boy home. Fortunately, the competition organisers tracked David down. "They came back and they said, 'Mr Helfgott is *prodigies.*' I won a special prize, because they said my special talent gave me an unfair advantage", David recalled with a wry smile.

A decade after that brave little feat, in a letter for a

submission to London's Royal College of Music, David referred to his performance of the *Polonaise* as "unexpurgated!!" and commented that he "didn't win the particular section; but was awarded a 'special' prize (I suppose for courage!)". He made no mention of the piano's moving.

Peter, too, must have been aware that his son's playing was in need of expurgation, and to this end he attempted to find him an appropriate teacher. In this, he succeeded when he met Frank Arndt, who agreed to teach not only David but also his sister Margaret, for free. This was just as well, as Rachel was pregnant again and Peter could never have afforded the lessons.

During 1958, David studied, expanding his repertoire and polishing his technique under Frank Arndt's careful guidance, and by the following year was well on his way to national exposure when he represented Western Australia in the Australian Broadcasting Corporation (ABC) Talent Quest. Playing *Malaguena* by Lecuona, David won the semi-final and went on to the grand final with a performance of Liszt's *La Campanella*.

Still aged only twelve, David then entered the ABC Concerto and Vocal Competition with Bach's Concerto in D minor. In this, his first attempt at the most prestigious national music competition, he did not get through to the State final. However, thanks to the Talent Quest, his name and photograph were in the papers, and the music community was starting to notice the remarkable talents of the curly-haired, bespectacled little boy. David Helfgott's journey to stardom had begun.

Birthday Boy

"Possum!", I called to David and waved to him to come out of the swimming pool. The balding, sunburnt head and the pair of thick-lensed spectacles bobbed up from the water, and the swimmer accelerated in my direction.

I stood on the lawn by the public pool and waited for David, who, having finished swimming through a programme of Mussorgsky and Scriabin, had climbed out and was running towards me with a beaming smile, his arms stretched out wide. When he reached me, he gave me an enormous hug. "So, how did you go with the études?", I asked.

"I could've played it better", he replied in all seriousness and frowned for a moment. I handed him his towel and clothes, and he ran off to the changing room, with his one spare hand lightly touching the heads of the children he passed.

More and more each day, David would show his delight in my being with him. He told me he loved me about forty times a day and, if I went out without him anywhere, even for an hour, he would be overjoyed at seeing me on my return. With each week, he was becoming increasingly reassured that the love he was feeling for me was reciprocated, and, though I was still to accept his near-daily proposals of marriage, he was feeling significantly more secure.

Squeals of delight, children's giggles and David's loud "Aaaah! Ooooh!" laugh could be heard from the men's changing room. I realised that David must have forgotten his purpose for going there, as was often the case. By now, he was probably deeply engrossed in a game of splash-fighting with the kids.

Though I couldn't walk into the men's changing room, I stood at the entrance and raised my voice, "Possum! Come on, darling! We've got to go!", but to no avail. A young pool attendant caught my eye, smiled and said, "I'll get him." By now, all the pool attendants knew David, and were always kind and gentle to him.

The helpful young man reappeared with David a few seconds later. Contrary to my suspicions, David had remembered to change, but his clothes were inside out, back-to-front and sopping wet. It was his thirty-seventh birthday.

I had organised a small birthday party for that night. Though most of the guests were friends we'd both made at Riccardo's, some of them were friends of David's he'd known before I met him. This was actually more significant than it sounds. When I met David, both Chris and Dorothy gave me the impression that he had no friends or people who cared for him, apart from themselves. I was told that even his family, most of whom still lived in Perth, wanted nothing to do with him. As David did not think to contradict these false notions, I was pleasantly surprised each time a 'new' friend turned up.

One such special friend was Frances Hebb. Like many others in Perth, she had known of David before he went to London and then, because there had been no local publicity, put him out of her mind. However, as soon as David had started at Riccardo's and his face had reappeared in the newspapers, she had got in touch with Chris and offered whatever assistance David needed. A fully trained nurse, she had been saddened to know of David's long incarceration, and decided to take him out on as many outings as she could. Frances would take David to the movies and concerts, for strolls in the park and Devonshire teas. David always looked forward to these outings.

I met Frances at Chris's house when she came to take David to the film of *La Traviata*. She immediately suggested that I come along as well, and offered to look after David any time I needed a free day.

Frances lived in a lovely apartment with a piano and extensive views of Perth and the Swan River. David felt very comfortable there. We always kept in touch and years later she would appear to David as an 'angel of mercy' on a sun-scorched outback road bearing gifts of icy, caffeine-laced Coke.

Another wonderful group of friends came from the Karrinyup Symphony Orchestra. The orchestra was an amateur group and the conductor just happened to be Frank Arndt. Frank, who hadn't seen David since his childhood, had tracked him down in the early '80s and suggested he might like to come and play with them.

I first heard about this association of David's from Chris, who was unhappy about the orchestra not paying David for his performances with them. When I questioned David about it, he said he was thrilled at the chance to perform with any orchestra at any time and was very grateful to Frank: "Frank believed in me, yes he believed in me. I read the music well, sometimes even brilliant, yes brilliant. It was terrific to play again. Frank was kind, he always believed in me."

At the time Frank made his offer, David's only opportunities to share his music were at church-hall recitals organised by Dorothy, and the rewards he received from playing with the Karrinyup Orchestra far outweighed any lack of monetary payment. The rehearsals and performances gave David a chance to be surrounded by fellow musicians, most of whom remembered him from his youth and showed tremendous respect and care for him.

The rehearsals were not far from Guildercliffe Lodge and the orchestra members would come and collect David, and often have him to dinner. David had begun to gain a feeling of acceptance from a whole group of people for the first time in a decade.

I had realised all of this when Mrs Cowan, a violinist from the orchestra, invited David and me to dinner. She told me she had always regretted not being able to offer accommodation to David when he lived at Guildercliffe Lodge, because she had a bad kidney and eleven children!

This birthday party was the first occasion David and I had to gather all these lovely and kind people together, although none of David's family was there that night. While I had met most of them briefly, I think they were still a bit wary of me, and I did not want to force things. Besides, there was not much communication between them and David at the time.

During the Passover in April, David had asked me to come with him to see his Marmena. When I met Rachel, and told her about my feelings for David, she was completely mystified as to why anyone would want to be with him. While she loved her son, his health at that time was a great challenge to her. Nothing in her life had prepared this quiet and simple soul for either her son's talent or his mental anguish. The sense of helplessness she felt at the sight of this cowering, dribbling and muttering creature, who was once so healthy and sharp, must have contributed to her mistrust of my motives, and there was an air of bewilderment about her. "I did not know how to handle him", she was to confess to me with sadness some months later. I reassured her that she was not the only one who felt that way, but it was still some time before she finally embraced me and said I was the best thing to happen to David.

What would have made it harder for Rachel to relate to me was the fact that, shortly after we'd moved to the Lathlain house, Dorothy had asked her to call David and find out if he and I were sexually involved, thus placing Rachel in a very uncomfortable position. This request of Dorothy's was a rather strange way to respond to a 'Get well' card David and I had sent her a few days earlier. At the time, David had plucked up some courage and bluntly told his beloved Marmena that it was none of her business.

I ignored the whole thing and sent Dorothy an invitation to David's party. Two separate replies arrived to this invitation, one addressed to David and one to me. In both, Dorothy declined to come, and in the letter to David she wrote that, because David's life had changed so significantly, she felt that she could no longer be a part of it. But she promised she would follow his career with interest and always come to his concerts.

However, before either David or I had a chance to respond, a new letter arrived from Dorothy. David opened it, read it in a few seconds, and started shaking. Suddenly there was silence; for once David was speechless. He waved the letter in my direction, his hand trembling. I took it and read it: "David, in the light of your recent change of lifestyle I want you to know that our friendship is now ended and I do not want you to write or telephone me ever again. I will send the money I owe you as soon as possible. Dorothy."

This cold rejection was not from a stranger on a bus, but from a very dear and special friend, and I had never seen David so upset. I tried to calm him, saying Dorothy was probably confused and in a lot of pain. That helped somewhat, but the overall effect of this incident was that for more than a year David was unable to open letters and always asked me to do it, saying, "I don't want a shock like that again, never again, darling."

I didn't want any more shocks either, but fate had other ideas. The next day, when I went to Rachel's to give her some tickets for David's upcoming comeback concert, I was faced with a woman whom I had never met, who started abusing me. The woman was Dorothy.

Rachel looked terribly embarrassed as a mass of unsavoury accusations flew across her kitchen in my direction. I don't think I had ever been so verbally attacked in my life, but what pained me the most was Dorothy turning on herself and admitting that she now felt dirty for ever having touched David. She was utterly confused in that she also displayed an attitude of total possessiveness towards him. Over the years I was to learn that a paradoxical attitude towards David was a common feature in most of his key relationships with people, no matter whether they were men or women.

However, standing there in Rachel's kitchen, I'd had enough. After twenty-five minutes, it was obvious that reasonable communication was impossible. I told Dorothy that, as she was a committed Christian, I suspected she would later feel remorseful about her words. I added that she was always welcome to come and see David at any time, and that we would always be grateful for her care of David. This was greeted with "Don't patronise me!" As Rachel was becoming increasingly uncomfortable, I left.

A few days later, I received a note of apology from Dorothy, but was asked not to reply. I greatly appreciated her gesture and left a pot of white chrysanthemums on her doorstep from David and me. I knew that Dorothy felt robbed of David, not just because of my appearance in his life, but also because of Chris and Riccardo's and all of David's new friends.

I felt I had to be honest with David and tell him about the incident at Rachel's. He listened carefully, nodded, hugged me and said, "Oh, you poor darling ... and, um, poor Dotty-Scotty." A few days later, however, it suddenly occurred to him what his intending to leave for a weekend with Dorothy had meant to me the day after I arrived. In his first-ever show of concern for me, he said, "Sorry, darling. I wasn't aware, but I should've been. How could I have done that? How could I? I didn't mean to hurt. I wasn't aware and didn't mean to hurt. But I must be aware, more aware, and I'd never do it again."

David was beginning to notice the needs and feelings of others, and consequently to see some clearer distinctions between the individuals around him and the difference between me and everyone else. For David, this was a small step out of "the fog".

"The fog" is one of the many terms he uses to describe his condition, along with "sore", "*dommage*", "sore *les yeux*", "the hook" and a host of others. "It's a foggy, misty sort of condition, darling", he would say, to explain what many psychiatrists have tried to define with a multitude of medical terms. In "the fog", everything looked, well, foggy, but what was worse was that everything, often including his own piano playing, *sounded* foggy.

While his mind swirled in a chaos of rambling thoughts and his soul was steeped in pain, external reality and everything and everyone in it were shrouded in a thick, cotton-wool fog – an incredible self-protection device manufactured by David's exceptional brain.

Rare and Prodigious

David's last 'fog-free' year was 1960.

In March, he started high school and, though separated from his best friend, Boris, who went to a different school, and feeling a bit lonely in his new environment, he wasn't unhappy. Too many exciting things were happening in other areas of his life.

David was about to turn thirteen and Peter was not going to let his prejudices about religion interfere with David's Bar Mitzvah. Though David told me he loved the experience, he was never naive about its purpose: "I had the Bar Mitzvah 'cause dad wanted to please those rich Jews and daddy wanted the money too." And in this Peter succeeded.

"I'm still very grateful to the Brecklers for making me a nice party with all sort of *gateaux* and *fixes*, and everything", David would say with the deepest sincerity. "The Brecklers gave me lots of presents and lots of money and it cost them money."

Though they did not have a high opinion of the Helfgott father, the Brecklers – and others in the Jewish community who could afford to do so – always supported the Helfgott family for the sake of the children, David in particular. The little pianistic prodigy was a prized asset of the entire community, and there is no doubt that this thought would have crossed Peter's mind when he took the prodigy to the synagogue.

But there was something in the whole experience that was more important to David than the money. For weeks prior to the big event, he studied with a kindly neighbour, Mrs Finkelstein, and revelled in the ancient melodies. "That music has survived for two thousand years! Has survived the Roman empire and the British empire unchanged!", he would exclaim with pride. "It's very melodious and very awesome and vast! You have to remember it all. Just magic, just magic! You have to sing it. My memory was brilliant. I did the Torah and everything and I could remember it all!"

Even though David has never been to a Bar Mitzvah since his own, amazingly he can still remember, and will occasionally sing, parts of it to me – though he will admit that, on the day, he remembered all the words and forgot some of the melody, the irony of which does not escape him. He occasionally laughs at the memory of the rabbi telling him, "Well, David, now we all know you're not a public speaker."

However, these memories are always tinctured with regret

at what, to David, was a rather futile aspect of the exercise: "I just learned it by rote. I just chanted and I had no idea, really, what I was saying. I sort of just learned it, like a parrot. I couldn't understand any word of Hebrew, 'cause father never taught me a word of Hebrew." Of course, learning Hebrew was not the point.

A few weeks after his thirteenth birthday, David again entered the ABC Concerto and Vocal Competition and got through to the State finals. This time he played two movements of the Ravel G major Concerto. Though he placed second, he earned favourable mentions in the press. The *West Australian* noted that he "brought the most sympathetic applause with his dexterous handling of Ravel's often difficult Concerto".

More importantly, David's performance in the State finals captured the attention of James Penberthy, a man who would a year later contribute fatefully to David's life. As music critic for the *Sunday Times,* Penberthy wrote, "With the appearance of 13-year-old pianist David Helfgott, Perth had its first sight of a rare and prodigious talent. His performance of the first and third movements of the Ravel Concerto was startling from one so young and small."

David was relishing his success. The press clippings were adding up, and he and his siblings were carefully pasting them into David's personal scrapbook, where decades later I would find them all.

The press clippings from 1960 tell of more concerts and David's ever-expanding repertoire. There is even an end-of-year report from school, with marks ranging from 94 in French to 47 in Woodwork, and a comment from the teacher that, "David has worked quite well throughout the year. He is a good class member, quiet and of pleasant disposition."

Rare and prodigious talent aside, David was not simply "quiet" but painfully shy. Though he adored performing in front of large audiences, always feeling buoyed by the chance to share his music, and though his little heart would fill with glee at the slightest hint of praise, his shyness always prevented him from showing his feelings. However, this shyness had a peculiar worth of its own; when mixed with David's deep humility, it made him so grateful for the privilege of being allowed to perform that he would never feel nervous about it, just overjoyed.

By the time he turned fourteen, David was every suburban mother's dream. At an age when boys tend to turn surly and unruly, David was portrayed in the newspapers as a perfectly charming young man. He was always photographed wearing a jacket and a bow tie, his spectacles and neatly cut golden curls giving a hint of earnestness to his sweet, open face. And then, of course, there was his magic talent at the keyboard. An article in a women's magazine reported David to be a "painfully modest" boy who "would be horrified to know that after he had appeared on TV many Perth housewives phoned the station to describe David's hands as the most beautiful they had ever seen".

Perth is one of the most geographically isolated cities in the world, and, at that time, had a rather parochial environment, where close-knit groups oversaw aspects of its cultural and social life. This was especially true of the Perth music world, where classical music was enjoying a particularly privileged and popular status within the community. The sudden arrival of David was a huge musical event for Perth and it is only too understandable that the power-brokers wished to have a major input into his career. The press, too, saw enormous 'human interest' potential in David's story and pushed it for all it was worth.

In late May 1961, David again entered the ABC competition, this time with two movements of the Mozart C minor Concerto, and got through to the State finals. By chance, two great American musicians, pianist Abbey Simon and violinist Isaac Stern, were in the country during the following weeks. It was customary at the time for the ABC to arrange for the country's young music stars to be heard by visiting celebrities. David was just such a star and, as Simon and Stern came through Perth on their respective tours, David was invited to play for them at the ABC. Among those present were members of the press and Frank Callaway, Professor of Music at the University of Western Australia. Peter, however, was absent on both occasions. David had played before many a visiting celebrity, and Peter was not in the habit of taking time off work for these recitals.

"There is no doubt that this boy is gifted and has a promising future", announced Simon to the press. But the private recital for Stern was to yield even greater results, and David has always considered that performance to be one of the two pinnacles of his career.

"That was great!", he would say unequivocally of his afternoon with Stern. "The ABC set it up for me and I was very grateful. Imagine that! The little me, without my father there! I just played the piano, Wolfgang's Concerto C minor, and Isaac just smiled all the time. He thought I was great."

With a total lack of self-awareness, David would add, "I wasn't nervous at all! By some great, good fortune I wasn't nervous at all. I was just nice and calm and relaxed and playing very well."

Though David had by this stage experienced many important musicians' approval of his talent, Stern's reaction held a surprise for the unassuming little pianist from the wrong side of the tracks. Without a hint of vanity, David recalled, "He could see some signs of genius and he said I deserve all the help I can get. He said something like 'I'll be your mentor in America', like he would look after me, and I didn't have to worry. He said, 'Would you like to go to America where music bounces off the walls?', and I said, 'I like tennis!'" David chuckled at the memory of his youthful witticism and then reassured me that this in no way spoilt his chances: "Isaac understood, and he thought that was great fun when I said I liked tennis. He took it as my assent. That was a perfect answer. He found that very charming and delightful."

The place where "music bounced off the walls" was the Curtis Institute of Music in Pennsylvania, and it was never assumed by anyone present at the private recital with Stern that Peter Helfgott would ever be able to afford to send David there, no matter how much his talent might have deserved the opportunity.

When David went home and proudly told his father about the conversation with Stern, Peter responded positively. And when over the next few days Perth's music-brokers and members of the Jewish community began to talk of a fund for David, that idea appealed to Peter as well.

Of course, there was no question of David's going any-where right away; he was much too young. "It worked for a while, it was all hunky-dory. What we decided was sensible", said David about his initial discussion with Peter. "Father said, 'We will raise the fund, and you'll go when you're ready. But first we'll raise the fund though. We won't say no to the fund, because that's money.' So it was all sensibly planned."

Peter told David that he would have to wait at least eight-een months, until he gained his Junior Certificate from school, before he could go overseas. Though the plan of going overseas was not something David would ever have been presumptuous enough to dream of before, it now took a firm hold of his imagination. In his boyish optimism, he could not imagine the dream not coming true.

In the meantime, David was about to receive more accolades. On 7 June he played in the State grand final of the ABC competition and won. He was then selected to play at the national finals in Melbourne later that month. This is when the press really took off, and David was on a high. He recalled: "When I was having my interview with Abbey and with Isaac and everyone was taking pictures of me, I felt like a star, really alive, you know. Everyone was making a fuss of me. Famous!"

But David's 'fame' was not meaningful to him alone. It had a great impact on the whole Jewish community. They had a young star in their midst and they felt proud. David would heartily laugh whenever he remembered the alleged reaction of mothers in the community: "I heard that when I won that com-petition in Perth I inspired all the Jewish *marmenas* in Perth to put their little *bubbies* on the piano, to try to catch up to David, to try to do the same thing. 'Cause they wanted to produce another 'David', they did! That's what happened! They all tried to beat me at my own game!"

An instant role model, no less. But there was a way of capitalising on this fame, and this is where James Penberthy's steady interest in David was about to come full circle.

chapter 8

Tear-jerker

A day or so after the State grand final of the ABC Concerto Competition in 1961, James Penberthy, whom David has always affectionately called "Lord Jim", came to visit the Helfgott household with the noble intention of doing everything he could to help David's career.

Penberthy, who was also a noted composer, genuinely believed in David's talent. Now he was going to build on the recent publicity generated by David's success at the ABC competition, and the commendations from the American celebrities, to rally the community together and fund David's education. His article, "Pappa Wouldn't Sell the Piano", appeared on the front page of the *Sunday Times* on 11 June.

Under a quarter-page photo of David at the piano, the piece began with a mention of David's appearance at the previous year's ABC competition. Penberthy described him as "a pale little boy with a coat too small and trousers too short", who "walked shyly on to the stage of the Capitol Theatre" and "was so small his feet barely reached the pedals of the concert grand. Seconds later the audience was startled as the 13-year-old pianist gave an amazingly strong performance of the difficult Ravel Piano Concerto."

When I asked David about this description, he shook his head and said, "Very colourful, very colourful, not true. Lord Jim was just trying to make a tear-jerker or a weepy."

The article went on to describe David's musical achievements and the need for him to study overseas. "But", wrote the genuinely concerned Penberthy, "this week I discovered that unless he receives a substantial scholarship, or unless a special fund is started for him, he will never go anywhere." And then he launched into a heart-wrenching description of poverty: "The Helfgott family is rich in pride, talent and happiness, but they have barely enough money for the necessities of life. Proud pappa, Peter Helfgott, a State Electricity Commission fitter, has a wife and five young children to support ... How Polish-born Peter and Rae [sic] Helfgott keep their attractive family happy, well-fed, dressed and educated in their Bulwer avenue, Perth, home is quite beyond me. Not so long ago Peter Helfgott fell ill, and at this time lost practically every stick of furniture in his humble little home. He told me: 'We wanted to maintain some life in the house, so we managed to keep up the payments on the piano.' The Helfgotts are, with justification, a proud family – they ask help from no-one. But only a wealthy family could adequately provide suitable education for such a boy as David. I believe he will one day bring honor to this city, so the community may well feel disposed to do something for him. Even now, there is something that can be done for the boy ... his piano needs a complete overhaul so badly it must be a nightmare for him to practise on it. And the stool he sits on to play? It's home-made."

The article had several very powerful and very different responses, most of which Penberthy never intended or foresaw, and never found out about afterwards. As far as he was concerned, the response was entirely positive, as his office phone rang hot for the rest of that Sunday with offers of money, piano stools and piano tuners' services for the poverty-stricken prodigy.

For the Helfgott family, however, Sunday 11 June was a day of tears. To Peter, who no doubt unwittingly pointed out to Penberthy most of the facts in the article himself, the words on the page amounted to a detailed description of his failure to provide for his family and, in particular, for his talented son, because "only a wealthy family could", and Peter's family was certainly not one of those. The article shamed Peter; it made him feel worthless and helpless. The piano for which he had sacrificed much, starting with its purchase while they lived at the warehouse, was a "nightmare" for David. Even Peter's honest efforts to build his "little prince" a stool were to be pitied and inspire charity. This was the first heavy blow to Peter's pride and more was about to come.

For David, the article had different, though also painful,

consequences. "The father was very *articulata*", he said. "Father said to me, 'David, don't read it, 'cause you'll weep.' But I disobeyed dad anyhow, and I read it anyhow and then I cried for days, cried for days. I did weep, because it said I was poor. I was afraid that my peers, if you know what I mean, the peers at school would make it tough for me because they would read about how poor we are."

The only comfort to David was Penberthy's kind words about his music. "I was very pleased at the same time, because I love what he wrote about my playing. It was wonderful what he wrote about me, and rapturous", said David.

But there was another group of people upset by the article – or, more to the point, by one sentence in it. "The Helfgotts are, with justification, a proud family – they ask help from no-one" had members of the Jewish community seething. What about all their financial help? What about David's Bar Mitzvah? How could the media be mentioning "their" David and not mentioning them? The article seemed to go out of its way to disassociate David from Jewishness, with his family's ethnicity denoted only by "Polish-born".

When Peter turned up at the synagogue for the next Sabbath, some members of the congregation let him know exactly how they felt. David stood nearby and observed how Peter's duplicity was finally catching up with him.

The memory of that day has always stayed with David: "The Brecklers helped us for a long time, and everyone thought that father should've said something when he talked to Lord Jim. Everyone said that he should've acknowledged the help and thanked them. And all those rich Jews they were furious, and they said to dad, 'We're gonna wash our hands of you, because, after all that help we've given you, then you say your proud family won't accept help from no one.'"

To Peter, being dressed down in this manner, and on this topic in particular, was salt on fresh wounds. The mention of the Helfgotts' pride in the article was Peter's only way of holding on to some sense of dignity in the eyes of the public, but in any future conversations with the press that resource, he was now told, must not be utilised. And why was all this happening? Because of David, the son for whom he had placed himself in this demeaning position in the first place.

However, if the Breckler family wished to "wash their hands" of the father, they had no such intentions towards the son and, during the week preceding that Sabbath, Alec Breckler met with Isaac Stern to discuss David's future. The meeting took place after a group of interested people from music organisations in Perth met to discuss how they could help David. The sum they believed would cover the costs of David's tuition and living expenses for five years in America was £5000. This group then approached Perth's Lord Mayor, Sir Harry Howard, and asked him to give his patronage to a fund for sending David overseas. Peter Helfgott was not invited to, or even consulted about, any of these meetings.

David was never to learn the precise nature of Peter's feelings on Sunday 18 June – the day after the dressing down by the "rich Jews" – when Peter opened the *Sunday Times* and read on page three about the meetings, and all the support and help which had been offered to David during the week. The article, not written by Penberthy, contained one sentence, in fact one

name, which would affect the rest of David's life the moment
Peter's eyes fell upon it. The sentence was: "In Sydney a meeting
of prominent businessmen was attended by pianist [sic] Isaac
Stern and Perth businessman Mr Alec Breckler."

To this day, David's crystal-clear recollection of the
moment of seeing his father read that article provokes in him
total bewilderment and pain every time he tells the story. The
first time I heard it, I also keenly felt these emotions.

"We said we'd raise the fund and I would go when I'm
ready. That was what we agreed on. And later the father suddenly turned around and said something completely *contraire.*
Father put the spanner in the works", said David in a surprisingly cold tone. "The article in the newspaper said that Isaac
Stern met with Smart Alec. And as soon as father saw that name,
just saw that name 'Smart Alec' and straight away, grrr, grrr . . ."
David attempted to imitate Peter's ferocious mood by making
grumbling noises. "And he cancelled the lot! *Parentally* and
abruptly. He said, 'No more fund. No more money. No more
America. No more nothing. And send all the money back!' He
got all *spiky-spitey* and spiteful. It was a word! It was just his
name! That name did all the damage! Just seeing that word!
That was the end, that was the end of it all."

"You mean, he cancelled the fund simply because of Breckler's meeting with Isaac?", I asked, incredulous.

"That's right. The Brecklers wanted to have a hand in
sending me to America. But then again as they'd been helping
us for years and years and years, I suppose it's understandable –
they all wanted me to go to America too. And I *needed* their
help to go to America, 'cause you *need* these rich Jews, 'cause it

costs a lot of money. But dad was so proud. Dad was so poor and so proud, too poor and too proud. Father shouldn't have had a problem like that with the Brecklers 'cause, after all, you should just accept the help. Just accept the help."

"But why would a name in the newspaper ... ?"

"Affect father so badly?", interrupted David, who has been asking himself this question for decades. He was becoming agitated, frantically trying to work it all out for probably the thousandth time. "Well, um ... What was the father's problem? Father must have been a bit of a tyrant ... perhaps ... Perhaps he was a tyrant. Dad never discussed it with me. We never sort of got it off our chests. Somehow, it was just festering, like a festering boil or something like that. He was so furious about the Brecklers and he just had this very bad sort of grudge, grudge-smudge."

"So, the only reason he didn't want you to go to America was ..."

"Smart Alec", David interrupted again. He seemed impatient to tell as much of the story as made sense to him at that moment, perhaps finally to solve it once and for all. "Dad had a grudge! All those years held a grudge! 'Cause Mr Smart Alec Breckler saw that I should be separated from my father. He implied father wasn't fit to bring up kids, 'cause he thought the father was destructive or something. And the Brecklers made dad weep when we were in the warehouse. And since that day father held a grudge, since that day never forgot that he held a grudge and I think Jews should know better than holding grudges. 'Cause I mean, after all, the Führer held those grudges against the Jews too, 'cause the rich Jews were a bit mean to the

Führer when he was a poor painter in Vienna. It's stupid! It's stupid! You shouldn't hold grudges, don't be like that, because life is too short."

David was now sad, and the sadness settled him somewhat. He shrugged and reflected for a moment: "So, I think my father was a bit foolish, really, just to let a name like that affect everything and change the course of history and the whole world. When I played the *Chimes* and the *Campanella* for Julius Katchen in '62, he said to dad, 'Anyone who goes to America on an Isaac Stern scholarship is very well looked after. Why didn't you accept it?' And dad said, 'Because they hurt me.' And all these great American concert pianists thought it was a waste of time talking to dad and that I should've gone anyway. And all this money they spent to correct this wrong. It's a *shamus* really, 'cause it was really mindless or stupid or something."

But David didn't solve the mystery behind Peter's extreme reaction when he first told me the story. He didn't solve it the tenth time or the fiftieth, either. He wasn't exaggerating when he said that it affected "the course of history and the whole world" – it did for him, and it would take him many more years and many more such discussions to put all the bits and pieces together.

Money and Jealousy

The moment David's father saw Alec Breckler's name in the paper was the culmination of many complex and frustrating thoughts and feelings which Peter had been experiencing for years. It was the moment when he realised that he'd had enough of other people controlling his son's life, even though that was the precise nature of his unspoken understanding with them. After all, David the genius was his son. The genius did not belong to the media, to the Jewish community or to the Brecklers.

However, he, the father of the genius, had not even got to meet Isaac Stern, and Breckler had. He did not go to meetings and have a say in his own son's future, because he did not have money. And though Breckler was not the father of the genius, he did have money and, therefore, power. He could control the genius's life if he wished to do so for any personal reasons – like his name being mentioned in the newspaper, for example.

Peter's poverty made front-page news. His name appeared only in the context of being the helpless, hopeless, sickly father who could do nothing for his son but provide him with a rickety piano and a home-made stool. Breckler, on the other hand, was associated in the newspaper with successful businessmen and a glamorous overseas musical celebrity.

Due to a succession of business failures and ill health, Peter's dignity and sense of self-worth would have been at an all-time low, and, to him, it would have seemed that all the public would now know that not only was he useless in terms of properly providing for his son, but that Breckler – the man who had once told him he was unfit to look after his own children – had had to step in and rescue the situation. What's more, the "rich Jews" were telling him that he should've been reinforcing such notions when he spoke to the press.

This was perhaps the moment when Peter discovered that having a genius for a son did not equal power and glory – only money did. And he knew, by that stage in his life, he would never have much money. So what then was the use of a genius son?

David has often said that it was all about "money and jealousy" – Peter's jealousy of the money he did not have, and of the power which that money could buy for those who did have it. But there was a way in which Peter could indeed put the spanner in the proverbial works, even if it did mean thwarting his own long-held desires, and those nascent ones of his son. He could just say no.

Even though Peter continued to encourage and support David afterwards, this moment was no doubt one of the contributing factors in the diminishing affection between father and son over the following years.

For the time being, however, Peter's rage was known only to David, and, to begin with, David took it to be just one of daddy's usual temper tantrums. He simply could not believe that such a wonderful dream could be shattered so suddenly and senselessly.

Regardless of all the dramas at home, David still had a very important performance scheduled, and on Sunday 25 June he and Peter flew off to Melbourne for the ABC Concerto and Vocal Competition finals. When the Brecklers sent an encouraging telegram to wish David well, Peter must have felt a bit haunted; what was worse, David loved receiving it. "That made a tremendous impact on me reading that telegram in Melbourne. I felt really flying high. I felt so privileged", said David. Then, after a pause, he added, "Of course, that's when we were still getting on with them."

On 27 June, the night of the national grand final, David again played the Mozart C minor Concerto, but this time he did not win.

"Did you not play as well as you could, because you were sad about not going to America?", I asked.

"No, I still played quite well. They thought it was perfect playing!", David replied, slightly indignant at the implication that his not winning the grand final had anything to do with his playing. Then he decided to elaborate: "See, I just sort of accepted and it didn't seem to affect me badly. It took a long time, it was just gradual, it was a gradual sort of thing." But it was not long before David finally realised that he really and truly was not going anywhere.

On the following Sabbath, the unwitting Alec Breckler came up to Peter at the synagogue to tell him the happy news that fund-money was pouring in and that he had arranged for "a nice Jewish family to look after David in America".

"That", David would say emphatically, "was the last thing father wanted to hear!"

First, this American family was "nice" – and to Peter, in the state he was in, it could have meant that Breckler, yet again, was implying that Peter did not have a 'nice' family. Second, they were "Jewish", and Peter, as we know, was not into 'Jewish' in any genuine way. He would not have wanted David to have the chance to discover, during his five-year stay with the family, that 'Jewish' was better than 'communist' – if that ever happened, all those hours, days, weeks of political discussion might have been wasted and the son might take on the deluded beliefs of his rabbi grandfather.

"My father's all muddled up about Jewishness", David said as he attempted to explain Peter's reaction to the "nice Jewish family", but he was getting all muddled up himself. "My father was too proud to be Polish, he wanted to be Russian, but he was really a Polish Jew. He was a proud Jew and a poor Jewish communist. So it's all very complicated and of course father said that all Americans are gangsters anyhow. So father's very extreme and you should be all different altogether." Suddenly David interrupted himself in order to plead with a ghost: "Don't be so fanatical father! 'Cause it's a *shamus*, you know." Then he leant close to me and whispered, "I think daddy's a bit confused, not consistent."

Confused or otherwise, after deciding once and for all that David was not going to America, Peter came up with two 'official' reasons for this. During the following week, he told the people in charge of the fund that as David would still be too young to go overseas on his own, even in eighteen months' time, the idea of the fund would have to be postponed indefinitely and that all the money should be returned to the donors. At home, however, Peter told his family that he had just received news that not enough money was coming in, and that the fund would have to be stopped.

As the media's interest in the life of the Helfgott family and the musical adventures of David had been whipped up significantly, Fred Dunhill, a reporter for the *Sunday Times*, went to see the Helfgotts the following Saturday to find out precisely why David was now not going. Before he arrived, Peter told David what to say. David has endlessly told me, "I always obeyed daddy", and on this occasion he did exactly as he was told.

"Father put the words in my mouth. Father put the words in my mouth" has been a common repetition in David's chatter ever since I met him. It refers to the moment when David, coached by Peter, said to the reporter: "I will certainly go on with my music. But I could not leave my family and go away. I don't know whether I want to go overseas eventually or not. I know I don't want to go away now."

This quote appeared in the *Sunday Times* the next day, in Dunhill's article "Pianist Will Stay in W.A.". The article said that David "seemed dazzled by the publicity", and that when "the idea of a fund was first suggested he thought he would probably be ready to go away in a few years". However, it said, that "since going to Melbourne for the vocal and concerto grand finals he had realised his family meant so much to him he could not think of leaving them yet". A bit of a *shamus*, it would seem, as the article began by reporting that "Several large sums of money had been promised – and given".

"And you know what?", David once quipped when telling me about that article, "I didn't even realise my family meant so much to me."

At the time, however, David did not find the experience amusing at all. It was, in fact, the first in a series of increasingly devastating 'last straws'. When David saw his father's ideas being attributed to himself in the article the next day, the reality finally sank in. "I did myself in and my father did me in, because he stabbed me in the back and betrayed me", David has said of that incident. To David, it was a betrayal of his trust in his father's love for him, and a betrayal of all the dreams he and his father had shared, and of all the career ambitions Peter had spent years instilling in him.

Fury? Frustration? Sadness? No, for David these would have been far too overwhelming. So, instead, it was numbness. "I sort of accepted", he told me with a sigh. "I had no option really. I really had to accept, because what option did you have at all? The sadness came in after days, later, later."

But the day after his big realisation, when David arrived

at school, he noticed that something very strange had happened to his usual environment. "It was like a light had gone out of the world", David told me, moving his hand in front of his face in the gesture of drawing a curtain. "Everything looked different. It was all dusty, everything looked different altogether, it was a very bad school. The school had not a single *l'arbre*, there wasn't a leaf of grass. It was one of those warehouse sort of schools, and it wasn't very nice, because I had to sit all on my own in the classroom and the teacher yelled at everyone, but I wasn't scared 'cause the father could scream louder than anyone. I felt rejected, actually. I felt friendless, I felt forlorn and bereft, I felt completely isolated or something, and it was a disaster."

"What happened, David? Why do you connect the school not having any trees with not going to America?", I asked, completely unprepared for David's inimitable logic.

"Well, 'cause if I would've gone to America, well then I would've gone to a different school and I would've been in a different situation altogether!", he replied, frustrated by my inability to see something so obvious, his voice filled with pain. "I would've been different and the world would've been different! I would've been different, wouldn't I if I would've gone? 'Course I would've been!" David paused and then quietly added, "Somehow, it seems the damage was done then."

At the age of fourteen, the world as David knew it stopped making sense to him. Reality was so baffling it literally became unbearable. It was all just too much and that's when the world 'fogged up'.

His father's denying him the opportunity to study in America was to colour David's life for many years. Somewhere at the back of his mind a little voice was always whispering, "Why didn't you go to America?" He was convinced that if he had gone to America the years in the psychiatric wilderness would have never occurred. He told me that during his time in Graylands Hospital he would often look around the room and Isaac Stern's words about music "bouncing off the walls" would come to taunt him.

We spent hours, days, years talking of David's anguish at his father's decision, and always with exactly the same outcome. I would remind him that it was impossible to know what might have happened if he had gone. It was a question that could never be answered. But David would find little consolation in this. He would leave the subject alone, without resolving it, until the next time, when he would start the conversation all over again.

Unique

My 'foggy' friend was lying on his stomach, on the dressing-room floor. Dressed only in his underwear, David was doing his peculiar brand of nonstrenuous push-ups and looking through the music books which were spread on the floor all around him, engrossed in a dialogue with himself.

He was highly excited: outside the door, the auditorium of the Octagon Theatre was packed with eager and curious music lovers. David's comeback concert was about to start. I paced up and down the dressing room, concerned about how he would get through the recital without cigarettes and coffee.

So far, his 'rehabilitation' was proving successful. At

Riccardo's, he was no longer smoking or drinking coffee while performing, and his overall sugar intake had been significantly reduced.

However, I had noticed that he was finding it difficult to wake up in the mornings. That, combined with his need for energy-boosting substances, made me wonder if his medication dosages were higher than they needed to be. I discussed this with Chris and a long period of dosage-adjustment began. I noticed that on higher dosages David was calmer and more coherent, but his playing was not as good – and not playing to the best of his ability always made him unhappy.

Since the day I decided to be with David, the fine balance of his medication and other aspects of his 'rehabilitation' have occupied much of my thoughts. He is an extraordinary human being, and it has been extremely difficult – in fact, almost impossible – to separate the special aspects of his personality from the unique aspects of his musicianship. Though there have always been aspects of his personality which we can work on together to make his passage through life slightly easier, I firmly believe that nothing must ever be done which might impinge upon his uniqueness as a person and as a musician. With medication, the dosage had to be such that it would enable him to unscramble his thoughts up to a point, but not dull his passion for life in general and music in particular.

David is incredibly, almost supernaturally, sensitive. He can often predict what someone is about to say or read someone's thoughts. He can be playing the piano with both the radio and the television blaring and still hear a quiet conversation in the next room. He also seems to know intuitively the precise manner in which each key must be touched on any piano, so that he can achieve the sound he desires. David is extremely short-sighted and rarely has his eyes fully open, yet he sees and notices things that by all estimations should be invisible to him. Great care has to be taken so that nothing hampers his uncanny abilities.

One also has to be careful when adjusting David's personality to suit everyday life. I once overheard a four-year-old girl query her mother, "Is David a kid or a grown-up?" Not an unreasonable question, as this aspect of David has puzzled not only children but many adults as well. David does have a childlike countenance and trust. Malice, jealousy, cruelty and deception have never been a part of his make-up, and his generosity and affection towards all around him is uncomplicated and bountiful.

David would gladly give away any or all of his possessions, if asked. I have had to stop him offering people our car, and in the past he has parted with much of his sheet music and cash. He does not understand the value of money, which leads to small disasters if he is ever let loose with any. One day, David had $50 in his pocket and went with a friend to buy me a birthday present. Remembering that I'd mentioned I liked pearl necklaces, he saw one for $5900 and said to his friend, "I want to get this for Gillian. Could you give me the money and she'll pay you back when we get home." Thank goodness he was not shopping alone with his credit card!

David's childlike qualities would also manifest in his untidiness, disorganisation and lack of practical skills. I once found him in the kitchen vigorously shaking a can of baked beans. He had made two small insertions with a bottle opener and was mystified that the beans were not coming out.

On another occasion, I saw him standing helplessly by the piano with a cassette recorder in one hand and its short cord in the other, gazing at the power point a few feet away. He looked up at me and, in a pleading, baffled tone, asked, "Oh, darling, can you help? Can you help, darling?" There was a special program he wanted to hear and tape while he practised. I went and got an extension cord, joined it up and plugged it in. He observed my actions with awe and, when I had finished, said, "Darling, you are so brilliant!" Never has anyone been so highly praised for so little!

However, such 'simple-minded' behaviour has never been the effect of a simple mind, as David is highly intelligent, and has immense general knowledge and a photographic memory – when he feels like using it. His brain is much like a vast library of facts and music, and these he can retrieve on demand. One can ask him to play a piece which he has not seen or played for years, and he will always respond with an instant performance. No one ever needs to search for historical, political or scientific data in books when David is around, because one just asks and receives an immediate answer. David is a dynamic partner in Trivial Pursuit, but does not have a competitive streak in this game and happily provides his opponents with information. There is no way to reconcile or explain his childlike tendencies with the maturity of his intellect. To use one of David's favourite expressions: "It's a mystery!"

His passion for music is also inexplicable, because it is absolute. It is not merely an inclination, but an obsession. He doesn't just play because it is his vocation; he plays because when he is at the piano he is ecstatic, and playing for others is especially gratifying. Whenever he can, he stays at the piano. He will eat and sleep at the piano if permitted. He would rather play than do anything else, and has been like this since he first touched the keys as a child. This passion for music is a divine gift. "I was put on earth to play, darling, to play", he would say. And what right do I, or anyone, for that matter, have to tamper with David's passion?

Yes, one could teach him the value of money and how to spend it with care. One could force him to perform a mass of routine daily tasks, and he would invariably obey, because, as he says, he tries to be "affable and amenable to all". One could give him enough medication that shops and restaurants and crowded streets would not bother him, so that he could conduct totally lucid conversations with strangers without first spending months learning to trust them.

In short, one *could* make him into a regular member of society, but then his time would be taken up with doing all the little tasks that regular members of society do, and he'd be robbed of his passion to play, each and every day of his life. It wouldn't be difficult to try and 'adapt' him to some arbitrary standard of normality, but then David would no longer be David and, by destroying the individual, one would risk destroying his magic.

One day at Riccardo's, after David had finished an extremely passionate rendition of a Beethoven sonata, a woman approached my table and, in a rather condescending tone, said, "I do hope you treat David as if he is normal." "I trust I never bring him down to that level", I replied. I will always fight for David's right to stay extraordinary and do whatever is necessary to protect him from any pressures to conform.

In the dressing room of the Octagon Theatre on the night of the comeback concert, I was but a novice at this task, and did not yet know how much I would learn over the years. There were no 'how-to' manuals for living with David. All I knew was that my intentions always arose from the love I felt for him, and all I could hope for was that my actions would have a positive outcome.

I have often been asked if I was nervous or anxious before that first professional concert, and I have never been able to describe the very peculiar mixture of tension and excitement I felt – and still feel before his every major performance. I had been watching David at Riccardo's, and was absolutely convinced of his power and mastery at the piano. I had also seen and felt the response to his music and personality from the audience at Riccardo's, and I hoped that it would be the same in the hall of the Octagon Theatre.

David had only one word to describe his feelings before playing that night: "Terrific!"

I felt very grateful to Mike Parry for giving David the wonderful opportunity to return to the professional concert platform after a twelve-year absence, and hoped that David would justify his faith.

There was something else I would be grateful to Mike for, but I did not know about it till many years later. Just hours prior to the concert, Chris Reynolds threatened to withdraw David should Mike refuse to renegotiate his fee. As it happened, Mike did refuse, but the concert did go on. Mike chose not to tell me or David at the time, and we were both spared what could have been a most unfortunate situation. This sense of protection was typical of everything Mike did for David, including how he handled press and publicity.

The concert programme itself was, as David put it, a "*compri*", a compromise between Mike, Chris and David. Mike and Chris had chosen the more 'popular' part of the programme, starting with Chopin's *Polonaise* in A flat major, *Fantasie Impromptu* in C sharp minor and *Ballade* in G minor. These were followed by three Rakhmaninov preludes: the G major, the G minor and the C sharp minor. David's choice, Balakirev's *Islamey*, was to conclude the first half, and Mussorgsky's *Pictures at an Exhibition*, David's choice again, was programmed for the second half.

The concert had quickly sold out and the ambience in the auditorium was one of great hope and support. Familiar faces from Riccardo's, David's family, his old piano teachers and numerous other well-wishers were all willing David to succeed. It was like being at a football stadium and feeling the crowd's desire for their team to win.

As David walked out onto the stage and took his seat at the Bechstein grand, we were all in a state of trepidation. The Chopin *Polonaise* spilled forth from the keys at a furious rate, and uneven phrasing resulted. The *Fantasie Impromptu* had moments of lyricism. When telling me about that piece sometime prior to the performance, David had said, "Some say there should be a miracle of spun gossamer and others say it's a storm. I reckon it's a *compri*, a *compri*, not too fast not too slow, it's just a nice balance." I was now listening to him search for that balance in front of 650 people.

In the *Ballade*, even more control was evident. The audience seemed to be inspiring David to play better. With his beloved Rakhmaninov, the preludes flowed with more confidence and beauty. Then he was into the Balakirev.

When I first heard David play *Islamey*, I suspected it to be one of the most challenging pieces of music ever written for the piano. "It is the most difficult piece in the world!", David confirmed. "Practically every pianist in the world says so. It's just so difficult to play. It's the greatest *toccare* of them all! *Difficile* beyond belief! *Difficile* beyond belief! Technically very difficult and temperamentally very difficult as well. Most pianists won't play it, because it's too *difficile*."

Technically, *Islamey* is a minefield for pianists, and the faster one plays it the more treacherous that minefield becomes. David started this work at such an incredible speed that Chris and I looked at each other and wondered if we should have encouraged this comeback. Was he back on the stage too soon? Would he get through this intact? What on earth had we been thinking?

However, this was to be my first experience of the true strength, courage and determination of David in a major performance. He pulled it back from what seemed a certain disaster, and held this perilous piece together, leading the *West Australian*'s music critic to comment that it "was thrown off without apparent difficulty" and that David's "very individual style revealed great technical mastery, by turns magnetically powerful and serenely lyrical".

After the first bracket, David came off the stage rather shaken. "I think by the time the Rak came everything settled down", he muttered, and lit a cigarette. It was not the nerves that unsettled him, though – it was over-excitement. In the dressing room, Chris had a quiet chat with David and told him to go out there and show the audience what he could *really* do in the second half. David inhaled deeply and nodded, "Golly Chris, all right Chris."

When David returned to the stage after the intermission, he proceeded to do as he had promised, and the true brilliance of his musicianship unfolded in a fine performance of *Pictures at an Exhibition*. He had got it all together and he knew it.

At the end of the concert, most of the audience were in tears as they erupted into spontaneous applause, followed by a standing ovation and cheering. After taking his bows, David stood in the middle of the stage and soaked up their affection and appreciation. Joy, pride and love all combined in me, along with a sense of enormous relief. From my position backstage, I could not see if David had tears in his eyes; I certainly did.

Slowly he lifted his hands and put them over his face, as if he were reminding himself, or the audience, that the *dommage* was still there. Or, perhaps because the joy of the occasion momentarily broke through the 'fog', he was shielding his eyes from a world which suddenly looked too sharp and beautiful. After a moment or so, he put his hands down, clenched his fists and, in a little gesture of triumph, lifted them up, just a few inches, and held them there for a moment. His humility and disbelief at such a success prevented him from lifting his hands any higher and truly claiming the victory.

A Mouse and
a Lion

"I put myself on the hook when I battened down the hatches and stopped talking to daddy. If I'd only kept talking it would have been better." This was, and still is, David's way of explaining the effect and cause of his condition. The imagery in this description did seem to me to be rather abstract at first, but as David filled in the details of the saga over the years, I began to see that it was logical, simple and obvious. In fact, there could hardly have been a better way to describe what had occurred in the years following Peter's refusal to let David go to America.

Surprisingly, the first reaction to the refusal did not come from David, but it did affect him. The members of the Jewish community who had generously invested their time and money in David's future were rather bewildered by Peter's stance. What made it even worse was Peter's telling David to publicly reject the fund in the newspapers. His off-loading of all responsibility for his irrational action onto David angered the Jewish community even more. "Of course, those rich Jews knew better", David would say. "They knew it was the father talking not me and they were very upset. And Mr Troy, he was sort of one of the foundation members, he was very furious about that."

No one will ever know what really finally happened between Peter and the "rich Jews", but David remembers that on one Sabbath in 1961 his father, for the first time, did not take him along to the synagogue. When Peter came home later, he had a strange story to tell David. "Mr Troy gave dad a killing look, a killing look, gave him an 'Oooo' look", David recalled. To support his story, David tried to reproduce the ferocious look. "Just like that! He didn't even say anything! He just sort of said with that look, 'You should've let David go.' I think that's what he was angry about."

Peter then swore that he would never return to the synagogue. "And dad never went ever again", David continued. "Just like that! After all those years of going to synagogue! I think that's a bit stupid, just 'cause he got a bad look. But looks can kill, I suppose." David chuckled, then sighed: "Still it was nice to go to the synagogue. We used to enjoy ourselves listening to all that soothing and gentle and glorious music. It was a beautiful time, really, and it's a shame it all had to end, but never mind." And thus David became cut off from the support and care of his community.

Meanwhile, the fog was thickening and David was gradually cutting himself off from his entire microcosm. "I used to hibernate", David confessed. "I used to stay all on my ownsome and I was sort of lonesome. I was unresponsive, like nature. It's wonderful but it's aloof. It seems nice, but there's really a ferocious struggle for survival going on out there, like spiders and all sorts of things. So I wasn't talking to anyone at school, nor to father neither. But everyone liked me. I knew everyone, but no one was really my friend."

Then, as he does with everything in his past, David tried to connect his behaviour to why everything went so wrong: "So that's when the damage was done. I couldn't help myself with those kids, I was a reject and that was that, and there was nothing I could do about it. If no one would sit next to me, well, what could I do about it? And the teacher screamed and screamed and screamed. It was damaging, damaging, because you see it's very important your acceptance by your peers, you see, by your siblings and peers. That can make all the difference to your mental health. And that's why I got sore."

However, he paused and tried to reclaim some responsibility for the situation by reprimanding himself: "So, I reckon, you should've been a bit different. You should've had more chutzpah." For a moment, he became very serious and leant close to me, as if about to share a great secret. "I think I got reclusive or something, and it's a bit of a job to break out of it now." He burst out laughing.

This new, reclusive David, unresponsive and clouded, was not easy for anybody to deal with. His siblings took it as arrogance, a conclusion anyone might easily have come to after living for years with a genius, who also happened to be the preferred child in a family of four others. Even though by that stage all the siblings played musical instruments (except for two-year-old Louise), it was only David who got new clothes every time he played at a concert. "I always got a brand-new suit, and it made me feel brand-new", he once told me, and laughed. It was only David who, on Peter's insistence, had a hot bath to relax him before every performance – a rare luxury in a house with no hot-water service. It was only David who didn't have to do any chores in the house because all he had to do was "to play piano for father". Family myths also abound about David not tying his own shoelaces, lighting burners or cutting bread, all because he had to protect his hands. And now this "little prince" was becoming withdrawn, a demeanour so difficult sometimes to distinguish from haughtiness.

The change in David's personality was annoying Peter, also. After everything he had just been through with the fund, the media and the Jewish community, the last thing Peter needed was David's strange new behaviour. Though David did not stop talking to his father entirely, he began to break little routines the two had shared for years. He remembers Rachel saying to him, "Look, you don't read to your daddy no more", as one of the most symbolic moments of that period.

Though Peter and David had not always agreed on every-thing in their intellectual discussions, an added mistrust of motives appeared in their dialogue. Peter's actions with regard to the fund were slowly destabilising the foundations of David's respect for his father, and he seemed no longer able to believe or wholly respect daddy's every word. This shocked, dismayed and angered Peter, and eventually most discussions turned into fights. According to David, these fights could be "about anything". But as politics was Peter's topic of choice, this became the vehicle for venting frustrations. "Mainly they were about communism in Russia and China", David recalled. "There was a big sort of split of scale and my father hated Nikita, when Nikita got into power. My father's fussy, fussy. And he made me cry, made me weep. Every time I stood up for Russian communism, he used to stand up for China. But I didn't always stand up for Russia. Sometimes I changed sides. But whatever side I took, father always took the other side. Spite! Just deliberately."

This, of course, was in no way improving David's affection for his father. As Peter couldn't reclaim David's love by either spoiling him with special favours or yelling at him, he tried other tactics, like envy: "I was the favourite son, but he would play us off, one against the other, like the Roman empire and the British empire. Father played me off against Margaret, father played me off, and it was very cruel of father to do that." However, this had little effect on David, who is incapable of envy. All he noticed, with not a little degree of disappointment and surprise, was that, "Father got hostile. Just like that, out of the blue!"

Around that time a new routine developed in the Helfgott household, something that David has nicknamed the "hate nights". After years of analysing the reasons behind them, he came up with a more or less plausible explanation: "Dad probably had a frustrating time, poor dad, with Rachel and with the work and everything. It was like he was boiling and he sort of had to explode or something." Apparently "these hate sort of lessons, these horror sessions, these hate nights" occurred "about every three months". Peter would come home from work and "get all sort of very pressured. The pressure, the *press*, was just beyond belief! It just went on and on. It was about all different things and, well, father was a bit of a screamer. If you didn't play that piano well, dad would just scream, 'cause heaven help the underachiever in a Jewish household. We were all sick in my family and we all copped it. Of course, I think I copped more than my fair share."

The favourite son was becoming more and more the favourite target, though no one escaped Peter's moods entirely. "If Margaret didn't play well, oh God! She got punished severely", David said. "Father was cruel to her verbally and aggressively too. He used violence! Father was very mean of spirit to Rachel too. Father always circled around like an angry lion and Rachel always cried."

One time, when talking about his father and mother, David started to tell me the story of yet another incident. He was totally indignant: "Fancy waking up in the *matinata* and seeing Rachel rushing out into the front yard! In front of all the traffic! Poor Rachel, screaming, screaming and yelling. Wow! And what a mood father's in! I think it's not very nice, 'cause I mean, what a way to wake up!"

"Why? What happened?", I asked.

In response, David just shrugged, his indignation dissipating: "I don't know, I was in bed reading the newspaper. I never heard, 'cause father always brought me the newspaper in bed, he always brought me the *West Australian* and the *Daily News*.

But I think that father shouldn't be so mean of spirit to Rachel, because I reckon you should be nice to her. Poor old Rachel had to go through hell to get to heaven."

I must have looked as surprised as I felt, so David had to explain: "Father was pretty good too, he could be very nice and very loving too. Father loved me dearly, but very stern at the same time. 'Cause father had a sort of a devil in him, and an angel in him, and all my life it was like that. Dad always had a devil and an angel all his life. It's a sort of a dichotomy, a split of scale. And I should've stood up. I should've said, 'No, dad. It's time you stop this. It's time you stop this, dad', shouldn't I? 'Stop this nonsense'. But I didn't, I just stopped talking. I was just a little mouse, a mouse."

However, David didn't entirely stop talking, not just then. Feeling friendless at school and increasingly confused by the family conflicts, David was rapidly losing his points of reference in the world. But there was, and always would be, one thing to rely on: music. Ironically, it was Peter himself who told David, when he first started teaching him how to play, that even if one day David had no money or friends, he would always be rich and never be alone if he had music. And thus David continued to practise, increasing his repertoire.

He performed at recitals and concerts, and the newspapers continued to follow his progress. In September '61, he flew to Sydney for an appearance on the 'Bobby Limb Show', then the most popular television variety show in the country. More photos of the boy at the piano, more notices and praise.

In October, David sat for his first official music examination, bypassing entirely the grades system, and at the age of fourteen presented a programme for the Associate of Music diploma, considered to be the second-last step to being officially recognised as a professional musician. With an easy performance of Bach, Mozart, Chopin and Debussy, he gained the highest marks on record, and won a prize for being "top candidate in Associate diploma examination".

The various recitals and prizes were proving a lucrative venture, and over the year David managed to save £100, a great sum for a boy his age who had never had a penny of his own. And this is where the near-daily disputes with Peter came to a climax.

Sometime towards the end of the year, the Helfgotts moved to a bigger, though much less cosy, house. The children were growing up and the family needed more space. And even though Margaret had by now left school, stopped playing the piano, and was working and supporting the family, any extra money was always welcome. But not as far as David was concerned: "I wanted that hundred pounds for my school, for my next year's education. And dad said, 'I want the money for the family, for the house', and that wasn't very fair, I thought."

I was shocked by the seeming selfishness of David's attitude. However, it was perhaps indicative of how far he had withdrawn from his father and family by that stage. I decided to check whether, withdrawn or otherwise, David had any understanding of Peter's motives. "Darling," I asked, "why do you think your daddy wanted the money?"

"Well, you've got to get your priorities correct, don't you? Perhaps father thought that having money for the house was more important than *livres* and he thought that David could somehow survive. So he took the money anyway, he completely ignored me and took it anyway. I think my father was being a bit selfish, but then again none of us comes out of it very well, none of us."

David paused, took a deep breath and confessed: "I thought that the only way I could retaliate was . . . I was foolish, I was very foolish. That was silly of me, I know. I still should have kept talking, but I didn't realise I was putting myself on the hook when I stopped talking to father. So there we are."

So David's withdrawal was not a gradual thing after all, but the peculiar imagery was still a mystery to me. "But darling, how do you explain . . . ?", I began, but, as always, it was something that David must have already asked himself numerous times: "How do you get on the hook when you don't talk to father? Well, that's a bit of a mystery. Perhaps the punishment put me on the hook. The punishment was so stern, so stern."

I swallowed hard. "What was the punishment, possum?"

The Pinpoint

In the first few weeks of 1962, David really and truly stopped talking to Peter. Apart from the most perfunctory of exchanges, David completely shut himself off. What few discussions they had were mainly about a new music teacher for David, as, along with all the other changes in his life, he could no longer study with Frank Arndt, who became unavailable due to personal reasons. David began to have lessons with Stephen Dornan, and though he was learning major new pieces, like Liszt's Concerto No. 1, his memory of these lessons is vague. The 'fog' had greatly increased by that time and only the most dramatic of events from that period would remain etched in his mind forever.

For David, the entire sixteenth year of his life is really only distinguished by a single occurrence – the father's "punishment" – which, in David's estimation, "exacerbated the damage, 'cause father wasn't aware that I'd already been damaged".

In the trajectory of his mental 'alteration', David has clearly marked that one event as "the turning point" or "the night of the tragedy". Before he launched into his detailed account of that night, he reassured me that it was not just unpleasant for him alone: "All the family was terribly upset, they all suffered. The whole house was in chaos that night. See, I was in the bath and dad was at work . . . " It was a typically quirky beginning, but I knew that in a minute, or a year, it would all make sense.

"Dad had been boiling and boiling, and stewing and simmering for a long time, for days and days, 'cause his prince wasn't talking to him. When he came home and slammed the door, I knew there was gonna be trouble, and his screaming never stopped."

David's usually half-closed eyes were now wide open. He was staring into the space in front of him as if watching a movie of that night. The memories were still so clear he shuddered. "I was scared to death and . . . Ah, but I can hardly remember that night! Too scared to remember that night!"

David gulped and then continued: "I think he must have come into the bathroom. I think he just yelled. He shouted and shouted and shouted! He threw things around and he screamed and screamed, and it was absolute chaos! I'm not sure what he screamed about. He said, 'I'll see you in the gutter and yo, ya, ya, ya!' We both wrestled with chairs." To demonstrate, David held up his hands in a deflective gesture, as if there was still a chair looming towards him, just slightly above his face.

"But I never fought. I was trying to stop dad from bashing me up. I was just trying to protect myself. The funny thing is I talked to him after that, at the concerto competition."

David turned to me as if trying to explain the most obvious thing in the world. His voice momentarily calmed down and he said: "I still had to play the concerto that night, the Liszt, you see. It was the night of my concerto competition and Margaret said she was gonna go for the police 'cause . . . "

Suddenly David's eyes filled with tears, and he began to find it increasingly hard to keep going. "If dad locks the door, the front door. He said, 'I will lock the doors and I'm not gonna let you go to the competition.' Because he was furious, father was furious, he said . . . his prince . . . oh, never mind . . . it was one of those things . . . happens in the best of families . . . " David gulped down his words as tears streamed down his face.

Always searching for the positives, I clung to what was at hand. "Oh, darling, wasn't it good of Margaret? She stood up for you!", I ventured in my most cheerful tone, and indeed this seemed to work for the moment.

"Margaret was gorgeous! Margaret was gorgeous! Margaret was super! She looked me straight in the *les yeux* and said, 'I'm gonna call the police if dad locks that front door.'"

"Ah, that's wonderful of Margaret to have done that!"

"Wonderful of Margaret, I know." David choked into tears again. "Yes, yes, I'm grateful, I'm grateful", he whispered, and suddenly smiled. "I'm jovial or joyful, *joyeux, parce que* Margaret stood up for me that night wonderfully. So anyway it was a *shamus* really. So that's how someone gets damaged and the father was all hung up and I was doomed and I was doomed."

By that stage I must have looked a teary mess, so David decided to reassure me. "But then it all settled. We both dressed and caught a cab to the Capitol Theatre."

"And you played well anyhow." I was doing my damnedest to stay cheerful.

"And I still *won* anyhow. After all that! Imagine that!"

"Still won!?" Given the circumstances, I was trying hard to imagine it, aided by David's roaring laughter at the bleak hilarity of it all. "What a star! What an unbelievable star you are!", I said and held him close. But as the final tones of his laughter died down, I became aware that he was also uncontrollably weeping.·

"I know", he whispered and wept.

Tears come to David quite easily and just as easily vanish. In a few moments he was happily sniffling and smiling. "Never mind, I likes to . . . I loves this to run!", he exclaimed, pointing to his eyes, "'cause I think then you smiles better! You smiles better when this runs!"

David's mood following "the night of the tragedy" was not laughter and tears, however. It was just pain. Though he had won the State final, he was not selected for the national final, a blow on top of a blow. The stress of that night further fractured David's already fragile mental condition, and a new symptom appeared: "the hook".

"I didn't even have an adolescence, so I missed out. I'm

still trying to catch up, I've got a lot of catching up to do!",
David would quip occasionally, to explain his juvenile tendencies, and laugh. But sometimes his perception of his own emotional level would be quite serious: "I've stayed on the hook at
a fifteen-year-old level. That was the pinpoint of the damage,
that's when the hook got into me."

"What is 'the hook', David?"

"Well, it's a soreness, it's a sort of soreness in the *les yeux*.
I could feel it myself. Somehow it seems that the damage got in
my *les yeux* then." David said, lightly touching the outer corner
of his left eyelid with his left hand, a gesture which, over the
years, has become his 'trademark', with a multitude of publicity
photos depicting him in the act of gently prodding his *dommage*.

"I wasn't actually depressed when I had that though!", he
continued. "That was the funny thing. When I had that, I was
really quite relaxed, except that I couldn't hear the piano
playing."

"Why couldn't you hear the piano playing?"

"'Cause it was sore, that's why. Everything was focused on
this", David said as he touched his eye. "It was a sort of
dommage. There was a little point there. It wasn't actually *in* the
les yeux. It was just in that corner, just in that bit there. It just
happened."

David became pensive. "It takes a long time to happen and
it takes a long time to cure", he said with a bittersweet smile.
"It all got exacerbated, it was a whole constellation, like a com-
pendium. It was all sorts of licorice all-sorts, it was all sorts of
things. It wasn't exactly painful, it was sore in a sort of emotional
way."

Slightly in awe of his own condition, David elaborated: "It's a bit of a mystery! It's very unusual and rare! Of course, I spent all my life denying it. I would never acknowledge it, because I reckon I'd always pretend that it wasn't sore. It was easy 'cause, when you're a bit sore, you're actually less het up, less *agitato*."

Very unusual and rare indeed. By the age of fifteen, David's heart could no longer ache and so his mind transferred all the anguish into a little point of pain in the corner of his eyelid. His shutting off from the world, surrounding himself with the 'fog' and focusing solely on the 'soreness' of the *dommage* in his *les yeux* prevented him from any further emotional pain, and, consequently, any further emotional development. On the 'hook' he was caught like a fish, trapped in the age of fifteen.

The little point of pain came and went. However, when David was about eighteen and a half, it lodged itself permanently and made him acutely aware of its existence every waking minute. By dubbing it "*dommage*", which in French means 'pity', but using it as synonymous with the English word 'damage', David simultaneously defined and commented upon his own illness.

However, while still fifteen, David worked hard at pretending that nothing was wrong and continued to play the piano. For as long as his playing was great, it seemed that nothing else would matter to anyone. And his calculations proved right, because even though his playing dramatically decreased in quality immediately after the ABC competition – even staunch supporter James Penberthy noted this in a review of David's performance of Ravel's Concerto in July '62 – it was generally believed that he needed better guidance from a music teacher.

At a reception for a visiting music celebrity at the ABC studios, David was introduced to Madame Alice Carrard who, according to David, "Just like Mae West, said, 'Come up and see me sometime.' " As at the time Madame Alice was fifty years David's senior, he appreciated her sense of play and gladly took her up on her offer. Peter did not object, no doubt feeling quite honoured.

Hungarian by birth and a former student of Béla Bartók's at the Liszt Music Academy in Budapest, Madame Alice had long been one of the great musical assets of Perth, and for David she was going to fulfil his long-held dream of learning the secrets of Rakhmaninov's Third Concerto. As well as that, with Madame Alice's help, David would add Beethoven's *Waldstein* Sonata, Liszt's B minor Sonata and Mussorgsky's *Pictures at an Exhibition*, and prepare his programme for the Licentiate of Music diploma, the final official examination. This massive expansion of repertoire and an introduction to many new ideas and techniques required a year's break from performances and competitions, and it was not till June 1964 that David would again perform a serious piece of music in public.

Life was quite pleasant for David. Protected by the complex structure of his own mind's making, he felt at peace with the world, except that he was "Deaf, of course. Dead and deaf. I had some singing mudcake or something", he once told me as he put his hands over his ears.

When David resurfaced in the public eye, it was with a spectacular performance of the first movement of his beloved

'Rak 3' at the ABC Concerto Competition. This huge piece, so demanding for a seventeen-year-old, simply flowed from him. He played as one possessed and, though he might have thought himself "deaf", he heard every note and had a sense of achievement he had not experienced before. A win was assured and he was then chosen to play in the grand final. Sally Trethowan, a Perth music critic, wrote, "Under his talented hands this work exploded in a display of aural pyrotechnics that brought long and enthusiastic applause from the large audience." One judge, Frank Hutchens, said it was "A performance of magic, excitement, colour and continuity." In David's appraisal, it was an all-out "Triumph!"

But there was something even more unusual and special about that night. "Dad gave me a *potchnagoola*", David recalled. "That night, when I played the Rakhmaninov concerto so well and exploded in a display of fiery pyrotechnics, father gave me a kiss. So it wasn't all tragic. I think it was the only time he ever gave me a *potchnagoola*. It was very rare, very rare. So you have to treasure these rare times." It would seem that at least some rays of happiness managed to sneak through the 'fog'.

Three weeks later, on 4 July, David was in Melbourne rehearsing with the Victorian Symphony Orchestra. After the rehearsal, Henry Krips, the conductor, said, "Play like that tonight, David, and you could easily be the winner." But it was not to be. "I wasn't ready", David recalled. "It was a disaster. Triumph turned into tragedy. When Would-if-I-could won, I said to him, 'It's a blood sport.' ... Of course, there was no disgrace to lose to the best."

Officially, it was nothing like a "disaster". David played

remarkably well, losing by only half a point to Roger Woodward, whom David has always cheekily and affectionately nicknamed "Would-if-I-could". Under the headline "Questions Awards", Melbourne music critic Adrian Rawlins, writing in the *Age*, found the placings by adjudicator André Cluytens to be "dubious", commenting that giving the first prize to Woodward for "a fiercely technical performance of Prokofiev's Concerto No. 3" was "ill-advised: the work is showy and pleasing but by no means a test of mature musicianship".

Whereas, Rawlins found that David had played "the far more complex and demanding Rachmaninoff D Minor Concerto with great sensitivity and insight" and the Rakhmaninov being "a more difficult work, making greater demands on understanding and requiring just as much facility – though of a less demonstrative sort – it would seem more appropriate to have given Helfgott the prize." However, with only a half-point difference, Cluytens' decision was clearly not flippantly made, and Woodward has rightly gone on to a celebrated career.

For David, a distress quite unconnected with the actual quality of his playing loomed so large that, as far as he was concerned, it must have affected his performance, and consequently resulted in the loss. On this occasion he had come to Melbourne with Rachel, who went shopping with her mother and left David standing in the street outside, where he froze in the blistering July wind, which in winter sweeps through the city as if straight from the Antarctic. "Imagine, before the performance!", he would say, to this day quite astonished at his mother's 'negligence'. He would usually add that "Father would never allow that. Father would have seen that I was resting and

I would have had my *mangare*. I would have had my lamb-loin chops, and I would have been looked after." It took me years before I felt I could point out to him that this was not necessarily the case.

David's uncle, Johnny Granek, with whom they were staying in Melbourne, loved his nephew dearly and David remembers that, after the loss, "Johnno was nice to me. He took me to a milk bar and he solaced me and said, 'Come to Melbourne and we'll look after you. I'll look after you. Don't you worry.'" What Johnny offered to David was to come and live with him and his wife, and be supported by them, while studying at the Melbourne Conservatorium of Music with the great Russian teacher, Jasha Spivakovsky.

When David arrived back in Perth and relayed Johnny's offer to Peter, Peter's response was not a surprise. "Father was quite indignant", David recalled. "'The nerve! The chutzpah!', he said. Father said all mean things about the relatives in Melbourne, because they've got the money and he hasn't, and he's jealous." More "rich Jews" were trying to steal his son. Would it ever stop? And Peter had done nothing to deserve this, but had given David all that he possibly could.

However, the forces at play were against him, and it was not long before David would finally break free.

c h a p t e r   1 3

Mentors

The first thing David did after his "tragedy" in Melbourne was to quit school, without completing his Leaving Certificate. Ostensibly it was done so that he could concentrate fully on his music, which he did, often starting his practice before dawn and continuing for most of his waking hours. He would also occasionally attend music lectures at the University of Western Australia, by special permission of Professor Frank Callaway and other professors who believed in his talent.

"There was a different reason why I stayed home from school, of course", David finally revealed, after years of going along with his family's version of how it was all for the sake of music. "It was 'cause I was a bit sore."

Though he was coping less and less with the world not in the immediate vicinity of his piano, he kept up appearances to the contrary and continued to give recitals. He also passed his Licentiate of Music, but found his marks too low for his liking. "Disgraceful!", he commented to Professor Callaway on his Licentiate score, in a letter a year later. He failed to mention that his score was again the highest that year, and that he had again won a prize.

As there was still some talk about David going on to tertiary musical study, he was advised to return to school to get his Leaving Certificate. He listened to the advice and entered Leederville Technical College in February '65. Somewhere, somehow, he also found the courage to enter the ABC Concerto Competition again in May. When I pointed out to him that it was rather brave of him to do so, considering all that had happened, David was surprised and completely failed to see the logic behind my suggestion. "Why not? I had to keep trying, keep trying. The point was, if you win you can't enter again. And if you get to the grand final, you can keep entering, and you can keep trying! Isn't it wonderful?! And you get the chance to play with the orchestra again! And poor old Would-if-I-could had to go over to Poland, and take them all by storm and set the world on fire at Carnegie Hall. The point was I got to the grand final anyhow. If you don't win it doesn't matter; like the Olympic Games, it's all about trying and struggle."

In a letter to Professor Callaway at the time, David also wrote: "Most of my musical development is intimately connected with the Concerto Competition; this gave me a great deal of opportunities which otherwise I would have missed."

The 'Rak 3' might have been 'triumph turned into tragedy' the previous year, but David's innate sense of enthusiasm for life – damaged or not damaged, "deaf" or not "deaf" – was not going to stop him from attempting to turn the tragedy back into triumph. He did not know it yet, but the oscillation between these two, and the "trying" and "struggle", would occupy the next twenty years of his life, and he would need every ounce of that unyielding Helfgott optimism.

For the moment, though, the first movement of Chaikovsky's grand Concerto No. 1 was on the agenda. David easily won the State final, and again was selected for the national final. Two days after the State final, on 30 May 1965, James Penberthy, who was genuinely concerned for David, wrote an article in the *Sunday Times* with a thinly veiled message to all parties interested in the future of David Helfgott.

Penberthy opened his piece in a commanding tone from which he did not refrain: "It is now time that Perth's inner musical circles stopped conjecture about the merit of young pianist David Helfgott. From the time he ambled on to the stage in 1960 to play Ravel, until Friday night's Tchaikovsky at the 1965 Concerto and Vocal Finals, I have believed in his rare talent. Young Helfgott is, and always was, a pianist."

Penberthy further commented that David's "performance of the Tchaikovsky Concerto – first movement – was of concert pianist standard. He made more mistakes than usual, but his interpretation, spirit and command would have been acceptable from a visiting celebrity."

Penberthy concluded: "What is Helfgott's future? He seems to be in good hands. Let his present mentors decide. One thing is certain, it should not be difficult to find assistance if it ever be needed. All the world seems to love a pianist and this one has natural public appeal."

Penberthy's message was heard and heeded. The "present mentors", including Frank Callaway, agreed that it was time to ask themselves what indeed was "Helfgott's future" if he did not go to study overseas. As David was now eighteen, the 'mentors' felt he was capable of contributing to the discussions about his own career. Besides which, "Something had to be done", David pointed out to me. Switching into a dialogue with himself, he continued, "'Cause they thought you were really good pianist, you deserve, so richly deserve, to get the finest tuition, and have a wonderful professor and improve."

Thus it was decided that an application should be made to the Music Council of Western Australia for a Bursary towards David's expenses for studying overseas. David applied and was almost instantly granted the Bursary of £500 "towards living expenses and tuition fees in a course of studies at an Institution overseas approved by the Council" for one year. The conditions of the Bursary also stated that "consideration will be given to a renewal of the Bursary for a further year or years" subject to the "Council receiving satisfactory reports from the Authorities of the Institution" on David's progress during his first year of study.

The founding chairman of the Music Council just happened to be Professor Callaway, who had, by that time, been succeeded by a close colleague of his, Professor Fred Alexander. In consultation with David – "It was a partial compromise, it was sort of a bit of this, a bit of that. We just talked" – the professors decided that the best "institution" for the boy was the Royal College of Music in London.

"It was my idea, father was opposed", David recalled, but then admitted that "Frankie-boy helped with it. I think it might have been Frankie-boy's application, but of course I agreed, I more or less accepted." For David, there were no doubts about the rightness of the plan, and for the rest of his life he would be utterly grateful to "Frankie-boy", of whom he invariably speaks with the highest esteem and much love.

All these great schemes were being initiated around the same time as the national final of the ABC Concerto Competition, which David still had to attend. He flew to Adelaide to rehearse the 'Chaik' with the South Australian Symphony Orchestra. John Hopkins, the conductor, was also one of the adjudicators of that final, and, though he thought much of David's talent and skill, David did not win.

This time, David took the responsibility for the loss entirely upon himself. "I was too fast, so I did myself in by my breaking the tempo", he acknowledged. "Breakneck tempo in Adelaide. And you shouldn't because you have to be *ensemble* with the orchestra, you can't run ahead. You gotta stay with the orchestra." However, with the prospect of going to London filling his imagination, he did not mind his loss too much this time. "When I got a chance to go to London, I felt privileged and I was very pleased, 'cause father was pressuring me beyond belief!", he explained.

David's agenda had changed significantly by that time, as the circumstances at home continued to deteriorate. Peter was demonstratively disapproving of any plans for David to go anywhere – more powerful folk meddling in his son's life – and was becoming increasingly 'hostile'. Even Margaret had "changed and didn't stand up for me", remembered David, mystified to this day by the reason for her altered attitude. Losing the love and protection of his elder sister had driven an extra wedge between the already withdrawn David and his family.

There seemed to be little choice but to rely on the support of his 'mentors', who were not only securing for David the finances and admission to one of the most prestigious music institutions in the world, but were also going to arrange for him to study there with the highly esteemed Cyril Smith. "They thought that Smith was the right one for me, they thought he was a very good pianist. And Frankie-boy went to London 'specially!", David recalled with true joy at the memory.

During his trip to London in September '65, Professor Callaway held discussions with Keith Falkner, Director of the Royal College of Music, about the possibility of David's studying with Cyril Smith, and other issues pertaining to his admission to the college. David, it seems, had to take very little responsibility for anything connected with his future studies at that time. Which was just as well, as Peter, having never encouraged independence in his son – in fact, having always striven for quite the opposite – had produced a young man who wouldn't even have known where to begin to take care of himself in these, and most other, matters.

But David's 'mentors' at the university were not the only people in the world he had to rely on, as by that stage he had formed an extraordinary friendship with a very special woman.

When they met, Katharine Susannah Prichard was eighty-one years old and David had just turned eighteen, but they found in each other something that no one else in the world could provide for them.

David first saw the woman whom he has always called KSP "at the Anglo-Soviet thing. She was wearing this very great flouncy dress. The poor darling, she'd just been desperately ill." Having grown up in Perth's 'communist' world, David would occasionally perform at the various meetings. This time, "They wanted to send me to the Soviet Union, 'cause they were all determined that I should go overseas", recalled David. Apparently frequent 'attempts' at this were made, even, it seems, by those whom Peter trusted to know better.

KSP was just getting over a debilitating stroke and had come down to town from her home, Greenmount, in the hills behind Perth. The famous – or infamous, depending on who at that time was talking about her – author and social activist adored music, and David's performing magic instantly endeared him to her.

She had had a tumultuous life, filled with struggle and tragedy. By a bizarre twist of fate, several men who were important to her in her life committed suicide, including her father and her husband, Hugo Throssell, an Australian soldier who had been awarded the Victoria Cross for his acts of bravery in World War I.

A prolific writer, KSP cared deeply about social issues and passionately believed in the socialist cause. Troubled by the plight of the Aboriginal people, poverty and a multitude of hardships suffered by the common man, she was fervently anti-Fascist and in 1943 became a member of the Communist Central

Committee. Enduring denunciations of her work because of her widely known political beliefs, and persecution from various 'Red-menace'-fearing authorities, she continued to fight injustice and write. She also became the seventh Australian member of the World Council for Peace. Generous to a fault with any income she made from her writing, she lived in stark simplicity in a tiny, dilapidated cottage surrounded by nature, and it was in this house that David came to know and love her.

David remembers that at least one aspect of their friendship was greatly influenced by Peter's actions the very first time he and KSP met: "We went up to KSP and father said, 'If I had David's chance, I would've been the world's greatest. I would've done this and I would've done that. I would've been the world's best in this, and I would've been the world's best in that.' And KSP was listening, and perhaps she was impressed and that's why she then said to me, 'You must be very grateful to your poor father, because he sacrificed himself for you. He's kept you alive, be grateful.'" From that moment on, David was never to summon up the courage to contradict KSP's view of his father. For her, Peter Helfgott was that 'common man' who had to sacrifice himself in order to provide for his children.

Apart from that, David's friendship with KSP was one of the sweetest, most precious things that ever happened to him. Every Friday night, he would catch a train to Greenmount and spend the evening with her. It became a ritual which David refers to as "KSP's Kaddish".

"Everyone always let me go", David recalled, slightly bemused by the situation. "Funny thing, even Mrs Luber they used to grudge me, but they always let me go to KSP."

David paused and for a moment tried to analyse by what strange logic he was never prevented from seeing KSP, considering he was forbidden to visit Mrs Luber-Smith, the President of the Council of Jewish Women of Perth. After a moment, a cynical smile appeared in the corners of his mouth and he said, "You know what? All my mighty buddies always used to let me go to KSP because they didn't feel threatened. They all let me go to KSP."

It was just as well, because "KSP was wonderful!", David would often say. "She just accepted everything, just gentle, gentle, gentle and kind and quiet, and let me light up a cigarette. We used to read together. We used to have lovely talks at sunset about French writers like Gide, and there were these lovely roaring log fires, and there was a tame magpie called Caruso, isn't that wonderful?" David sighed with delight at the peaceful memories of those Friday evenings. "We used to read the Cantos from the *Divine Commedia*, tragi-comedia, and it was a bit of a tragedy in a way, 'cause I was a bit sore there." David pointed to his *dommage* and chuckled at his own pun.

But mainly David would play to KSP, for hours. "She loved Chopin", David would often comment. "I used to play that a lot. She thought my Chopin playing was very good. I played the *Appassionata* too. It reminded her of Hugo, the hero of the First World War. He was like a songbird ... he suicided while she was in the Soviet Union. She said she'd never come to terms with it, she never understood it, but she just kept writing anyhow, just very lucky to survive at all."

However, KSP would have her moments of sadness and this was when she found not only David's music, but his soothing nature, of great comfort: "KSP'd say, 'Oh, I never look in the mirror any more. It happens to all of us', and I'd say, 'Oh, don't be silly KSP, don't be silly.'"

"She said I was a pretty young thing", recalled David and squirmed with delighted embarrassment at the memory. "She liked my gentleness, my kindness, my niceness. I was nice in those days. Once she came to me and she gave me *potchnagoola* on the lips and she started talking about love, just once. And she said I meant the world to her, I meant the world to KSP. I think she kind of fancied me, in a lovely way, in a sort of lovely, loving way, and I'm very proud of that." David sighed and, feeling gratitude for the friendship and sadness for its fleeting existence, pondered aloud, "Was that one of the best things in my life, in a way? Great privilege, it's a huge privilege."

Often on those Friday nights, David would become so involved in his conversations with KSP that they would both lose track of time, and David would miss the last train home. Then, he would leave Greenmount and in the middle of the night run all of the 20 kilometres home. "Well, it was good exercise, anyway" was his way of justifying this.

However, when telling me about KSP on another occasion, David could perceive the inconvenience of the situation and said, "I should've stayed the night, shouldn't I? But KSP said I had to go back to dad." Then, perhaps thinking that KSP was not coming out of this reasoning as entirely sensitive, he added, "'Course she had no idea what was going on at home, no idea that I was sore and that daddy was being all very very snitchy. I never told her. I pretended with KSP, but I should've talked. KSP said, 'Be grateful to your father' and I just accepted what she said. I didn't want to talk about it in those days. I didn't want to burden KSP. Why would I want to worry KSP? So she had no idea." But this triggered another memory and David's eyes opened wide with disbelief: "And you should've heard the father's language about KSP! He said, 'She lives in a hovel', and all sort of things ... My father's funny. I thought the house was quite nice."

Though the ritual of "KSP's Kaddish" lasted only about a year, his visits to Greenmount provided David with a much-needed escape, and this was also one of the reasons why he would not have wanted to bring his problems into KSP's home. Instead, he always came away from her with renewed strength and courage.

David uses one of his most special words, *potchnagoola*, both in memory of and in tribute to KSP. Meaning 'a kiss' or 'kiss me', it is an amalgam of three titles of Prichard's collections of short stories, which in order of publication date are: *Kiss on the Lips and other Stories, Potch and Colour* and *N'Goola*. "I constructed out of that a sort of symphony, a synthesis", David said.

Away!

"I was accepted at college-knowledge! Everyone else had to present a sort of a recording, but I didn't have to 'cause I was in a privileged position. Frankie-boy got me into there! They accepted me without hearing me!", David once told me about the incredible circumstances of his acceptance into the Royal College of Music. After a pause, he could not let the opportunity slip by without another pun about his 'fog'. "It was lucky in a way, 'cause I couldn't hear anyhow", he added and burst out laughing.

On 21 December 1965, Professor Callaway had received the current college prospectus and admission form, and an accompanying letter in which Mr Stainer, the Registrar, wrote: "We will certainly accept David Helfgott on your recommendation and I will correspond with him directly when the application form comes back. There is no need for a tape to be sent. It should be possible for us to allocate him to Mr. Cyril Smith."

However, there were two possible hitches to the plan: the funds provided by the Bursary were insufficient to pay for David's travel and day-to-day living expenses and, as he was not yet twenty-one, a parent's or guardian's signature was needed on his application form. Professor Callaway wasted no time, and immediately arranged for a meeting with Peter the very next day.

"The professors called father to the university and me as well", explained David. "And Frankie-boy pressured father. All the professors pressured father too. They all said to father, 'You gotta accept. Let David go, 'cause David wants to go. You gotta sign your name to this, so that David can go.' They asked him to sign his name, that's all they did, just sign the name. And poor old father didn't say anything, he just accepted. He accepted very grudgingly. I remember dad writing his name down at the meeting."

"And how did your father feel about all these men pressuring him and telling him what to do with his son?", I asked.

But David ignored my question: "Well, I reckon father was in the wrong anyhow and he wouldn't talk."

On the way home from the meeting, David feared that, even though Peter had signed the forms, he would not, in the end, let him go to London. So David alternated between expressing profuse gratitude to his father and pleading with him to be allowed to go.

"I tried to talk to father, I talked and talked to father, but father was all sooky and sulky and he wouldn't talk", David remembered. "Of course I was happy that daddy accepted. Daddy accepted me completely, yes. Of course I was happy 'cause I wanted to go to London and I was grateful to the professors." Even though David still did not believe he would be allowed to go, his seeking of Peter's approval was so desperate that he equated a signature on a piece of paper with a show of real affection.

David kept pleading and Peter kept saying no. The Christmas period of 1965 continued to be a tense time in the Helfgott household. After literally being forced to 'sign his son away', Peter's mood darkened and he became even more resistant.

The new year brought further emotional tension and strain when Rachel's father, Mordecai, feeling that he was coming to the end of his life, decided to visit his daughter in Perth, accompanied by Johnny. The family differences between Peter and Mordecai, which were as old as they were complex, inevitably surfaced. But among the stories that David remembers, there is one he finds particularly amusing: "Father said that Djadja, grandfather Mordecai, took a hundred pounds from dad – just the same amount of money that dad took from me. That's why it's so fortuitous." David chuckled and continued: "And then he paid it back in dribs and drabs and father never forgave that, and always made a big point about how good he was to give him the hundred pounds and always held a grudge against him because of the way he paid it back."

Peter was not thrilled with having to welcome his father-in-law, but Mordecai had his own problems with the situation.

"Djadja and Johnno were sorry for poor Rachel, 'cause they could see the father was being a bit mean", remembered David. Indeed, Mordecai could hardly believe the poverty in which his daughter and grandchildren lived, but could do little about it as Peter would not, of course, accept charity. Mordecai left with a heavy heart, determined to do something for David whenever an opportunity arose.

Peter was in for more 'meddling' in his family's life when, at the end of January, a group of Jewish women, including Mrs Luber-Smith, turned up on his doorstep to propose a charity concert for David to help top up the money from the Bursary. This visit was to contribute to Peter's frame of mind in much the same way as Alec Breckler's news of a "nice Jewish family" did back in 1961. Peter's answer to Mrs Luber-Smith was not just an outright "No"; it was delivered in such a way as to discourage her from any further communication with Peter.

David remembers that, in the days following her visit, "Mrs Luber used to wait in the car until dad went out – she was scared to death of the father – and then, very cunning, she would come rushing into the house quick, and talk to me about taking me to London. But of course it was a very explosive situation, 'cause evictions can end fatally and I was very lucky to be alive."

"Evictions? Who got evicted?", I asked, puzzled.

"Well, I did of course! 'Cause dad threw me out. It was a hell of a night, a hate night. Father got all sort of fierce, and aggressive, scream and scream and scream ... and scream and scream and scream, and he said, 'Don't go to London, 'cause you'll forget things.' He said he had contacts all over the world and everything and he could arrange it all himself. But the father was lying. Father didn't even have a single contact in Perth.

"Father said 'Don't go' and I never argued", continued David in a calm tone. "I never argued with anyone in my life. I'm just too scared to argue with anyone. I'm a mouse. I just smiled. I just accepted. You see, the point was the father was so hostile, so I thought, 'Well I have nothing to lose anyhow.' I went to London as soon as I could, really, 'cause what did you have to lose?"

David dutifully packed a little suitcase and left his father's house, to which he would not return for years. Accompanied by his brother Les, whom David has dubbed "Barmy-on-the-army", and whose love and support he has always treasured, he went to a phone box and called the only person he thought might take him in at the time: Mrs Luber-Smith.

Though Mrs Luber-Smith was not overjoyed at the prospect, she kindly agreed for David to come and stay with her and her husband. David recalled she "kept saying to me, 'Are you sure your father won't change his mind? Are you sure your father won't take you back?' But I didn't have much option at all really."

Mrs Luber-Smith must have soon realised that she could do much more for David's future if he remained with her, so she began to organise the practical side of his trip to London. With the help of the Council of Jewish Women, she was able to arrange her proposed farewell recital for him.

David also appealed to Djadja Mordecai and Uncle Johnny. "I wrote this letter to the relatives in Melbourne, after dad threw me out," recalled David, "telling them all about the father and Margaret. This woeful, woeful letter sort of thing and they supported me anyhow. The relatives in Melbourne gave a lot of money, and everything."

As well as the fund-raising, Mrs Luber-Smith also found it was necessary to teach David some manners and etiquette. She was horrified when she discovered that he had no idea how to use a knife and fork. "I had to start using knife and fork, because Mrs Luber insisted on it", recalled David. "It's more civilised, I think. They had to get me ready for London", he explained, and his words in the sleep-out at Chris's about Mrs Luber-Smith's getting him ready for London suddenly made sense.

For the next three months, David continued to practise – both his piano playing and his table manners – and visit KSP, of whom Mrs Luber-Smith was not fond. "Mrs Luber thought she was a terrible, terrible communist," recalled David, "'cause communism in those days was considered very unvegetarian."

To everyone around him, David seemed to be a frenetic, brilliant and slightly eccentric young man, who had a few problems with a particularly strict parent. In truth, he was very unwell, and not at all happy with his playing.

However, the farewell recital had been arranged, and an article promoting it and David was published in the Jewish journal, *The Maccabean*. On 17 May, in the Government House Ballroom, in the presence of His Excellency the Governor Sir Douglas Kendrew, and Lady Kendrew, David played a mammoth programme: Beethoven's *Appassionata*, five Chopin études, Liszt's *Dante Sonata* and Mussorgsky's *Pictures at an Exhibition*. Even though David was dissatisfied with the standard of his playing, the critics, including James Penberthy, admired his performance. They did complain, though, that the ball-room's piano had the tonal qualities of a "bathtub".

The recital raised £400 and Mrs Luber-Smith arranged for an additional sum from the Phineas Seeligson Trust, to which Mordecai had anonymously donated some money for David, not wishing Peter to know that he had helped his grandson.

None of David's family attended the recital, but KSP made a rare trip down from Greenmount. She also gave David a gift of "these wonderful gloves", which he has never forgotten. "'Cause she said London is gonna be very very cold, and you gotta have these wonderful fur-lined, very costly gloves."

David was now all set and the money from the Seeligson Trust made it possible for Mrs Luber-Smith to also buy him a complete new wardrobe, suitable for any student at the Royal College. However, David's planned departure by ship was delayed by a seamen's strike, and for a while it looked as if he might have to fly to London to get there in time for the academic year's Christmas term.

The strike finished just in time, and on 14 August David was on the wharf about to board the P&O *Himalaya*. He remembers that "Madame Alice came and she contributed a metronome and Mrs Luber came and I said bye-bye to Mrs Luber with lots of kisses and cuddles."

Not a single member of David's family came to say *bon voyage*, as he hadn't even told them that he was leaving.

Revelations

People were pouring into the dressing room at the Octagon Theatre after the comeback concert, and David was overjoyed at all the congratulations and hugs. The tiny figure of Madame Alice Carrard, who had been in the audience, emerged from the crowd and David quickly enfolded her in his arms. There were tears in her eyes, and the sight of this grand old lady of music sharing her pupil's courageous return was a very emotional moment for me.

A few minutes later, however, the teacher in Madame Alice surfaced and she told David that, though his *Pictures* had been wonderful, his Chopin was not good enough. She then turned to me and said, "Bring him to me and I will help him." Though eighty-seven years old at the time, she still had plenty of energy, and a determination to ensure that her favourite student displayed nothing but the very best of his talent to the world.

A month or so earlier, David had announced that he wanted to see "Madame" and he was going to give her a call. This was the first time I had heard of Madame Alice and, after David explained who she was, he added, "She's always been there for me, always, always." When he then spoke with her on the phone in a relaxed and happy manner, I realised how close they were and how much David trusted her. He asked her if we could come and see her, and a couple of weeks later we went to her home, where she had organised a soirée.

Arriving at Madame Alice's was like stepping into a European home: embroidered curtains, Hungarian mats on the tables, Persian rugs on the floor, and music and books everywhere. Music permeated the whole house. A portrait of Béla Bartók hung above the Musica piano, which had a Steinway as its companion. When I queried her about Bartók, she said that she remembered him as a stern man with sad eyes, so absorbed in his compositions that his students were merely peripheral. His music, she told me, had always stayed close to her heart.

Madame Alice was one of the few people in my first challenging months with David who accepted me unconditionally. She told me that she believed David to be a special human being for whom she cared very much, and thought that things could only improve for him now that someone was looking after "my David" full-time.

In the dressing room of the Octagon Theatre after David's comeback concert, Madame Alice's words were a great support to me, and I thanked her for her kind offer.

After leaving the Octagon, a group of David's friends and supporters proceeded to a party to celebrate his comeback. While the champagne was flowing and everyone was feeling rather elated, Chris asked Mike Parry if he would be interested in taking over David's management, as Chris felt he had neither the time nor the experience to do justice to David's evolving career prospects. Over the next few days the idea was endorsed by David, and Mike gladly accepted.

Right from the outset, Mike was determined to present David as a serious concert artist. "David's dignity deserves to be respected and he ought to be treated with the same deference as any other artist", he assured me. Mike was acutely aware that it would have been all too easy to present David as an 'act', given his eccentric demeanour. Thus, every recital he arranged for David was a formal occasion, with no deviation from what he believed to be the standards of 'normal concert practice'. In the following years, he would proceed to impose this condition on other presenters as well.

Though it was very late when we arrived back at our cottage after the party, David went straight to the piano. It is one of his little routines to immediately start practising anything he has been unhappy with during a performance. For me, this had been David's first proper concert, and his attitude amazed me. However, I did understand that there was no time for David to rest on his laurels, as he did, in fact, have only four and a half weeks to refine Rakhmaninov's Concerto

No. 1 for a recording with the ABC, and six weeks in which to polish Rakhmaninov's Concerto No. 2 for a performance with the Nedlands Symphony Orchestra.

The recording for the ABC had been arranged by Gerald Krug, the musical director of the West Australian Opera and Arts Orchestra. A frequent visitor to Riccardo's, Gerald had long admired David and often compared him stylistically with Svyatoslav Richter. Some months earlier, he had commented in an article in the *West Australian* that David was "a genius musical talent. His technique is equal to the greatest in the world." In the same article, he pointed out that it was "a tragedy that a man like David with world-class talent is not able to give concerts", and promised to donate his time to conduct any orchestra David played with. Gerald followed through on that promise when he insisted to the ABC that David was the perfect choice of soloist for their recording of Rakhmaninov's No. 1 with the West Australian Symphony Orchestra, which he was conducting for the occasion.

For David, the offer came through at fairly short notice. It was to be his first full concerto performance for recording in many years and, though he knew the No. 1 well, he had never performed it before. He had also never performed the No. 2, which Mike Parry had organised for him to play.

In the next few weeks David almost never left the piano, except to go to Riccardo's and to swim. One day when I heard him doing the same passage for well over an hour, I asked him if he didn't get tired of playing it. He looked astonished at the naivety of my question and said, "But, darling, I have to get it right." I was a slow learner, but I had been rather thrown in at the deep end. It also occurred to me that, even though he had been stuck "on a hook at a fifteen-year-old level", David was still a mature and dedicated professional.

Madame Alice's offer to give some guidance to David was a timely one, and I took David for lessons with her on Rakhmaninov's Second Concerto. They were on familiar ground with the 'Rak', as Madame Alice was the one who had originally introduced David to this piece. He still had his old score and must have played it a lot as it was in a very battered state, as indeed was most of his music. Madame Alice was a teacher of great strength and insight, and she did not allow David to get away with any careless notes or phrasing. Gerald Krug had talked with me at Riccardo's about David's phrasing needing greater attention and about the need to "hold the line more". Madame Alice worked on these aspects with David.

During the lesson I sat with them, fascinated by it all. When my children were little, I took them to music lessons to learn piano and violin, never intending for them to learn anything more than some musical appreciation. Now, being close to a music teacher and student of this calibre, I found the attention to minute details quite enlightening. Madame Alice was happy with David's interpretation of the work; it was the 'tidying-up' that absorbed their time. I then realised how important it was for David to have the guiding hand of discipline, and Madame Alice was supplying precisely that.

Many years had passed since he last had regular lessons with Madame Alice, and I wondered how he would react to the process. Looking at them, I was shown the answer. Teacher and pupil were locked into the music, extraneous things of no interest to them as they dedicated themselves entirely to Rakhmaninov. It also dawned on me that, quite apart from David's natural passion for the piano, there was also an enormous amount of practice required of a professional concert pianist to get the work up to standard. I gained a new perception of David's complete dedication and his professional needs. Over the next seven years, David would return for many more lessons with Madame Alice.

The recording of the 'Rak 1' with Krug and the WA Symphony Orchestra took place in the ABC's Basil Kirke Studio in Perth on 11 July. Many of the musicians knew David, but at the end of the recording one of the double-bass players, who was from overseas, said that he had not heard playing like that in years and asked why on earth he hadn't come across David before. Many in the orchestra were in tears.

Everyone involved in the recording thought it went very well and it received coverage in the press, but disappointment was to follow. The ABC inexplicably chose not to air it, despite great public interest. This saddened David, but he had little time to stew over it. Not only did he have another concert to play at the end of the month, but a television program, 'The Willesee Show', had decided to do a feature story on him in the meantime.

The 'Willesee Show' brought Kirsty Cockburn into our lives. She was a highly motivated television journalist with thorough research skills and tenacity. We spent many hours with her talking about our lives and the changes that had occurred. She was intrigued by David's swimming and preoccupation with water, and seemed to have genuine respect for his talent. Kirsty and her partner, George Negus, one of the leading political journalists in Australia, became firm friends of ours, and many years later introduced us to the place David and I now call home.

The filming for the television show was done over several days and it was fascinating to watch David's love affair with the camera. He was a true performer, and relished every moment the lens was on him: no shyness or reticence, just complete co-operation. This was a side of David I had not experienced before and I was greatly relieved to see that the media would not be a problem for him. But I also chuckled at his vanity. The same man who but two months ago was constantly trying to hide his head in a stoop, aided by a mask of cigarette smoke, was now preening and flirting with the camera.

The final shoot for the show was done during his performance of the Rakhmaninov No. 2 in Winthrop Hall at the University of Western Australia. A huge crowd turned up for this, David's first concerto recital in over a decade. The audience consisted of not only Perth's concert regulars, but also many people who had discovered classical music and David's magic at Riccardo's and were now keen to see him in a concert-hall setting.

Having survived the nail-biting comeback concert, my mind was now filled with new apprehension. Playing with an orchestra is always more of a challenge for a soloist than playing alone. When by himself on the stage, David could afford to be a bit 'creative' with tempo, mood and dynamics; here he could not afford to be the least bit wayward. He was so thrilled at the chance to play with an orchestra again that no pre-concert nerves could break through his happiness. Something in my face must have revealed my anxiety, because David hugged me shortly before going on stage and said, "No worries! 'Cause when I get on that stage and see the audience I feel really alive. Just relax, just relax." Easy for him to say!

This time I was in the audience during the performance and Chris sat next to David on stage, turning the dog-eared pages of the score to which David hardly referred. Chris found sitting in such proximity to David during a performance to be an extremely powerful experience, one which he said he would remember all his life. The power of David's passion radiated from his body and enveloped whoever was nearby. I have often since had the experience of sitting next to David during a performance myself, and find it to be simply electrifying.

Rakhmaninov's Concerto No. 2 is the most romantic and best loved of all his concertos and the response from the audience was tremendous. After rising to their feet and applauding David at the end of the performance, they sat down as one, and for a few moments Winthrop Hall was filled with complete silence. Music critic Jan Shepherd, in the following month's issue of *Music Maker*, suggested that the strange silence was the audience's search "for another way of showing their tribute". Backstage, David was again feeling "Terrific!" He hugged me and said, "See, darling, when I saw the audience I felt like a leaping lion! A leaping lion!" I confess it was heartwarming to note the shift in his zoological metaphors.

After the concert there was another party. David, of course, went straight to the piano, where he proceeded to play duets with Bill, an American friend he had met at Riccardo's. There were many people there, including many friends from Riccardo's, and after supper David was in a great mood, running around the room and chatting with everyone.

I remember someone had put on a recording of Brahms's B flat Piano Concerto. As people gathered to listen, David was doing his usual round of hugging everyone and telling them they were "the best". In gatherings of friends, he could not bear to leave anyone out of his field of affection; as he could never stop himself from hugging or kissing one person, he then had to do this to everyone else in the room.

"You're the best. You're the best", David said as he continued his journey from embrace to embrace. But suddenly he stopped. As if some great new revelation had just dawned on him, he looked at the person he was hugging, then he looked at me, and after a moment he said, "You are the best, but Gillian is extra-special." After another quick grin in my direction, he proceeded with his "You're the best" routine.

I could hardly believe it: for the first time David had shown he could differentiate between his feelings for me and those for all the other people in the room. It was an enormous breakthrough.

Over the preceding couple of months, he had continually asked me to marry him. Even though I felt that it was right for us to be together, it had always seemed better to hold off any marriage plans. This, however, was a major confirmation for me that David's proposals were genuine, and that he was fully conscious of his feelings for me.

After that night, I seriously started to consider the possibility of marriage. I was slightly amazed at my own thoughts, as marriage had not been on my agenda. I did not think it necessary, at my stage of life, to take that step and wondered why I was suddenly seeing it as a wonderful idea. I had not the slightest doubt that my love for David was all-abiding, and that marriage was not needed to give our life together any more love and affection than we already had – it was not really possible, anyway. So why was I now seriously considering his marriage proposals?

I then realised that I really wanted to be his wife, that I would be very proud to be 'Mrs David Helfgott'. It was not very 'feminist' of me, I know, but announcing to the whole world that I had given up my name for David's was going to signify something quite different in our situation. I was a mature woman and not just thoughtlessly following tradition: I was making a determined choice.

It was obvious that not everyone in the world could understand or accept David, and more understanding and acceptance were always desirable. By marrying David, I would not only confirm his trust in my commitment to him, not only make a gesture of validating him as an individual wholly accepted and loved by at least one person on the planet, but go further and declare that I saw David as so special and important that I was happy to give up my own name for his.

I'm still not quite sure, though, exactly what it revealed about our society when my intuition proved to be correct. After our marriage, the way in which people in general perceived David became significantly more positive.

Made in Hell

David was totally *joyeux* about my decision to marry him; he had been mentioning the subject almost daily for months, and now he was going to have his wish come true. We must have informed Kirsty about it in a phone conversation after her shoot, because, when the segment about David screened on the 'Willesee Show' in late July, the program's presenter, Mike Willesee, announced on national television that he had just received news about our wedding plans, and added that David was promising to invite all the Riccardo's patrons.

I had spoken to Chris about our decision and he said he too now believed that David seemed sure of his love and commitment to me, and he agreed to be best man. When I told my friend Barbara Brackley, she immediately said, "Come and have it at our home", and David and I took her up on her generous offer.

But first, the perfect date had to be found for the occasion, so I did many astrology charts to find the best aspects, not only for the day but also for the exact time for the wedding ceremony. I came up with 11.57 am on 26 August.

As we thought about who to invite, David began to mention people who had not been part of any story he had told previously. He usually began with "Oh, darling, 'course there's also . . ." and out would come a nickname, some strange personal title of David's own construction, based solely on private references, word games and puns. This would be followed by many questions from me, and finally a person and a story would emerge, bringing with them various associated new characters. I was rather shocked by some of the stories and saddened by others, but grateful to discover that David had even more friends who had cared for him over this last, darkest decade of his life than I had ever suspected.

The cast of characters mainly emerged from the WA Opera Company, with whom David had worked as repetiteur in the early '70s. Among them were the soprano Elaine Flint and "George", who turned out to be Georg Tintner, the former musical director of the opera company.

Though I was unable to meet Georg at the time – he had moved to Queensland to become musical director of the Queensland Theatre Orchestra – I joined in the prolific correspondence between him and David, and we thus made our acquaintance. David always spoke of "George" with warmth and gratitude, but the real evidence of Georg's enduring care and affection for David came not only from the letters he wrote to me about David, but also from the multitude of letters he wrote to David from Queensland throughout the entire time of David's on-and-off hospitalisations. Georg always worried that his decision to move to Queensland meant he was not able to look after David in Perth.

All the letters began with the words "My dear friend David" and were followed by heartfelt apologies for not writing sooner or more often, which was particularly touching as David received letters from only two or three other correspondents and Georg was the only one who wrote with devout regularity. Though work commitments prevented Georg from being with David in person for more than a few days every year or so, he ensured that David would always feel he was with him in spirit. In all his letters Georg inquired about David's practising, as if David were not in a hospital at all but ensconced in a comfortable home with a grand piano. But then there were also phrases like, "I think the world misses a lot while you are in [the hospital]. I think you must try hard to get well because you have a lot to give!" and "Naturally it would be better if you did not need to be in Hospital and let's hope that soon you will be out again."

One day, when a letter arrived from Georg, David read it and an hour or so later came up to me in the kitchen with the letter in his hand. He muttered, "She hated the guts of him, you know."

"What are you on about, possum?"

"She was jealous of George. You know what? Clara had a trick, she made me wear a beard, you see, because, you see, she thought if I looked twenty years older then George won't love me no more. That was mean trick, because Clara is a bitch, the best bitch in the world, the world's greatest bitch."

I knew that Clara was David's first wife because, on the second day after we met, and a few minutes after proposing to me, David found it necessary to 'confess' to a previous marriage, but then assured me that he was not 'responsible', saying, "I did not ask her. She took me off to be married."

At the time, considering I had just been proposed to by a man I had only known for a few hours, I found this all a bit daunting to comprehend. Later, as we began our life together, I realised that David would only ever speak about what he wanted to, and there were many areas of his life – particularly the more devastating periods in the '70s – of which he did not want to speak at all. I was very conscious of not asking him about things that I suspected might really upset him, believing that when he was ready he would share whatever he wanted of his own volition. And I was right. It was now the time for the story of Clara, and those associated with that period in David's life, to come out, though it took many more months, and the words of many other people, for it to make complete sense.

It all began in 1971, when, after being discharged from his first four-month stay at the Charles Gairdner Hospital in Perth, David found himself in reasonably good health, feeling quite strong and rather independent. Mrs Luber-Smith generously took him in again, but, after a few weeks or so, David moved

David and his friend, Boris, outside Highgate State School, Perth, in the late 1950s.

David outside the Helfgotts' Bulwer Avenue home, about 1960.

Peter Helfgott with Les and Suzie in 1961, outside Highgate State School.

David, Suzie and Peter Helfgott, about 1964.

DAVID HELFGOTT FAREWELLED
BY LLOYD LAWSON AT A STUDIO
RECITAL ON WOMENS PROGRAMME.
ON AFTERNOON OF HIS DEPARTURE
FOR LONDON — 1967. (SEE OVER)

On the eve of his departure for London in 1966, David gave a recital at Channel Nine's Perth studios, on a program hosted by Lloyd Lawson.

David at the piano in London, about 1967.

BELOW: David receives the Marmaduke Barton Prize and the Hopkinson Silver Medal from the Queen Mother at the Royal College of Music in 1969, while Sir Keith Falkner looks on.

The Helfgott family in 1967: from left, Peter, Suzie (kneeling), Margaret (at piano), Louise (sitting), Rachel and Les.

Gillian and David at their house in Lathlain, Perth, 1984. (Photo by Tony Ashby, courtesy The West Australian*)*

David and his cat, Rakhmaninov, at Lathlain in 1984. (Photo by Tony Ashby, courtesy The West Australian*)*

ABOVE: Gillian and David on their wedding day in 1984, with Dr Chris Reynolds.

The happily married couple with Gillian's daughter, Sue, and son, Scott.

David at the piano in the Treasury Lounge of the Intercontinental Hotel, Sydney, 1987.

out to stay with the Harrises, who were good friends of Madame Alice's.

Cliff Harris was then president of the Music Council of Western Australia, and he and his wife, Rae, took a special interest in David. They ensured that he stayed with them until he gathered enough confidence to live on his own, and then rented a flat for him close to their own house. In this way they could keep an eye on him, as each day he would come over to practise on their grand piano and have his meals with them.

Cliff also undertook to raise funds so David could, once again, concentrate on his musical studies full-time. The ever-supportive James Penberthy wrote an article about David and the fund-raising in the *Sunday Times* and the money started to roll in. The Harrises also organised small musical functions for David to perform at. It was at one of those functions that he met Clara.

A mature divorcée with four children – some close in their age to David's – Clara was quite well known in the Jewish community; she was also an acquaintance of Madame Alice's. Of striking appearance, she came from a wealthy Hungarian family who lost everything in World War II. Thrown into a concentration camp as a teenager, she was eventually rescued by the Russian army and ultimately made her way to Australia.

Clara showed great interest in David, and, as with age he had become even more of a 'mouse', she found him to be extremely malleable material. David was flattered by her attention and soon allowed her to guide him. Though the Harrises and the Luber-Smiths were gravely concerned about this friendship, they were powerless to stop it from developing.

A few months later, David again entered the ABC competition, playing the Brahms B flat Concerto, and again won the State final. Around this time, Clara asked him to marry her.

"I kind of was forced", confided David. "I was more or less cajoled, coaxed and friendly persuasioned. I didn't have much option at all really, 'cause Madame Alice said to marry her. Of course, Madame Alice was all taken in. Clara was sort of like two-faced. She fooled Madame Alice, and I just obeyed Madame Alice's orders."

At the time, Madame Alice thought it would be beneficial for David to have full-time companionship. But others were not so pleased. "Mrs Luber and her husband tried to dissuade me", said David. "Mrs Luber kept saying, 'I know Clara.' The Harrises said the same thing, the Harrises warned me. They all said it was the greatest mistake in the world." As David was far from close to his family at the time, he did not even inform them of his plans.

Within days of marrying Clara in July '71, David knew he "had just made the greatest mistake, but what could I do? I had made the mistake."

After hearing the story of the Harrises' generosity, I contacted them and asked if we could meet. When we met, they revealed further details of David's marriage to Clara. They told me they had been deeply hurt by it, as after the wedding David had immediately moved out of the flat they had provided for him and from that day on more or less ignored them.

When David eventually did come to see them, he turned up with Clara, who demanded that they give her the money raised for David – a sum substantial enough to ensure that he could live and practise in comfort and peace for several years. The Harrises refused, and said it was raised for David's use only.

On that day, even David, showing rare courage, turned to Clara and rather firmly said, "It is not yours, you cannot have it."

For David, this was not the first glimpse of the true nature of his new wife. Some weeks prior to the incident at the Harrises', Clara had found out that David was not selected for the national final of the ABC competition and she had been furious. David, who was not exactly full of self-confidence at the time, was made to feel gravely embarrassed for failing to provide his wife and her children with the prize money.

Having alienated himself from the Harrises, David was faced with a new problem: no piano to practise on. Richard Cleaver, who was a Member of Parliament and also the founder of Swan Cottage Homes for the elderly, somehow heard of David's problem and organised for the residents of Swan Cottage Homes to take up a collection in order to buy an upright for David. The piano was delivered and he could now get back to practising. This he did for a few days only, as, upon coming home one day, he found that the piano had vanished.

"She sold it just like that! And didn't consult me! Imagine that! And whose piano was it anyhow?", he recalled, astonished to this day by Clara's actions and still reeling from the acute feelings of loss and injustice he had experienced at the time.

When I heard this story I was absolutely horrified, and, when Richard Cleaver wrote to us asking David to come and play at Swan Cottage Homes in 1985, we were delighted to offer this service free. David then played at the Homes on several other occasions, both of us feeling it was the least we could do.

As David's relationship with Clara deteriorated, so did his financial situation. And though he did manage to do a few recitals, it became necessary to find a day job. This is when Georg, who had heard David perform many times and truly admired his talent, invited him to work for the Opera.

Elaine Flint had met David and Clara during a production of Verdi's *Masked Ball* and, when I finally got in contact with her, she told me that her memories of David at that time were very sad ones. Clara would publicly ridicule and bully him, and displayed a marked possessiveness of him, resenting his friendship with the members of the opera company.

In particular, she had problems with David's friendship with Georg, and this was when she forced David to grow a beard. Her reason for this, as David had told me, was to 'sabotage' the friendship, something he always found quite bizarre.

Clara's problems with David's friends manifested in other ways as well. If he wanted to go and hear any of the Opera's performances, he had to creep out of the house and then creep back in again. He did not have sufficient cunning, however, to remove the ticket butts. Clara would go through his pockets and discover them, and "She'd hit the roof!", David once told me. "Those Hungarians got pepper-straw tempers! Oh God, did I get punished! Oh God! I got punished severely. The language, the language that ensued! You'll have to imagine it, I don't even want to say . . ." David shivered at the memory.

One day, some people came up to me at Riccardo's and told me that they recognised David from the early '70s, as they had lived next door to David and Clara. They told me that they had often seen him crawling around his backyard on his hands and knees. Little was done, it would seem, to alleviate his suffering. By 1972, David's performing career had nearly ground to a halt, and his health had severely deteriorated. By 1973, he told me, he was basically confined to bed, and rapidly spiralling downwards.

At the beginning of 1974 Clara had to have an operation, and, as she was afraid to leave David alone at home unsupervised, she admitted him to Graylands Hospital for two weeks. When she came to take him home, he chose to remain in the mental institution rather than go back with her.

When Peter turned up on one of his occasional visits to Graylands, David told him he wanted to divorce Clara and asked Peter to retrieve his music scores and all the medals he had won in various competitions, which Clara still had. Peter went to see Clara and pleaded with her to return them, but she refused, denying she had them.

"It was a marriage made in hell and consecrated by and presided over by the Devil" was David's ultimate comment on that relationship.

Though I realised that, in those years, David was barely capable of being sensitive to the feelings of others, I was determined to mend the hurts that had been so unjustly inflicted on the Harrises. When I found out that Cliff was a professional marriage celebrant, I had great pleasure in asking him to officiate at our wedding.

Small Miracles

Wintry sun was filtering through the trees, and the round fountain in the Brackleys' garden was filled with pink camellias. Though Barbara and Peter had decorated their house with flowers just in case it rained, the sunshine meant it would be a garden ceremony, which was what David really wanted. It seemed my astrological calculations were right.

My children, Scott and Sue, had come from interstate, as had Doris Greaves, my astrology mentor. Rachel and David's siblings were there, with the exception of Margaret, who was in Israel. Madame Alice had also come, along with many of our friends from Riccardo's. I suspect the guests were wondering how David would behave at the ceremony; I must admit I had the odd thought about it, too. Would he stand still for this one special occasion? Could he be quiet during the ceremony? Or would he wander off to hug and kiss everyone present?

A friend from Riccardo's delivered us to the ceremony in his vintage car, which he had decked out with ribbons. David was dressed in a new cream suit, and walked into the garden all straight and proud – a complete contrast to the cowering figure I had met nine months earlier. He had a red carnation in his buttonhole, and a permanent smile on his face. I wore a peacock-blue dress with a matching hat and felt rather *joyeux* myself.

Cliff Harris commenced the ceremony at precisely 11.57 am, and everything seemed to be going perfectly to plan. However, it was not long before the whole thing became something of a two-part canon, as David repeated every word of the ceremony just a beat or so behind Cliff. I stood with my arm through David's and held on tightly so that he did at least manage to stand still, without hugging or kissing anyone, until it was time to kiss the bride.

For our wedding march, we chose the 'chorale' section of the Liszt B minor Sonata. In this work, Liszt captured a sense of the majesty and triumph of life and love. It was truly inspiring to walk through the garden with this uplifting music playing at the culmination of the ceremony. When it was all over, David was free to run around hugging and kissing all the guests, and this he did until we all left to go to the reception, for which Chris had very kindly offered the use of Riccardo's.

Chris also supplied the wine, and friends from Riccardo's prepared the food. My children and astrology students tended the bar and served the guests. A long table had been set with flowers and Frances Hebb brought the wedding cake, which was aptly shaped in the form of a crotchet note.

As soon as we entered Riccardo's, David made straight for the piano. For the next few hours the bridegroom provided the entertainment, stopping only to cut the cake and give hugs. Then it was time to farewell the guests and drive for 75 kilometres to Mandurah, south of Perth, for our two-day honeymoon at the Atrium Hotel.

I realised this was going to be a long drive, and was worried about how David would deal with the prolonged confinement of the journey. But I hoped that, with the excitement of his wedding day, it would not bother him too much. My hopes were realised, as David was much too happy to notice the length of the journey. From that time onwards, his passenger skills progressively improved.

When we arrived at the hotel, David was thrilled with its plush luxury, constantly mumbling, "This is all for me! Especially for me! I'm lucky, lucky! I'm privileged!"

Our room overlooked the sea, and the next morning we went for a stroll along the sand. But as there was an indoor pool at the hotel, David spent most of the time in it. He soon struck up a friendship with a Member of State Parliament, Pam Beggs, and her two little daughters, who were splashing in the water with him. I sat by the edge of the pool and mused about the ease with which David was relating to these people. He was chatting without too much agitation, but then he was in the water, and the water was not only calming him but improving his social interaction. It seemed as though life would be much easier for my husband if he could only stay immersed.

As the evening approached, I wondered what David's reaction would be if I suggested dinner at the hotel's restaurant. I knew it would be a major decision for him. We had never eaten together in a public restaurant and his fear of being confined to a table could be a problem. And though we had been practising the use of cutlery at home, there was no guarantee that the added stress of using it in public would not have a negative effect on his newly rehearsed etiquette skills.

To my amazement, David agreed to dine with me. Warily looking about, he took a few hesitant steps into the restaurant. I was sure he was going to make a quick exit. However, he did not, and nervously sat down at our table. When the waitress arrived, David surprised me again by not leaping to his feet immediately to hug and kiss her. Though he still chattered at the waitress, he remained seated and the fear soon left his eyes.

When David's steak arrived he ate it with gusto, managing the use of the cutlery quite well, though, I have to confess, still not brilliantly. With David, I had been learning how to be grateful for the smallest of achievements.

After the honeymoon it was back to Riccardo's and our busy, chaotic life. David still needed at least two swims a day and, even with my great reserves of energy, I would at times feel utterly depleted. By the end of an evening I would often find myself sitting on the floor, searching for the energy to stand up and go to bed. David, who had become much more sensitive about such matters, would come to embrace me and say things like, "Darling you are music to my senses." Re-energised, I would face the next day without trepidation.

Fortunately, by late September David had begun to feel more centred in himself and said that one swim a day might now be sufficient. The first glimpse of free time had appeared. Before meeting David I had never known how grateful I could be for two free hours in a day.

In that same week, he wandered into the kitchen one day, poured some dishwashing liquid and hot water into the sink, and proceeded to wash the dishes. I was astounded, particularly as he seemed to be really enjoying his task. Though he had stacked the dishes in a rather precarious manner, and his generosity with the dishwashing liquid made it all look like an out-of-control bubble bath, it was still a heartening sight. Once David had his hands in the soapy water, I could sense that it was much like a swim or a shower for him. From that day onwards, he became enamoured of dishwashing and towards the end of a meal would become impatient, often grabbing unfinished dinner plates from under our guests' noses, muttering, "May I? May I? May I?", and would run with them to the kitchen before anyone even had time to blink.

Two days after his first dishwashing effort, David announced that he was going down to the shop, which was a few blocks from our house, to buy a newspaper, and, "No, thank you, darling", he did not need me to come with him. He took some money and walked out the front door. As I stood by the window watching him cross the road, I had a vague sense that something was missing, and then I realised: for the first time since I'd known him he had left the house without holding onto his portable radio!

When David returned with the newspaper and no change

in his pockets – he had, of course, spent every last cent on cakes and soft drinks – I felt like celebrating! But because I did not want to remind him that he had left his main security-blanket at home, I said nothing and instead gave him a big *potchnagoola*.

As David continued to overcome small obstacles on the personal front, his concert career was growing, thanks to Mike Parry. Mike's strategy at the time was to build a secure base in Western Australia on the foundation of two major concerts at the Octagon every year. These yielded fair earnings – no mean feat considering that, regardless of his job at Riccardo's, David's livelihood was still being supplemented by social welfare when Mike agreed to be his manager. Apart from the concerts at the Octagon, David would do 'outside engagements' like charity concerts, performances with local orchestras and country tours. These provided extra income and an expanded base of public support without the danger of overexposure.

Because of his experience in the industry, Mike was greatly concerned about overexposing David, and one of the conditions he imposed on hirers was that no public promotion in Perth was permitted. He did not want to see David's name splashed around the media every week. Dozens of concerts were thus staged 'in secret'. Many charities benefited and the two precious Octagon concerts remained inviolate. Over the next few years, David played to thirteen sold-out houses there.

Once a secure base had been established in Western Australia, Mike wanted to duplicate the process in the rest of the country by developing a presence in the capital cities and then spreading out into regional centres. It was crucial to build up David's concert experience and, through a rigorous schedule of appearances, demonstrate to the world in general, and concert promoters in particular – who still found it rather difficult to see beyond his infamous eccentricity – that not only could he take the strain of regular performances, but that he was a consistent and reliable performer. Regardless of David's talent, the process was never going to be easy or fast. Thus it was not till December '84 that he received his first touring engagement in Geraldton, some 300 kilometres from Perth.

Meanwhile, as my musical knowledge grew, I realised that David needed a grand piano to do him justice. I could now tell the difference between his playing on Chris's grand and our Yamaha U3 upright at home. Though he never complained – the Yamaha was a top-of-the-range upright, and the first new piano he had ever had in his life – I just knew it was no longer meeting his practice needs. But with our severely limited resources, my dream of a grand seemed to be just that – a dream.

I gave the matter a lot of thought, and decided that if it was absolutely right for David to have a grand piano, then it would just appear one day in our house. But then my grand plan met with another little obstacle: if this piano did appear one day, it would not fit into our cottage. So, with the optimism of a Sagittarian – what's the use of praying for rain and then leaving your umbrella at home? – I decided to look for a house which would accommodate a grand piano. Of course, anyone I talked to about these ideas thought I was a total kook.

Rental properties were scarce in Perth in those days, but, as I looked through the classified pages of the newspapers, I just knew that if the piano had to appear then so would a house. The words 'should', 'try' and 'impossible' were well out of my vocabulary by that stage. In early 1985, I saw an advertisement for a house in South Perth which backed onto the river. The location would be a paradise for David, I thought. If we got the house, he would have the whole of the Swan River to swim in, instead of the local public swimming pool.

The property turned out to be ideal. It had a huge lounge room and David and I could see the perfect spot for the grand: right near the glass doors which overlooked a beautiful garden. When we came in, there were about seven couples inspecting the property, and they all wanted it. The estate agent knew of David and his struggles, and I had told her we were looking for a house that would take a grand piano. After some consideration, the agent gathered all of us under the grapevine on the terrace and announced that she was giving the house to David as he needed it for his piano. The others were disappointed, but they had all met David and did not resent the agent's decision.

I was mortified. I went up to the agent and confessed that we did not have the piano yet, but added that I was confident we would have one in the near future. She assured me that was fine, and at the end of January we moved into the house.

A few weeks later, I was in Riccardo's when a couple of regulars, Malcolm and Dee Jones, who would often ask me to join them for dessert and a glass of Sauternes, called me over. As we were sipping the delicious wine, the conversation drifted to the topic of pianos and Malcolm said, "Of course, David has a grand, doesn't he?" I had to admit that he didn't, to which Malcolm simply replied, "Well, then, we will buy him one."

Riccardo's attracted all sorts of people who had made all sorts of offers which never came to fruition, and I wondered if this was just another one of those. However, the Joneses seemed to be sincere, and they proved to be just that.

First, Malcolm had to run the gift past his company's board. Then, after a chat with the manager of Riccardo's, Miles, he had to decide on the most appropriate model of piano. By 18 March, a Yamaha C7 was paid for and ready for delivery.

Elaine Flint had taken David out that afternoon so we could get the piano into the house. The Joneses arrived with their children and brought me a basket of white roses, with a bottle of Château d'Yquem in the centre. When David came home, he was not only speechless but his joy and astonishment at seeing this magnificent instrument in his own lounge room seemed to take his breath away. Of course, he immediately ran to the piano and began to play. Over the next few days, David kept repeating, "It's a miracle! I am the luckiest person in the world! I'm grateful! Grateful! Grateful!" What was particularly significant was that his gratitude was a joyous and honest one. He simply adored the feeling: if there was someone to be grateful to, it meant that they cared for him, and that was what mattered the most.

The Joneses had a property in the country and there they had established the acclaimed Brookland Valley vineyard. On the property, there was an historic drover's cottage by the side of the road, surrounded by vines. A week or so later, the Joneses invited us to the vineyard for a special celebration breakfast.

When we arrived, we discovered a grand piano had been transported from Perth and positioned on the front porch of the tiny cottage. It was a most incongruous sight, this fine instrument on an old wooden verandah, surrounded by large, colourful umbrellas, and guests gaily eating breakfast while David played *Gnomenreigen* and other Liszt pieces. The cars driving past literally stopped in their tracks to stare at it all and listen. Malcolm later said that the Chardonnay vines nearest the house were the ones that flourished the most over the next years.

A few days after our trip to the country, David and I were sitting on our terrace enjoying an unusually peaceful afternoon. The sun was filtering through our little grapevine overhead, and the bunches of ripe fruit were looking very tempting in the glow. David was rather contemplative, which was most unusual for him, and to be seated like this, doing nothing in particular, was equally unusual. We talked about going to Riccardo's that evening and I said it was nearly time to get ready. David was quiet for a moment, and then a strange look of enlightenment came over his face. "Darling," he said, "I think the fog is lifting. Yes! Yes! The fog is going, it is going."

Category 'B'

David's career opportunities were expanding, and early in 1985
he was invited to play at an outdoor concert at Leeuwin Estate.
Situated at Margaret River in the southwest of Western
Australia, Leeuwin was already producing some of the finest
wines in the country. Now its owners, Denis and Trish Horgan,
had had a vision of their vineyard becoming the setting for a
world-class musical event. A large sound shell had been constructed against a backdrop of giant ancient gum trees, which
gleamed under the lights at night, creating an enchanting
atmosphere.

Headlining this inaugural concert was the London

Philharmonic Orchestra, which was also performing at the Festival of Perth. David was asked to play for forty-five minutes beforehand at a piano placed on a large mound in the garden near the winery.

About 7000 people turned up with rugs and picnic baskets. Media interest was very high and, when David started to play, a helicopter zoomed down over his head filming it all. I felt quite dizzy from the sound and the rush of air, but David played on unperturbed. His habit of practising with radios and a television blaring, and his experiences at Riccardo's with all the toing and froing near the piano, appeared to have made him impervious to distractions.

At sunset, just as the London Philharmonic started to play, the local kookaburras – also known as 'laughing jackasses' – perhaps wishing not to be outdone, filled the air with their raucous cackle. They must have felt successful, because they returned every year to the concert for an encore.

David returned to Leeuwin Estate for the next nine years as well, supporting many great artists, including Dionne Warwick, Tom Jones, James Galway and Dame Kiri Te Kanawa who, in a display of total professionalism, continued to perform in the pouring rain. But the concert which I found most memorable was the one with Diana Ross.

David was in the middle of *Rhapsody in Blue* when the organiser of the concert came up to me and said, "You have to stop David playing. Ms Ross wants an announcement made immediately and, if you don't stop him, she'll cancel the concert."

I was furious. "That would be unfair to David, Gershwin

and the audience", I replied. The concert organiser pleaded with me and seemed nearly at his wits' end, as Ms Ross's demands throughout the day had worn him out. Very much against my will, I had to tell David to stop, which he did. Then the earth-shattering announcement came over the loudspeakers: "Please do not photograph Ms Ross during her performance."

Ms Ross aside, Leeuwin Estate was a great boon for David and, after his debut there, Mike decided to arrange performances in other States. The one obstacle was David's terror of flying. Driving thousands of kilometres from Perth to concerts in other capital cities would have been impossibly time-consuming and stressful. What to do? As David's fear of car travel had been overcome on the drive to his honeymoon, perhaps his fear of air travel could be dealt with in the same way. I suggested to him that, as our honeymoon had only been a rushed two days between engagements, we deserved a longer one. This time, though, I said, "I really want to go to Bali." David just could not refuse such an enticing proposition.

As soon as we arrived at the airport, he began panicking. However, the trip was booked and paid for, and there was no time to retreat as the boarding call was being made. After many reassuring hugs and reminders of the tropical paradise at the other end, David finally agreed to get on the plane.

As the jet taxied along the runway, his tension increased. He gripped the armrests with such force that his knuckles turned white. A trapped, anxious look in his eyes made me wonder if I had made the right decision. I plugged in his earphones and selected a classical music channel. Then, prying free one of his hands, I took it in mine and we faced the takeoff together.

Once in the air, David's panic gradually disappeared and the classical music soothed him for the rest of the flight. He barely noticed the landing in Denpasar, as he was too busy giving me a rundown on the past twenty years of Indonesian politics.

When we returned to Perth after five idyllic days of sun, delicious food and walks on the beach, everyone at Riccardo's was eager to know about our second honeymoon. Someone asked David what he enjoyed most about the trip and he merrily replied, "The flights! The flights!" Oh, the mystery of Helfgott! And he has never shown the slightest fear of flying since.

This was just as well, because a few months later Kirsty Cockburn, who had moved to join Ray Martin on the 'Midday Show', organised for David to perform on the program. This required a plane flight to Sydney.

David was to perform on two consecutive days and an interview with Ray was scheduled for the second day. It was an exciting experience for both of us, and it was the first opportunity David had to perform on national television since his late teens.

Ray Martin was a delightful interviewer, and David chatted to him in his usual eccentric manner, as if they were old buddies. During the interview, David must suddenly have realised what was happening and said, "Ray, are we on television?" "Yes", replied Ray, which brought out a "Golly, I guess I had better behave." Ray laughed and the audience loved it.

The television appearances continued when SBS came to Perth to do a twenty-minute documentary on David in the middle of the year. He was thrilled to be the 'star of the show' yet again, but the most noticeable aspect of that documentary was that it captured the comparative clarity of his thoughts and an overall improved coherence in his speech.

This was the time when Gerald Krug yet again showed his great commitment to David and arranged for him to play Chaikovsky's Concerto No. 1 with the WA Arts Orchestra in the Perth Concert Hall. After that success, Gerald invited David to be a guest artist in *Die Fledermaus*.

The operetta ran for thirteen performances and, in the scene where a guest artist makes an appearance, David played Liszt's *Hungarian Rhapsody* No. 15. This proved to be quite a juggling act on the nights when David was also playing at Riccardo's. Chris was most co-operative and we timed David's brackets so that the minute he finished the first one I whisked him off to Her Majesty's Theatre, where he would do his bit before getting back into the car and returning for his next bracket at Riccardo's. The wine-bar audience was hardly even aware of his little disappearing act.

Clearly, David had come a long way from playing to himself on a derelict piano at Guildercliffe Lodge, but he still had much further to go. Though we were both extremely grateful for the smallest career step in the right direction, everything was not as perfect as it seemed.

There were two main problems. The first was that the conservative factions of the music establishment in Australia, and in Perth in particular, refused to recognise David as a serious professional. His beloved ABC had declined to play his recent recording for them, and the organisation showed a distinct lack of interest in him. Equally, when we suggested to the Perth

Conservatorium that David do some lunchtime recitals for free, they coolly rejected our offer. No one, it seemed, apart from the general public who usually came in droves to hear him, and the occasional music critic who wrote a favourable review, wanted to believe that David was anything other than a 'performing freak in a sideshow'. This severely limited his career opportunities. What was even worse for him, in some ways, was that this attitude prevented him from genuine interaction with his musical peers.

This was our second problem. David desperately needed this interaction for the sharing of new ideas and inspiration, but his opportunities to do so were severely limited by people's lack of understanding of his personality. Performing at Riccardo's three or four times a week was keeping him on his toes and he enjoyed the close contact with the audience, but it was not exactly inspiring the sort of musical discipline one would need to play at Carnegie Hall. David's lessons with Madame Alice were invaluable, but she was eighty-eight years old, and there was just so much she could do. She was firmly convinced that David's having to work outside the cliquey music community in Australia was not healthy for him professionally, and that he really needed to be among fellow pianists – to hear them play, to have them hear him, and to discuss their work together. David also needed to polish up various aspects of his playing, which he simply could not do in Australia.

After a discussion with Chris and Miles at Riccardo's, we decided that it would be beneficial for David to go back to London for some further study. Mike Parry was in London at the time and made some inquiries about a teacher for David.

After much thought he approached Peter Feuchtwanger, a pedagogue whose reputation was mixed. Some regarded him as a god, others as a charlatan, but Mike thought that Feuchtwanger had the sensitivity and skills David needed.

Mike found Feuchtwanger to be a very approachable and gentle man. He gave Feuchtwanger some tapes of David's playing, and Feuchtwanger was so impressed that he said he would welcome David to England, and could work with him for four days a week. He added that he ran masterclasses in Europe which could be of benefit to David, as they would give him the opportunity of sharing with other musicians, in contrast to the private lessons in London. Thus it was decided that David would go to London for further study during the European summer of '86, subject to finance being available.

When Mike returned to Perth he lodged an application, on David's behalf, with the Arts Council of Western Australia for funding of $6000. In early December I received a call from the Arts Council regarding the application, and was asked if David planned to work overseas or just study. I assured them it was only a study tour. I was then told that as David had received a previous grant – the Bursary from the Music Council of Western Australia for his first trip to London – this would disadvantage his application. I pointed out that the previous grant was awarded in 1965, when there was no Arts Council. I could not understand how something that had happened twenty years ago could be a detriment to David now. The Arts Council man then told me, in a rather condescending manner, that David was only in category 'B' and he was near the bottom of that. I realised we were fighting a losing battle.

A few days before Christmas, the rejection letter arrived. Having had many rejections in his life, David just shrugged it off, but I was angry. When the grants were announced early in the new year, the main overseas grant was given to a pianist who had had a similar grant the year before.

The arrival of the bad news coincided with a Christmas-party performance David was to give for one of the big local mining companies. The mid-1980s in Perth were a real 'scene'. The West produced some of the most flamboyant characters in Australia. Dom Perignon was the lunchtime beverage of choice and locals would quip that money was flowing in the streets. The social set was buzzing and extravagant parties were thrown almost every week. Defending the America's Cup was on every-one's mind and David was even invited to play on the cruise ship *Achille Lauro*.

His Christmas-party performance was on the large terrace of the new and luxurious Merlin Hotel, which overlooked the Swan River. With the piano positioned beside the pool, the atmosphere was one of opulent confidence, an impression enhanced by the golden glow of the setting sun.

Allan Rogers, a senior business executive whom we had met socially at Riccardo's, came over to speak with me. I told him about David's recent misfortune and he was quite shocked. He then asked how much money we needed and I told him we had applied for $6000. In a laid-back but very confident manner, Allan said, "Leave it to me", and walked away just as David began to play some Rakhmaninov preludes.

A few minutes later Allan returned and calmly said, "Russell Smith, of Camon Mining, will give David $10,000."

I was stunned. It was incredible that someone could make such a generous decision in five minutes flat. I thought back to all those Arts Council forms we'd had to fill in and the time Mike had spent on them. All Allan requested was that we give Russell a brief outline of David's study program and that we have a photo taken of Russell giving David the cheque.

Mike prepared the outline and, a few weeks later, Russell presented David with the cheque – with an extra $2500 added to the promised sum. The *West Australian* came to photograph the occasion and published the whole story the next day, giving the arts bureaucracy a bit of a serve. And it was not unwarranted: David has never received a cent of government or Arts Council funding while re-establishing his career.

chapter 19

Works in Progress

Austin Prichard-Levy was a research astrologer whom I had met at various conferences and kept in touch with. Being also a proficient lute and guitar player, he was interested to meet David and said he would like to organise a recital for him in Sydney. Through his contacts in the Music Department at the University of Sydney, he arranged for the use of the Old Darlington School in February '86.

The Old School is an historic building of great charm and character which seats about 150 people. Austin soon spread the word and, on the evening of the performance, the recital received some coverage on the 7 pm television news on the ABC. Some people were so intrigued by the report they literally switched off their televisions, abandoned their desserts and hopped straight into their cars to come and hear David play. It was a wonderful sight to see all these people eagerly running up the pathway from the road to the School.

David really enjoyed playing in the beautiful setting to the capacity audience. Once the concert was over, chairs were stacked against the wall and we served wine and cheese. For the first time, Sydneysiders were able to meet David, who, of course, hugged them all and chatted with his appreciative, relaxed audience.

We were staying with my daughter, Sue, and, by the time we got back to her flat, it was quite late at night. It wasn't till I was about to go to bed that David suddenly realised that he was all out of chewing gum. Gum, much like cigarettes, coffee and sugar, was an addiction we were still working on. The cigarettes had been reduced to fifty a day, the coffee was not drunk at all while performing, but the gum was a constant companion, alleviating, no doubt, the withdrawal symptoms from the reduction of the other two substances.

In a way, this little confidence-boosting "prop" of David's was the most annoying of them all. Wrigleys Double Mint, PK and Juicy Fruit would be chewed till the last drop of flavour ran out, and then disposed of onto the floor, where it would invariably stick to his shoes; under chairs, where one would find it when moving furniture; onto plates, which he would then be too disorganised to scrape off before washing the dishes; and, in the worst scenario of all, into his trouser pockets.

We had had many discussions about this unpleasant habit,

but to no avail. So, in the middle of the night, we got dressed and went to find some chewing gum. But as Sue lived near the central business district, there were no little twenty-four-hour grocery stores or service stations open at that time of night. In vain we walked around the empty streets for an hour or so before I had finally had enough. I explained to David that his little dependence was ruling our lives, and, feeling rather exhausted himself, David agreed. "*Yash, yash*", he said, playfully imitating a mouth full of gum. "*Beshidesh*, it *shtopsh* you *shmiling* properly." And that was the demise of chewing gum.

A few days later my son, Scott, came to Sydney on business, and we all decided to go and have a family dinner at an Indian restaurant. I was happy that David agreed to come with us. Because we lived in three different capital cities, this was going to be the first occasion since our wedding that I would be in the same room with my children and my husband. Consequently, I did not notice that Scott began to experience some problems with David. It was only the second time they had met.

The next day, we decided to go for a family Sunday drive to the Palm Beach peninsula. When we stopped at an outdoor café for lunch, Sue, who has always been extremely sensitive to Scott's feelings, took David off for a walk, and this is when Scott finally opened up and confessed that he was simply not coping with David.

Scott told me that when he first met David at Riccardo's, the night before the wedding, he could not really get any sense of who David was, as David hardly left the piano and was always surrounded by other people. While understanding the importance of Riccardo's in the revival of David's career, Scott was saddened by the fact that some people there seemed to be treating David as nothing more than a "performing seal". At the wedding the next day, he could not get any closer to David, as David was again at the piano surrounded by a large group of people. "It was as if David felt people wouldn't care about him if he weren't playing", said Scott. "His running off to the piano all the time seemed as much a need for a secure place – a secure role – as a love of playing", he added, and this saddened him also.

Scott told me that he had spent the previous evening at the restaurant on tenterhooks. "I felt very uncomfortable when David tried to touch and talk to every person he saw", Scott confided. "It was okay when people responded warmly to him, but I was scared stiff someone would turn on him. I found the tension unbearable."

After we had come home from the restaurant, David seemed remote, content to mutter to himself while lying on the floor, doing his eccentric form of push-ups and reading. Scott simply could not connect with David and, though he could sense the love and warmth I had been telling him about, he just could not respond to it under these circumstances.

Driving up the peninsula, Scott found David's extreme restlessness and incessant talking difficult to handle. Scott was driving, and what was even more unsettling to him was David's habit of grabbing him from the back seat every few minutes – something he had always done and still does to every driver if he is seated in the back of the car.

When we stopped for lunch, Scott's discomfort merely grew as David, once again, tried to involve everyone in conversation, including the waitress. The waitress proved unresponsive and Scott was overcome with tension. All these sensations were further complicated by the increasing guilt he was feeling about them.

I told Scott that he should not be feeling guilt of any kind. Of course, even though David had made a significant improvement since I had met him, he was still disturbingly noisy, had no idea of personal space and could not really interact with other people in any manner that could be called 'normal'. I realised only too well that not everybody would embrace David the way I had and some people could not do so at all.

But I also knew my son, and believed absolutely that I would always have his support, even though he himself was not yet able to accept David fully. I told him that everyone, including him, must feel free to react to David in whatever manner was true to them.

After our talk Scott felt a lot calmer, but he continued to puzzle over why his response to David was not as positive as that of others.

Despite all manner of personal difficulties, our stay in Sydney was a marked career step for David. And, when we returned to Perth, we decided in consultation with Mike Parry that it was time for David to do a national tour before going to Europe. Arranging it proved to be a huge challenge for Mike. There was no touring structure in Australia to tap into, and he had to visit each State individually to set up venues. His great efforts paid off and David received four engagements: Adelaide, Melbourne, Sydney and Brisbane.

As David's commitments over the coming months were to be fairly demanding, a friend suggested that it would be sensible for him to have a medical check-up, and she arranged for an examination by a leading heart specialist in Perth. The doctor was a warm and friendly man who knew of David, and the two had a happy little chat about David's smoking and love of exercise. When the doctor asked David if he had ever had a chest x-ray, he replied, "Not for years, not for years, doctor", and was then immediately sent off to have one done.

When we returned the next day, the doctor had some unpleasant, though hardly surprising, news. He told David that there was deterioration in the top of his lungs and, if he did not give up smoking entirely, he would not live to a good age. David listened, nodded, said "Yes, yes. 'Course, 'course", and then, as soon as we were outside the doctor's surgery, lit up a cigarette.

I was worried, but as David had already made such great progress, I felt it would simply be a matter of time before he gave up smoking altogether. I have never smoked or drunk tea or coffee in my life – I have just never had a taste for them – and I wondered if I'd had an addiction to any of these things whether I would still approach David's problems with as much confidence in solving them. I also had no idea that nicotine addiction was the hardest of all to beat. So for the time being I decided that, with the national tour coming up, it was not a good idea to ask David to stop smoking completely, but made a mental note to do so at the first sensible opportunity.

Much had been written in the press about David's upcoming tour, and the Edmund Wright Hall in Adelaide, our first venue, was full to capacity. David was eager to show everyone his progress and readiness to take on the extensive tour, and was terribly excited. This was the first big concert outside his home town, and I looked at the unfamiliar, curious faces in the audience and hoped for the best, a strange, gnawing feeling in the pit of my stomach.

As it happened, David played well. Music critic Elizabeth Silsbury noted in her review in the *Advertiser* that David had "not only restored his technique but also ... pushed it to realms that can only be described as superhuman". Though she did not mind his "highly individualistic" interpretations, commenting that David treated the piano "like an orchestra, expecting and usually getting an unlimited supply of timbres" and behaved "as though he were not just one player, but a whole band of them, all of like mind and of equal capacity", she did find David's "intermittent, tuneless vocalised drone that sounded as though the Grand Prix had come early" quite irritating. I knew all about the "drone" and had held many discussions with David on the topic, but, when it came to actually going out there and performing, it all depended on his mood. Sometimes he sang away and muttered, and sometimes he didn't, and to this day one can never predict what he will do when left alone on a stage.

During the supper which we served after the performance, I was talking with a group of people when a tall, quietly charming man approached and introduced himself as Scott Hicks. He told me that he was greatly affected by David's playing, and intrigued by his transformation from the shambling, bent-over figure walking onto the stage to the passionate performer at the piano. Scott Hicks said that, being a filmmaker, he would be very interested in making a feature film of David's life.

Though surprised at first, I was impressed by his emotional response to David's playing and thought he seemed to be a man of sensitivity and integrity. David and I had had many hair-brained schemes put to us at Riccardo's, but this seemed to be something entirely different, and over the next nine years it proved to be just that. In the meantime, I asked Scott Hicks to put his proposal in writing, as we were leaving for Melbourne the next day.

The Melbourne venue was the Great Hall in the National Gallery of Victoria, and it was packed. It was to be David's first major performance in Melbourne since the night of his disappointing loss in 1964. This time, David's playing was simply electrifying.

This was also the first proper concert of David's that my son, Scott, attended. During the second half, when David began to play *Pictures at an Exhibition*, I could see that Scott was totally captivated. By the second *promenade*, he was weeping and could not stop until well after David had finished. When we went backstage, my son still in tears, David rushed up and hugged him, joyously exclaiming, "I made Scottie cry! I made him cry!" The two of them just stood there holding each other and, as Scott wept on David's shoulder, David was thrilled that his art had touched someone so profoundly. At least, that is what Scott and I thought at the time.

Over the years, David would repeat "I made Scottie cry" every time he saw him again. Whenever we would meet Scott at airports or see him driving up to the house, David would run towards him, arms spread out wide, always smiling and repeating, "I made Scottie cry! I made Scottie cry!" Every time the topic of *Pictures* came up in Scott's presence, David would again repeat the phrase, and we would always interpret his words literally. It was strange that David singled out that particular concert and that particular piece, because since then Scott has been to many of David's recitals and again been greatly moved.

It was only recently, after spending a fortnight with David, during which they had had various long conversations, that Scott told me he finally realised what "I made Scottie cry" really meant.

"David", said Scott, "must have sensed all along that I was having difficulties relating to him. And it was not till he played *Pictures* that time, and I cried, that he knew I totally accepted him and not only understood his musical greatness, but responded to the childlike purity and love which is his essence. When he tells me that he made me cry, he is really telling me that he knows I love him." Though David was not present when this conversation occurred, somehow, in the almost telepathic way that he has, he sensed that Scott now understood his message and has never repeated "I made Scottie cry" since.

The Melbourne recital was also memorable because it proved to be the best one of the tour. In Sydney, the organiser, Andrew McKinnon, managed to jam 600 people into the hall at Scots College which only had 550 seats. Thus the tiered auditorium had people trying to perch everywhere, including on the steps, and the crowd had a real buzz to it. What was most notable about that performance was that David had toned down the humming and the infamous "drone" to a more acceptable level, so it was more like a Mini Minor coming to town than the Grand Prix.

On the morning of the recital I had pirouetted on the slippery floor of the bathroom, falling in an ungainly heap on my right arm. It made a rather disturbing crunch but, after drying myself down, I thought it would be fine. However, when we arrived in Brisbane the pain had worsened, and a visit to the doctor was necessary. Yes, my wrist was broken and our pile of luggage was now a rather daunting sight.

To start the much-anticipated overseas trip with my arm in plaster was a considerable bother. But David still had the Brisbane recital to do and again the crowd responded wonderfully. He was on a roll, I was longing for bed and a few quiet days, but the show had to go on. My broken arm seemed a minor inconvenience to how David must have been feeling about the prospect of returning to London, the city which he had always perceived as the scene of his great undoing.

The Vintage Years

Sailing into the northern hemisphere on the P&O *Himalaya*, the nineteen-year-old David Helfgott experienced a rare new feeling: freedom. This, he soon discovered, came with another new feeling: aloneness. Though he was "sore" and rather "foggy", on the *Himalaya* he found a miraculous substance which numbed the "soreness", made the "fog" irrelevant and enabled him to carry off the pretence that nothing at all was the matter, with the greatest of ease. The substance was alcohol.

"I was often drunk on the *Himalaya*, drunk and happy", David recalled. "I went to the Captain's party and got very drunk and turned off all the lights. Everyone thought it was

uproariously funny. I was naughty, cheeky and mischievous."
David also performed for the passengers, who loved it, and
during the course of the journey made some friends. To most
people on the ship, he seemed to be a brilliant, eccentric, heavy-
drinking, but incredibly charming and vivacious young man
with an exciting and promising future. That trip on the *Himalaya* was to set the pattern for David's life over the next three
years.

David recalled that when he first saw London, "It was
foggy, but then the fog cleared and it was fine." But while the
notorious London fog might have cleared, the one in his mind
did not, and his recollections of his time in London have always
been, and will probably always remain, extremely vague.

Arriving at Victoria Station, David was picked up by a
contact from a Jewish organisation, B'nai B'rith, who took him
to its headquarters. He then caught a cab to Willesden, where,
by prearrangement, he was going to board with a Jewish lady,
Mrs Strauss.

Upon meeting Mrs Strauss, David presented her with a
box of chocolates and a ring, which he had bought especially
for her as a greeting gift in Ceylon on the way over. Brought
up to be nice and obedient, and with a natural tendency to be,
as he always says, "affable and amenable to all", David did not
deviate from his usual behaviour with Mrs Strauss, nor did he
do so the next day when he went to enrol at the Royal College
of Music.

David had just made it in time for the start of the Christmas term, and was told to go and immediately present himself
to his new teacher, Cyril Smith. Feeling extremely fearful and

David and Madame Alice Carrard (at 92 years old), 1989.

BELOW: David on the banks of the Swan River, in South Perth, writing his composedlies, *1990.*

David and Nils Ruben, Denmark, 1990.

David playing Liszt's handmade Bechstein piano at the Liszt House in Weimar, Germany, 1993.

David and Gillian at Portofino, Italy, 1994.

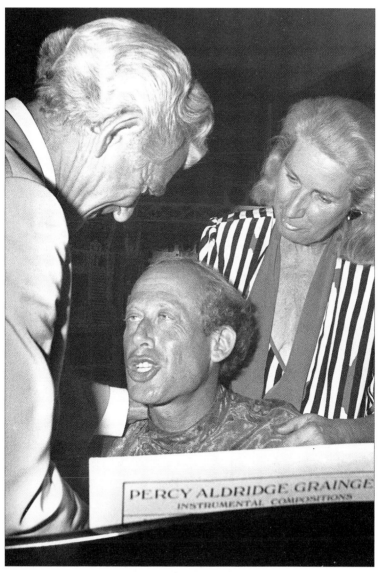

David and Gillian with then Prime Minister Bob Hawke at a naturalisation ceremony in Hobart, Tasmania, in the late 1980s.

David relaxes at a friend's house in Mackay, Queensland, with the cat, Sophie, in 1993.

Gillian washes sand off David after a swim at Bargara, near Bundaberg, Queensland, 1993.

Lizzie the blue heeler, in the Promised Land, early 1990s.

BELOW: David swimming at a friend's house in Bellingen, New South Wales, 1995.

David and Mike Parry, about 1993.

David and his brother, Les, 1996.

David with Rachel, Rachel's friend Harry, and Les's son Peter, 1995.

During the filming of Shine, *at the Adelaide Town Hall, 1995: from left, Suzie, Lynn Redgrave, Gillian, Louise.*

David and Lynn Redgrave at David's birthday party in Adelaide, 1995.

Geoffrey Rush, David and Lynn Redgrave celebrate David's birthday in Adelaide, 1995.

David and film director Scott Hicks, at the world premiere of Shine *in Adelaide, 1996. (Photograph: Martin Jacka,* The Advertiser, *Adelaide)*

shy, David stood outside Smith's door and tried to summon up courage. When he finally went in, Smith told him that he was late, but then David started playing and "everything soon settled. Smith smiled very indulgently and thought there were some quite brilliant passages", he recalled.

David quickly immersed himself in the hectic life of lessons with Smith, practising, attending college choir rehearsals and going to composition lessons. The microcosm of the college was providing a stable environment, from which David could set forth and explore the large and unfamiliar world of London, and the complex and just as unfamiliar world of himself as a private and now completely independent individual.

The first six months in London was a time of great expansion for David. Word soon spread around the college that he was particularly gifted and his peers' admiration was easily obtained. As the students became more familiar with him, they also found his childlike, mischievous nature and love of a good party just as appealing.

In contrast to the very remote and rather provincial atmosphere of Perth, David was overwhelmed with the frequency and standard of the concerts he could attend in London. "Professor," David wrote to Callaway, "I am going to as many concerts as finance allows; admittedly I have to miss some because there are 150 being held this month alone!! 150 imagine!! And some of them are magnificent!!" David would often sit through a concert completely in awe, and then dash out to buy the full miniature score of whatever he had just heard and study it in detail.

He was also enthralled by his own music-making. The great Cyril Smith, himself a renowned pianist, who ten years earlier had suffered a stroke and lost the use of his left arm, was opening new vistas for David, and the boy was soaking up every word of Smith's wisdom.

After the initial shyness had passed, David found he really liked his new teacher, and even though in December of '66 he wrote to Professor Callaway, "Mr Smith is a marvellous teacher – but he's terribly strict – every note has to be perfect!! He's always hammering away at the idea of 'discipline' which I am sadly lacking in", two months later David was writing to him that Smith was "a remarkable teacher; so sympathetic – I couldn't ask for better!!"

Overall, David's recollection of Smith is of a patient and supportive man: "In a way he was the most indulgent really, because first he would always let you play all the notes. First, confidence – that's the first rule. Then we'd take it apart, look at every corner, every nuance, and then we'd put it all together again."

Having instilled confidence in the boy, Smith set about changing David's practice methods. Quite apart from being a known believer in self-discipline, Smith was concerned about David's disorganised and disoriented manner, and the early signs of the chaos that was slowly taking firm hold of his mind.

"At the moment I am engaged in a complete overhaul of my piano playing – endeavouring to discipline myself and to play in the correct way!! I hope never to play another note; which hasn't been <u>thought</u> about", reported David to Professor Callaway in December '66. Some weeks later, in another letter, he confessed, "Of course the piano doesn't give up its secrets so easily; it's a long arduous road it seems. But I'm doing my best

(I hope)." By February, he had become quite an exponent of Smith's ideas on the topic and wrote, "It makes me feel awful when I think of all those wasted years mucking around at the piano!! But what's past is past; and I am very happy with my present style of practising; which is mainly great concentration and intense listening – apparently everything depends on the brain!! If you are thinking clearly you can't go wrong."

The struggle for clarity of thought in general was becoming increasingly difficult, no matter how happy or excited David was about being in London. The growing inner chaos had very little to do with external events; nevertheless, any bothersome or unpleasant situations affected him more than most people. Thus, he found his lodgings with Mrs Strauss and the routine she set for her boarders to be rather annoying, particularly when it came to dinner time.

Mrs Strauss would usually serve the evening meal at around the same time as the start of most concerts David wanted to attend, and for which he would often have a ticket. However, instead of going, he would have to sit and eat his dinner – otherwise he would starve, as he could neither cook for himself, nor did he have any money left over to buy any other food, having spent the food allowance in his all-up rent for Mrs Strauss. Having to miss these concerts upset David significantly enough for him to write about it to Professor Callaway and remember those frustrations many years later.

Also, David recalled that Mrs Strauss was "scared to death" of him and used to lock her door at night. This David found to be rather unfriendly, but there was an extra 'personality problem' he had with his landlady: "Mrs Strauss had all those

'Victorian' problems like the father. I soon found out father wasn't the only one. All those 'Victorians' have been damaged, they've all been damaged. They are all a bit repressive."

Having glimpsed freedom, David was not keen on any reminders of the sort of stern discipline he had experienced at home. Independence was beckoning. "That's why I went to the Irish," he explained, "because when I went to the Irish I could practise any time I liked and I could go to the concerts any time I liked and I could just look after myself and it worked for a while."

"Irish" is David's nickname for Mrs Clifford, into whose house he moved during Easter '67. Here, unlike at Mrs Strauss's, he had no piano and the room had very few comforts, but the rent was only a quarter of his previous one. "Irish" was kind and gentle, enduring many of David's growing eccentricities and allowing him all the freedom and solitude he craved. "I am happiest when I am on my own; and have my privacy to work undisturbed; and with full concentration", wrote David to Professor Callaway in March '67; "in any case, how else can one hope to progress!!"

Though the progress David was writing about was of a musical kind, his absolute independence meant he was now free to party and, consequently, drink as much as he liked. "That's what everyone did at college, it didn't seem to do much harm anyhow", David explained. "Everyone risked a bit of red wine and a bit of white wine, and it's good for you in a way. So I always used to drink *vino, vino* and apple cider."

Indeed, for the time being, the *vino* was not doing too much harm, as David's playing was improving and, in a rare display of self-sufficiency, he even managed to save £5 and acquire a piano. Though the instrument was a complete wreck – "all the pedals were broken and the keys as well!" – David did have enough gumption to call someone in to "get it tuned and regulated and needled and everything".

The drinking was also, so far, not interfering too much with his practising, and he would spend hours at the keyboard, leading Smith to note in David's end-of-year report that, "He has had bursts of quite brilliant playing." However, it would seem that all David's good intentions to concentrate and discipline himself were not up to Smith's standard, as Smith also wrote that David needed "a steadier application to some work and more attention to basic rhythmic problems". Bryan Kelly, David's composition teacher, was even less impressed. "A rather muddled year", Kelly wrote in the report. "A keen pupil but emotion dominates over mind and matter and the results are hectic."

Nevertheless, the authorities responsible for providing the necessary finance for David's tuition must have been fairly content with his progress during the first year, as he received further money to continue his studies.

David's summer holidays were spent practising and visiting friends, who were many and varied. By the end of first year, like most students of his age, David had become part of a little 'gang'. Four of its members he has remembered with much affection, though, of course, always referring to them by their nicknames. There was "Sir Simon", who studied piano and organ and was in no way a lord. There was "Immaculate", another piano student, who for a time was one of David's 'platonic' girlfriends, as was "Dr Connie Francis", who was not a doctor at all but a cello student. The only one of the group whom David called by his real name was a violinist named Ian. Together they went out to concerts, music competitions and parties, and, as the others always had more money than David, they would occasionally take him out to restaurants and movies.

Apart from these friends of his own age, David also kept in touch with some Jewish families, to whom he was introduced via his contacts with the Jewish community back in Australia. Though these people were caring and kind to him, after a while, as David developed more independence, he saw less of them.

One of the most important friendships that David formed in London through an Australian connection was with expatriate writer Jack Lindsay and his wife, Meta. A great supporter of Katharine Susannah Prichard, Lindsay, whom David has always called "Dr Jacko", welcomed the young Australian pianist to his home and David spent his first overseas Christmas with the Lindsay family. He would often go and visit Dr Jacko in Halstead, Essex, and play for him, their conversations reminding David of his time with KSP in Australia.

Apart from introducing David to Jack Lindsay, KSP, with whom David kept up a dedicated correspondence, also commissioned a portrait of David to be done by another expatriate friend of hers and sent back to her in Australia. "KSP wanted to have me for all time", explained David.

Overall, the years from 1966 to 1969 were near-perfect as far as David was concerned. "They were my good years, my vintage years", he would say.

One of the most important, but seemingly obscure,

moments of the "vintage years" occurred during a speech by the Director of the Royal College, Sir Keith Falkner (he was knighted in June '67). One particular phrase of that speech etched itself in David's memory forever – and, as David and I would later find out, in Sir Keith's as well.

The phrase was simple: "What's it all about?", asked Sir Keith of his students. At the time, David knew the context in which the question was asked, but apparently did not know the answer. Some twenty years later, when David had all but forgotten the context, Sir Keith would unexpectedly reveal the simple answer, and David would be amazed by the strange path his life had had to take in order to hear it.

Wild
Colonial Boy

In the spring of 1967, David made an extravagant and, by his own estimation, "extremely costly" birthday-present purchase of a pair of contact lenses. "But," he insists to this day, "it was worth it." Desperate to get rid of the ungainly, cumbersome spectacles which he had worn from the age of three or four, and which had always made him feel different and inadequate, he boldly and recklessly spent some of the grant intended for his living expenses.

Though the lenses were one of the earliest models, and were crude and rather painful to wear, their effect was instantaneous. "It made the world of difference", remembered David.

"It restored my *confiance* and improved my appearance and *posturepedic*. It made me happier and improved my playing." The new *confiance* must have also made him more attractive to others, a result that David had not quite bargained for, but which he found to be rather wonderful.

Due to poor eating habits, David had lost much weight and become rather willowy. This, added to his golden curls and a mischievous immaturity suffused with gentleness and charm, made him rather popular with girls, as was perhaps to be expected. What was not expected, however, and what David had no idea how to handle, was that he became rather popular with boys as well.

"Everyone at college fancied me", confided David, with not a little degree of pride and amusement. "I had plenty of girlfriends at college and boyfriends, I had them all. I nearly had it all! Admittedly, I was sort of a very wild pianist, that's what everyone said anyhow. When I was in my vintage years I was so incredibly good-looking, naturally everyone wanted to sleep with me!", David revealed with a self-deprecating chuckle. But after a moment he added, "Of course I didn't know about things like that. I was naive and innocent."

Indeed, craving attention and affection in any form, the 'wild colonial boy' was relishing all the propositioning and seductive suggestions, but, lacking any previous experience in that area, was unfamiliar with the protocols of flirtation. Mostly he opted for total passivity, and let himself be led in any direction anyone desired him to go. However, when it came to the crunch, David would bolt. To most who desired him, he would have seemed to be a 'tease', and of these there were surprisingly many – not only students, but also some members of staff and others he encountered in artistic circles.

"I used to always run away, you see", confided David. "I used to run away from the men. I was always running scared. I was lonesome and scared. It must have been a bit of a barrier, a bit of a shield." Women did not fare much better with him either; cuddles and kisses were all they got, no matter what they tried. David's behaviour would have mystified them: how were they to know that the twenty-year-old in front of them was, in fact, stuck "on a hook at a fifteen-year-old level"?

Immaturity was not the only "shield", however. By his second year at college, alcohol was no longer blunting David's emotional pain sufficiently, and he was finding it necessary to keep increasing his intake. "I was stupid", David acknowledged. "I used to drown my sorrows in drink, in *vino*. I just drank and drowned." By the end of a dinner date or a party, he was rather useless to his companions. To David, they would look pretty 'foggy' to begin with, but with the addition of an alcoholic haze they would become almost invisible.

Nevertheless, David was becoming even more respected by his fellow students. During his lessons with Smith on *Islamey*, they would mill outside Smith's room, occasionally peering in, listening to David's playing with a great deal of admiration. On 17 October, he performed *Islamey* at a chamber concert at the college. "*Islamey* went off very well", he reported in a letter to Professor Callaway. "I've had a lot of favourable comment on it from my fellow students and in spite of a few wrong notes etc; it was alright because I wasn't a bit nervous on stage!"

The lack of nervousness during a performance should not

have been a surprise to David, as this had never been one of his problems. A mind slowly spinning out of control, lack of finances and an increasingly chaotic lifestyle, however, were.

Sometime in the first weeks of 1968, David found himself particularly short of cash. Due to Christmas and New Year holidays, and the various delays of the postal system, his cheque from Australia was late. Most of his friends were away, spending the winter break with their families, and David found himself alone and starving. The feeling of panic about his financial situation made him agitated and more than ever aware of the 'soreness' in his eyelid. His thoughts racing wildly out of control, David walked through London in the cold winter wind, desperately trying to figure out what to do. Wandering across Hyde Park Corner, he was approached by a friendly young man; in fact, as David recalled, "a German Jew. Imagine that! One of my own!"

The young man started talking to David, but must have found him to be gibbering and not terribly coherent, as David can remember being told, "You're talking too much." The young man then offered to take David to a restaurant.

"I was destitute and I was hungry, so I had to accept some help. I couldn't really turn down a bowl of soup", explained David and sighed. "Then it just went like that, and I just wanted to see how far it goes, and I was very grateful for the help. It was the first time I accepted." This time, for a reason that still mystifies him, David did not run away. Unsettled by the experience, he discovered with not a little degree of amazement that, "The next day I was fine!"

However, intimacy frightened him, and he continued to

run from anyone whom he knew well. Complete strangers, though, did not seem to be so threatening, "It was just that way", David would sadly chuckle, pondering on the reasons behind his behaviour in those years. "It just happened to be lopsided, it was sloping." At the time, his little ventures to the wilder side of life caused him a great deal of confusion; they were just about the last thing his fragile mind needed. However, after a couple of decades of thought and self-analysis, he reached an understanding and acceptance of his actions and would become quite forthright on the topic: "Of course, in those days it was all swinging London – anything goes, anything goes. Well, almost, almost. We tried everything, practically everyone did. But I reckon when you're in your vintage years, you should explore and enjoy yourself. Because if you don't have fun in this world, you're silly. You gotta go for it and take all the risks because life is so short and you ought to have fun and enjoy yourself."

In his utter naivety, David did not realise that some areas in life which might well be safe for others to explore were not so for him. By the second year of living alone, David's expedition to the inner world of his private and independent self was leading him into uncharted waters, and he was beginning to flounder. However, as always, he could return to his port of call: music. David continued to play at college recitals and competitions and, under Smith's guidance, again started to work on Rakhmaninov's Concerto No. 3.

"He has an extraordinary pianistic talent", wrote Smith in David's report for the second year, "but his work is ill-organised and spasmodic." That Smith held this opinion would have come as no surprise to David, as he was well aware of his teacher's concerns for his future.

"Just from his observations of me," recalled David, "Smith thought that I was very good at playing the piano but I had no common sense in other things. He thought a lot of me and was grooming me for international stardom, but he said that I better be a very good pianist because there is nothing much else I can do. Smith told me that everyone's got an Achilles heel and he thought I was risky. There was gonna be no *compri* he said. I was going to be the top cat or else the least."

Smith's wise words only confirmed what David had already proven to himself. In order to earn some much-needed cash, David found employment at a London hamburger restaurant. He started in the kitchen making up the raw burgers, but gradually, as his first day on the job progressed, his boss kept demoting him to more menial tasks, until David was sweeping floors. And even though the kindly boss took pity on the hopeless youngster and promised to find him something to do if he came back the next day, David declined the offer. "I am better at the piano playing, that's what I do best", he told me, by way of explanation for his early retirement from the burger industry. "Besides, it was *raw* hamburger meat!", he conceded, squirming at the memory.

Also, Smith was not the only one who was no longer thinking that David was merely childish and eccentric. As David became more disorganised and forgetful, failing to turn up to or arriving late for lessons, rehearsals and college events, other teachers were beginning to notice that the young man was experiencing some problems. One day, when David missed a crucial rehearsal for a concert recital, Sir Keith had to step in and plead David's case, so that he would be given another chance. The few older and more sensible friends whom David was still seeing were also becoming aware of his problems. He recalled that a middle-aged Jewish lady friend of his "saw that I was fretting and took me to her GP".

When the doctor asked David why he was fretting, David burst into tears – for the first time in almost a decade – and started telling the doctor that all he wanted to do in life was "to play piano for father". David was inconsolable: he just wanted life to be like it was when he was little, before Peter threw him out of the house, before the chair-wrestling incident of '62 and certainly before anyone had suggested David go to America. David wanted his daddy to love him, to protect him, to tell him he was once again his "little prince" and to be very, very proud of his piano playing.

The doctor listened carefully and prescribed Valium. David went home and took the medicine, but a few weeks later decided that this was not enough. And so, for the first time in his life, he began to look for a psychiatrist.

When David told Smith about his intentions, the great master was totally opposed. As with everything else in his students' life, "Smith expected you to discipline yourself, look after yourself, you see", David explained. "'Cause he thought you could cure yourself. And I reckon that Smith was a good teacher, but Smith was not wise. I was calling out for help, see, I needed help with my soreness."

Even seeing a psychiatrist was not going to be an easy matter, as, quite apart from Smith's opposition, it took a while to find the right doctor. "I tried all different doctors – the cost was phenomenal!", remembered David. "I went from doctor to doctor until I finally found Dr Lupin."

For a while, everything more or less settled down. David continued to study and practise and attend regular sessions with Dr Lupin, whom he really liked: "It seemed to do me good. We just talked. He made me feel much better." Around this time, David's piano playing began to show rapid improvement.

All RCM students were graded according to their standard of musicianship, and when David first came to college he was placed in grade IV B. He was dissatisfied with this position and from his first days in college dreamt of achieving grade V. Finally, after playing *Pictures at an Exhibition* at a college competition in third year, he was not only upgraded to V, but was also awarded the Marmaduke Barton Prize and the Hopkinson Silver Medal – the third-highest medal for piano playing. David attributed all these achievements to his sessions with Dr Lupin.

To improve his general health and fitness, he would go swimming, either at the Marshall Street swimming pool – when he could afford it – or, as was more often the case, in the murky waters of the Serpentine in Hyde Park when he was low on pennies. The physical exercise seemed to have little effect on his weight, as, along with everything else in his disintegrating metabolism, it began to fluctuate wildly, leaving him reed-thin one month and pudgy the next.

David was still drinking copious amounts of *vino*, and his diet was poor. Most of the time, he was more inclined to pay extra money for good seats at a concert, where he was able to see the performer's hands, than buy himself a decent meal. To keep up his energy, he drank coffee and gallons of Lucozade. In fact, his colleagues and friends would comment on how inseparable he was from his bottle of Lucozade. Little did they know that at home David was becoming just as inseparable from his little bottle of Valium: the more he took, the more he needed.

In the early summer of 1969, David made one of the most unfortunate mistakes of his life, an act which he has always regretted. Though he cannot remember the reason for his most uncharacteristic behaviour, he made a rude comment about "Irish", his wonderfully kind and patient landlady. The comment was apparently about her appearance, which was even more uncharacteristic of David, who rarely noticed how anyone looked. Understandably offended by his comments, Irish told David that her family needed the extra room and asked him to leave. Once again, David packed his suitcase and went to a room in a shared student household. "I was all right with the Irish", David would say wistfully. "But I was cruel, and I sort of shot myself in the foot, and after that it all went bad, except for my great Rak performance of course."

The change in living arrangements could not have come at a worse time, as David was preparing for the most important performance of his twenty-two years: on 17 July, he was to play the entire Rakhmaninov Third Concerto with the RCM orchestra at the college concert hall.

This was going to be his last great effort in London. After that David just wanted to go home, as he could feel himself falling apart. For now, however, he was going to pull all his mental and emotional resources together, concentrate and prepare to the best of his abilities.

"The college didn't know what to do about me, they were in a dilemma", acknowledged David, and it would seem that the solution they came up with was rather different from David's plans. The most prevalent notion about his state was that, though he was a pianist of enormous potential, he was not as yet properly 'grown up', and some extra time in the security of the college environment would be beneficial for him before he went out into the big wide world to display his talents on his own.

A few days before the Rakhmaninov recital, "Mrs Luber had come especially all the way from Australia to organise me!", David recalled. Travelling with her husband, Mrs Luber-Smith kindly decided to look into David's affairs and found his financial situation and mental condition wanting. She arranged for an interview with the college bursar and another one with Cyril Smith. As a result, the college granted David the Leverhulme Scholarship, which provided enough money for one year's tuition and some living expenses. David, however, was not to know of this until four days after his recital.

On the morning of 17 July, he woke up feeling rather 'sore'. It just happened that way; some days were 'foggier' than others and the 'soreness' was worse. At 2.30 that afternoon, he was to attend a rehearsal with the orchestra. In order to concentrate his thoughts, he decided to go for a swim. In the water, he more or less lost track of time, and consequently was late to the rehearsal. Dashing into the hall after the orchestra had already begun playing without him, David leapt onto the piano stool and, immediately picking up the first movement of the concerto in the right place, proceeded with the rehearsal as if nothing had happened.

Though unnerved by their soloist's behaviour, everyone present at the rehearsal "forgave me, because I played so well", remembered David. "I was sore, sore, sore, but everyone thought the rehearsal was going quite well, they told me that was the feedback back from the college", he continued, but then confessed that there were some concerns: "You know, they said they weren't sure if I was going to turn up that night at the college concert. Smith said to me, 'We're not sure what you're going to do, David.' But the fact was, of course, I would turn up at the college concert."

Hardly aware of his reputation for erratic behaviour, David did not find out till seventeen years later that, just prior to the concert, Vernon Handley, the conductor, turned to Sir Keith and, taking a deep breath, said, "It's going to be hazardous and it may be brilliant."

chapter 22

Risky Business

Following his stroke in 1956, Cyril Smith wrote *Duet for Three Hands* and, according to David, "absolutely insisted that all his students read that book, 'cause it's motivational and inspirational".

In the book, Smith wrote of the difficulty for even the most dedicated pianist of achieving "more than ten consecutive seconds of absolutely perfect playing a year", and executing even one single phrase of music to their "complete satisfaction".

By the time David took his seat in the RCM concert hall to play Rakhmaninov's Concerto No. 3, he was well acquainted with Smith's beliefs. Also, as David once told me, he had come to share Smith's opinion that perfection is only achieved by a pianist when there is "a balance: hands, mind and soul have to be even, and then the circle is complete and you feel satisfied".

Though David started to play the concerto a touch too slowly, he soon settled. "I really gave it all", he proudly recalled. "That was the only thing that mattered. I just decided to concentrate and I was fine."

"Playing the piano", David once mused, "is a risky business, but you gotta take risks 'cause life is a short trick." Therefore, he concluded, "You have to know all those notes so well that you can play them blindfold. When I played the Rak that night, I knew every note blindfold and I was actually quite safe. I was aware that it was magic, 'cause I was so inspired that night. I was in nice balance. I really did feel satisfied. I felt complete. I succeeded beyond my wildest dreams."

When I read Cyril Smith's book, I asked David if at any stage that night he felt he achieved the "ten consecutive seconds of absolutely perfect playing".

"Yes! Yes!", he replied, "It was perfect playing for *all* of that time!" Considering that David usually completes the 'Rak' in approximately forty minutes, "all that time" in this case was definitely beyond his wildest dreams.

But David was not dreaming; he really did play so remarkably well that he received a standing ovation, and not just from the audience in general, but also from the professors of the RCM – an extremely rare occasion in the history of the college. However, David does not remember seeing the crowd or hearing their cheers and applause. "I was told about the standing ovation afterwards", he said. "I was only aware that everyone was pleased."

"Why didn't you see them? Did you leave the stage?", I asked.

"No," he replied, "I kept walking up and down the stage. I walked back and forward, up and down, and I just sort of looked up. Perhaps I was feeling tremendously excited and elated and relieved, relieved. I knew it was a success." After the adulation settled, David recalled that "Smith was very pleased and he gave me his hand! It was the only time he gave me his hand! It was pretty unique!"

David's performance was considered to be the best performance of a concerto by an RCM student that year, and for this he won the Dannreuther Prize of £13. The following Monday he received the cheque and an accompanying letter, telling him that he had won this prize and had been awarded the £500 Leverhulme Scholarship. Suddenly, David found himself in a quandary.

He knew that the scholarship was a rare honour. He had now proven to himself that great musicianship was his destiny. He knew, too, that there would now be recital opportunities at some of London's most prestigious venues. However, he was also keenly aware that he was moving dangerously close to the edge.

"I should've come home in triumph", David would mutter when in a sulky mood. "I knew the fourth year was gonna turn out to be a disaster, but what could I do? I had to obey the college because they spent all this money on me and they insisted that I stay. They wanted to put me on at the Albert Hall and the Academy. So, I was in a dilemma. I was caught in a trap, in a steel trap. But I should've put my foot down. I should've followed my own *intuitive*."

Given the circumstances, it would have been extremely difficult for David to follow his *intuitive*. He could look out of the windows of the RCM and see the Albert Hall beckoning – a great honour for a twenty-two-year-old Perth boy who began his musical career on a home-made piano stool. There was Smith and Sir Keith and "Frankie-boy" – men whom he admired tremendously, men who had supported him, and whom he now had the chance to 'do proud'. Moreover, there was this great sum of money and, after all he had been through, how could he possibly refuse this privilege? Thus, David decided to stay for the fourth year and, by his own admission, entered "a hell of a time", as "After the Rak it all went chaos. It all went absolutely foggy and misty, foggy and misty."

David's mind was no longer successful at restricting his emotional pain to the corner of his eyelid, and it began to spread, insidiously moving towards his heart, and finally nestling into his soul. In order to combat the agony, David drank and drank and took more Valium. "But," as he soon discovered, "that was not a solution either.

"I was just trying to alleviate the soreness and I thought it would help", he explained. "But of course it doesn't. It's a vicious circle. The point is all those medicaments have side effects! They make you drowsy. A smidgen of medicament is not so bad, but I took too many and I had no idea I was too excessive. I overdid it. I always overdo things. I took handfuls! I did a 'Judy Garland'! Imagine, I could've killed myself! Alcohol and medicaments is a killing combination – now, that's really doing yourself in.

"You must not consume yourself", continued David. "You must have that reserve of health to carry your intention to the audience, mustn't you? And Valium made it difficult to concentrate – those medicaments are a bit *unpredicaments*", he chuckled. "And then I couldn't play so well. Imagine that! And I'd played so well for three years."

The months following the end of David's third year in London have vanished into oblivion with the exception of one clear memory: asking Dr Lupin to admit him to a psychiatric hospital. "I was desperately crying out for help, 'cause by that time I would've been sore for a very long time. I've been carrying this *dommage* with me ever since fourteen really, and when I went to London there was already something amiss", explained David. "I begged and begged Dr Lupin, 'cause it was very painful."

Though objecting at first, on the grounds that David was insufficiently unwell for such radical measures, Dr Lupin finally agreed, and by October '69 David found himself in Halliwick Hospital. As is the case with all his other hospitalisations, David has few memories of being there. However, his Halliwick stay was marked by such a tragic occurrence that it has singled itself out from all his other hospital experiences.

One day, when a nurse brought David his mail, there was a little package from Australia. The nurse came back after a few minutes to check up on David and found him sobbing. The package contained his correspondence with KSP and some other little mementoes. Throughout his time in London,

David had received strength and courage from his friendship with KSP. Though she may have been on the other side of the planet, her regular letters, containing, according to David, "All sorts of loving things, wonderful loving things; wonderful poetry and wonderful prose", were the one and only unambiguous and limitless source of affection he desperately needed. Now there would be no more letters, and there would be no more KSP, even if and when he did return to Australia. KSP was dead.

The nurse took David in her arms and held him tightly. "She told me I was beautiful, I could cope. She consoled me and said the pain would go, it would go", he recalled.

But it didn't go. It was merely temporarily dulled by chemicals less common than Valium. And when it seemed that it was dulled sufficiently, David was released from hospital, just in time to make it back to college for the annual visit of the college's president, at that time the Queen Mother, and be awarded the Hopkinson Silver Medal by her.

By December, he somehow managed to be organised enough – no doubt with a great deal of help – to arrange accommodation at the new RCM hostel for male students, the Robert Mayer Hall.

David's condition hardly improved, as on 31 December he wrote to Professor Callaway, "I attempted the Brahms 2nd Concerto last week – and it could have gone much better, unfortunately. I was in a very bad mood ... what shall we call it? 'End-of-term malaise?'" However, in the following term there was no need for him to describe his moods: the deterioration of his mental health was quite evident in his prolific underlining and eccentric punctuation in the simplest and shortest of notes he wrote at the time.

Nevertheless, David continued to practise and perform. There were not as many scheduled lessons or rehearsals at the college in the fourth year as there had been in the previous three. Though the structure and support of the institution were still available to him, he was now expected to learn how to become much more independent. But the sort of self-organisation which was extremely difficult for him at the best of times had now become impossible. Sometimes he would forget to confirm engagements or sufficiently prepare for them. And, even when critics or audiences responded positively, he abhorred his playing.

On 24 March 1970, David performed the Rakhmaninov Concerto No. 3 at the Duke's Hall of the Royal Academy of Music, and by all accounts the performance was "embarrassing" and "histrionic". Cyril Smith was mortified, commenting to a friend, "I did not teach him to play like that." Though David was aware of the poor quality of his playing, there was little he could do about it as he had become completely 'deaf'.

The 'deafness' worsened when, a month later, he bowed in front of a capacity crowd at the Royal Albert Hall, and proceeded to play the fateful Liszt Concerto in E flat – the same one he had performed once before after the "hate night of all hate nights" with Peter. Though the critics were, in his estimation, "kind", and the crowd responded well, he was extremely disappointed with what little he could hear of his own playing. "Of course I was sore that night when I had to play the Liszt E flat in Albert Hall", explained David. "And at that Rak 3 at the Academy I was sore as well."

"His life has been so disordered & chaotic", wrote Smith in David's final report at the end of the fourth year, "that pianistic progress has been allowed a sporadic opportunity. Nevertheless, such fantastic hands have sometimes produced almost unbelievably brilliant passages."

Sir Keith, who had great admiration for David and who was deeply saddened by one of his favourite students' unfortunate fate, added, "You have had many ups & downs. Some brilliant & some less so. I hope you will have found success & be able to stabilise your life & work. Keep in touch."

As the academic year was coming to an end, so was the money and David's capacity to endure the pain. "When I said I wasn't well; of course I was referring to the 'psycho-trouble' – it's a terrible thing, you know, and its really not my fault", wrote David to Mrs Luber-Smith on 5 July. "My chances for the moment anyhow, at the [major music competitions] have been affected by this illness; what an awful thing this is ... I'll have to get a job just like anyone else (who isn't rich); or at least try to get one. And keep music for a hobby for a while; when I'm really healthy I could always go over to New York or Philadelphia etc. I've always done my best you know; but when you're unwell one's best simply isn't good enough for the very high standards which prevail today ... I may have to leave Robert Mayer Hall soon and a winter in London without a roof over my head doesn't appeal to me – I must come back to Australia."

Four days later, David sent a desperate plea to Professor Callaway: "I am writing to find out if I can come back to Australia as soon as possible. I cannot survive out here ... I am starving; I have no money; no job; nor any accommodation after next week." David waited another four days and, on 13 July, cabled Professor Callaway: "I want to come home now please. David Helfgott."

David did not know that Professor Callaway was out of the country at that time, and his desperate pleas reached only the professor's secretary. She kindly organised for David to be sent a sum of money to tide him over until Professor Callaway returned and could take care of the matter properly. Mrs Luber-Smith also rallied David's old supporters: the Seeligson Trust, Alec Breckler and Johnny Granek. And thus, by the end of the second week of August, David had a flight back home booked and paid for.

Rushing around his little room at Robert Mayer Hall, constantly stumbling and agitatedly babbling to himself, David threw a few odd socks into his suitcase, then a couple of sheets of music, a book, a pen and ... But, no, there was no time to pack anything else. The cab was waiting. David rushed out into the street, jumped into the car and asked the driver to take him straight to Heathrow.

part 2

A Foggy
Awareness

"Life is a journey, a journey a day. Every moment is precious."

Ghost Dance

"Jenny darling, may I have some Coke, just a smidgen more of Coca-Cola, or coffee. Coffee's just as fine, Jenny, or Coke or coffee or ..."

"Coke's no problem."

"Thank you, Jenny. Thank you. I'm spoilt, spoilt, privileged."

The passenger next to me was muttering. David. Where am ... ? Plane. Oh yes, we're on a plane. What was that about Coke? God, how many has he had? How long have I been dozing?

I woke up. No, it was not a dream. The nice young flight

attendant was on her way to our seats with a can of Coke. I had a few seconds left to ask the vital question. "Possum, how many have you had?", I said, tapping David on the knee with my plaster cast to attract his attention.

His face lit up in a grin, hands busily removing the head-phones: "Just a few, darling, only a few, very rare, rare and *prodiguy*, scarce, scaredy, scared, mustn't be scared ..." The hyperactive chatter continued. There was no time to waste. I smiled apologetically at the flight attendant and told her that we were sorry to bother her, but, no, we did not want any more Coke.

David and I were on our way to Europe, our first really long overseas flight together. Apart from the small hitch of a slight caffeine-and-sugar overdose, David was coping well. He had worked out a special aeroplane routine during our Australian travels, and had never deviated from it since. Upon boarding the plane, David would look at the name tags of all the atten-dants in the doorway and immediately memorise them. For the rest of the trip he would call them by their names, and chat to them as if he had known them all his life. He would charm them into plying him with an endless supply of Coke, coffee and lemonade – heaven for him, particularly if I was not awake to stop him.

Hearty farewells would always be exchanged at the end of the trip, the attendants being extraordinarily sweet and kind to him considering the bothersome passenger that he could some-times be. They became even more enamoured of David when I realised he should always have a window seat. If he sat on the aisle, then every time an attendant walked by David would engage them in conversation, try to hug them and present himself as a generally disturbing element. Safely ensconced in a window seat with his earphones plugged into some classical music, David's travelling manners improved even further with the addition of pen and paper for his *"composedlies"* – a very important part of his life.

When I first started going over David's music books in order to repair them, I noticed that he had written tiny pieces of composition across some of the pages. I asked him what they were and he told me they were his *"composedlies"*, which he had written long ago. He then told me about his love of composing and said he had written some works before he went to London, but, as he had not done well in this field at college, he had not written anything since.

However, as the 'fog' started to lift, David told me he was able to hear the music in his head again and then the notation started. He would be playing the piano when suddenly he would jump up, grab a pencil and scribble a chord or sequence on whatever bit of paper was at hand. Sometimes he would sit up in the middle of the night, jot down the *composedly* and go straight back to sleep. In fact, he would do it anywhere, any time, sometimes jumping out of the swimming pool and, dripping all over the page, smudging the ink with his wet hands as he wrote. It was crucial for David, it seemed, to make a note of a *composedly* the moment it was heard, before it vanished into the labyrinth of his thoughts.

Of course, problems arose when there was no manuscript book or clean paper at hand. David has left special signs on most of his music and books, making random choices for the recording of his "fragmented masterpieces". Liszt's *Marzeppa* had been completely covered, the brilliant Liszt notes struggling for any recognition. One of David's favourite books, a biography of Horowitz, received three pages of *composedlies* over its first chapter. In fact, David would 'compose' on anything. Serviettes, envelopes, letters, paper cartons, newspapers, magazines – all would bear testimony to his impulsive urges. I bought him manuscript books, but he would fill them up very quickly and often lose them, returning to the random scribbling attacks on his library.

The manuscript books are a bonus, not a necessity, as David has refined his notation technique. He simply draws the required length of staves and writes the notes on them, often without bothering to record the clef. Usually, out of a dozen *composedlies* on a page, only two or three have any connection with each other; everything else is as random as most of David's other thoughts. As he has never bothered to keep any of his *composedlies*, a complete work is unlikely to be finished any time soon.

After our visits, friends would find telltale signs of David's presence in their home long after our departure. "When are you going to write a complete composition, David?", they'd egg him on. "In God's good time, when I concentrate. So I might have to wait", he would reply, and then become quite defensive. "It's still got value to me. If I write something, it keeps me alive, it makes me more positive. Writing things settles me", he would say. "Mainly my thoughts go for symphonies", he once revealed to a friend who then quipped that, whereas Schubert had written the 'Unfinished' symphony, David was writing the 'Unstarted' symphony!

The thought of our imminent arrival in Moscow must have been quite inspirational for David, as the airline's safety instructions card in front of him was thick with *composedlies*. He pointed out a couple and, after singing something quite incomprehensible, told me he was particularly proud of them.

As I did not know precisely how David would react to London after everything that had happened to him there, we had decided that a brief visit to Russia prior to his lessons with Peter Feuchtwanger might be a good idea. I hoped that David's love of Russian music might make this visit a particularly happy experience, and so it was.

The grandeur of Moscow, with its imposing buildings, huge boulevards, and the Chaikovsky Piano Competition in particular, captivated David. From one of the scalpers outside the theatre, we managed to buy tickets for one session of the competition and, sitting in the great white hall of the Conservatorium, David absorbed every note. Afterwards, we also managed to see a few other sessions on Russian television and David was thrilled. He could not imagine how anything that was to follow on our little tour could possibly top that.

However, David was to remain in a constant state of 'wow!' as we headed to St Petersburg, which in 1986 was still called Leningrad. To walk the same streets that Balakirev and Mussorgksy had once walked, to see the same sights as Chaikovsky and Rakhmaninov had seen, were precious experiences for David. We visited the Leningrad Philharmonic Hall and heard a brilliant young violinist play Khachaturian. David wanted to see the bridge open over the Neva River and wandered off by himself at 2 am. The demise of communism had not yet taken effect on the country and it was still reasonably safe for him to roam the historic city on his own. Also, as it was June, the night was 'white', and David walked through twilight, not darkness. Of course, a swim in the Neva was also necessary, providing a fitting finale to our stay in Russia.

Then, on to London. The feeling of unease about David's possible reaction to the place once again descended on me, and I asked him how he was faring. However, it seemed that the memories of his ignominious retreat from the city, which had seen his first nervous breakdown, did not trouble David as much as I had feared. He reassured me that he was in fact very excited and even longing to revisit the college, and eager to meet Peter Feuchtwanger and begin his lessons.

Friends had recommended that we stay at the Rudolph Steiner Lodge in Hammersmith, and their suggestion turned out to be ideal. The large Georgian house – the oldest residence in Hammersmith, tucked away between the Odeon Theatre and the overpass – had a surprisingly serene atmosphere. There was a beautiful rose garden, and flowerbeds glowed with summer blooms against a backdrop of shady trees. Upon our arrival, we were greeted by Dr Evelyn Keppel and her husband, Bert. David immediately felt at peace with the place and the people – which was just as well, because this was to be our base for the next five months.

There were two grand pianos for David to choose from: one in the dining room and one in the chapel, and David would often entertain the other Lodge guests at dinner time. Living at the Lodge was akin to living in a large family home, with groups of different relatives visiting all the time. The friendliness of the

Steiner visitors, and their understanding of David, made for a very rewarding and happy time. Steiner teachers and people interested in Steiner's philosophy and educational methods came to the Lodge from all around the world, and we made many new friends during our stay.

Evelyn, a very efficient, clever, strong and determined woman, whom some people might have found challenging, had a great rapport with David. But while she was caring and kind to him, she would not let him get up to any of his tricks. He was, of course, completely dedicated to raiding the communal sugar and tea supplies, and Evelyn was quite firm about his naughtiness. On the other hand, she made him cups of tea and took him for outings in the garden, and I was grateful there was someone else to help contain his pranks.

Prior to leaving Australia we had corresponded with Peter Feuchtwanger, and David felt very positive about him from his letters. A tall and slender man, with beautiful hands and a gentle manner, Feuchtwanger made David feel completely at ease right from the beginning, and David seemed quite excited to be starting on this new musical adventure.

Feuchtwanger's studio was in a mews in Knightsbridge and it was a cluttered space. There was just enough room for the three of us and the piano, which was almost buried under a heap of music and sketches by an artist friend. Feuchtwanger asked David to let him hear some Chopin, and David played the *Ballade* No. 1 in G minor. Feuchtwanger listened with an appraising look on his face and, at the end of the piece, said, "That was very interesting, David, but there was too much Helfgott in it. Now I would like you to play Chopin."

After an hour and a half of detailed analysis of every single chord and dynamic, Feuchtwanger asked David to play the whole piece again, but this time to concentrate a bit more on what Chopin might have wanted. As he played, the piece unfolded with a completely different message and, I must confess, I liked it better.

The lessons continued in the same manner, two or three times a week, covering much of Chopin, and Mussorgsky's *Pictures at an Exhibition*. As David gleefully undertook the new method of playing and his overall sound improved, I knew we had made the right decision to leave Australia for a while.

Feuchtwanger's mews was within easy walking distance of the college, the Royal Albert Hall and Kensington Gardens, and, after our lessons, David began taking me on little tours of his old haunts. Through our correspondence with Sir Keith Falkner, a visit with the new Director of the RCM, Michael Gough Matthews, had been arranged, and David was feeling very "privileged" that he was expected. I was grateful to Sir Keith for his thoughtfulness, and knew that to be accepted back by way of introduction from this great man would chase away any ghosts which might have made it difficult for David to enter the premises.

I rang and made an appointment, and a few days later we set off for the college. As we approached the Albert Hall, David began to run, dashing past it towards the college entrance, where he suddenly came to a complete stop. He was terribly agitated, gazing up at the imposing building, muttering away about everything at once and passionately gesticulating. For a few minutes I stood quietly by his side, allowing him to calm down and collect his thoughts. Then we entered.

David looked around and did not seem to be too unsettled. We inquired about the Director and were soon shown to his office. Mr Gough Matthews immediately told us that Sir Keith had been in touch with him and how pleased he was to meet us. We had afternoon tea, and David chatted about his years at the college in a slightly more frenetic way than usual, but this did not seem to phase the Director.

There was a grand piano in the office and Mr Gough Matthews then asked David to play. Having just spent much time on the Chopin *Ballade*, David chose to play it. Unfortunately, his vocal cords were also in fine form that day, which somewhat marred the performance, but Mr Gough Matthews was very gracious about the playing. He told us of an upcoming music competition at the college and David said he would love to hear some of it. As we said our farewells, David promised to return for the competition.

Later, when I asked him if he were confident the experience would not prove to be distressing for him, he assured me that nothing could make him happier. Absolutely all my worries, as it happened, had been for nothing, because David was reacting to his return to London with the most unexpected and abundant – even for him – joy, enthusiasm and sense of adventure. Yes, the painful events of the past were part of his life, but it seemed that, as the present was gradually 'de-misting', it was the pain of the past that was beginning to 'fog up'.

The following week, we arrived early for one of the sessions of the competition, so that David could take me on a thorough tour of the college. As we walked around the grand old main building, David proudly pointed out the board where the notice of his memorable Rakhmaninov performance had been pinned up. The next stop was the hallowed portals where his lessons with Cyril Smith had taken place. Gently patting the door to Smith's old room, he said, "They would all put their *les oreilles* here, darlinka, just here, and listen to my *Islamey*. They were terribly impressed."

Most of all, though, David was keen to show me the concert hall where he had played his 'Rak'. We walked up the stairs and opened the doors to the auditorium. "See, it's so awesome and vast! Awesome and vast!", exclaimed David, pointing to the high ceilings of the fairly large auditorium. There were many paintings of famous ex-students on the walls, Sir Malcolm Sargent and Ralph Vaughan Williams among them. As we walked around the empty hall, David told me something about each of the people depicted in the portraits. Slowly I began to realise that David was unequivocally proud to have attended this great institution, proud of having been one of the many people whom he greatly admired, who were a part of it at some point in history; and so very proud, too, of having once played here so well.

David went up onto the large stage and explored the grand piano, all set up and ready for the start of the competition. Could he see himself sitting in this place some seventeen years ago? Could he hear the distant echoes of applause? Could he feel a tingle of the relief and elation he had experienced that night? Or had it all vanished into the 'fog', leaving behind a light, warm glow of achievement and triumph?

David's reverie at the piano was interrupted by some

bright, enthusiastic voices coming from the entrance to the hall. Young men and women were coming in. These were *their* "vintage years", and every good thing in the world was still possible for them.

David scurried off the stage and ran towards me with a smile, soaking up the vibes of their excitement and anticipation. As the hall gradually filled, a certain amount of tension was also palpable. One by one, the students came out and played their set works, and all the contestants were of a uniformly high standard.

Between the performances, David kept chatting to me about the pieces that were being played and how well everybody was doing. The environment must have stirred up memories of his own youth, because soon David began to reminisce about his peers and the competitions that had been staged when he was a student, and I was amazed that he could still remember who had played what, when they had played it and how. There was not a tinge of pain or regret in his voice.

As it happened, John Lill, an old friend and fellow student of David's, was performing a Beethoven concerto in the Albert Hall the following week. We bought tickets for one of the boxes and David had an uninterrupted view of the soloist. He had been in this hall so many times and heard so many marvellous musicians, having often sacrificed several meals for a ticket. Also, he had played on this stage once himself, with disappointing results. But now all that was behind him, and he was thrilled with the performance. Afterwards we went backstage, and David gave John one of his enormous hugs. As we left the hall, David walked with a bounce in his step, merrily singing some passages from the Beethoven. That was the melody for today.

The Answer

The music one plays can be quite different from the music one listens to – or so it is with David. "Rak", "Chaik" and "Modka" – that's Mussorgsky to everyone else on the planet – are among David's favourite composers for playing. However, when it comes to listening, "Uncle Ralph" and "Edward" are very close to the top of his list. Put on a good recording of Vaughan Williams' *London Symphony* or Elgar's *Enigma Variations* and David will be enraptured, entranced and, therefore, quiet for the entire duration of the piece – and often for many repeat plays.

Thus, when some friends invited us to visit them in the

Malvern Hills near Worcester, an area where Elgar spent much of his life, we immediately hired a car and ventured westwards. As we approached the white farmhouses nestled in the green fields at the foot of the hills, David animatedly recounted stories of first hearing Elgar's music on the radio when he was a young boy and falling in love with it. He talked about the choral traditions of the area, and the famous Three Choirs Festival, with which Elgar was involved in his youth.

After two delightful days with our friends, it was time to drive to Suffolk for a special reunion with Sir Keith. A scholarship student of the RCM himself, Sir Keith was a distinguished baritone. "The loveliest singer in all of England, that marvellous, marvellous voice", David would often comment. The RCM had never had a singer before as its Director, and Sir Keith's appointment in 1960 had raised a few eyebrows, but he soon won everyone over.

A wise, kind and gentle man, Sir Keith has been described by Herbert Howells as having "rare gifts of sympathy and disciplined equanimity", and he well understood that his position was really "a combination of psychiatrist, public relations officer and civil servant".

What most impressed David while he was at college, however, was Sir Keith's seemingly infinite patience. Sir Keith had been very supportive of David's acceptance into the college, and he always took a special interest in the boy during his time there. This did not change after David returned to Australia. Throughout his years of hospitalisation David would often write to Sir Keith, and always received prompt replies. Even after his retirement in 1974, Sir Keith continued to correspond.

When David told me this, I thought it utterly remarkable that a man in such an important position, with so many time-consuming duties, a man who during his directorship had seen some 3000 students pass through the college, would always remember and unfailingly find time to write to an ex-student who was tucked away in a mental institution, in a city on the other side of the world.

"I am still in Hospital, but your cards and letters act like tonics; and I am sure I shall be out soon", wrote David to Sir Keith in 1975, a comment typical of most of the letters he wrote to him. David would also often write of the music he was trying to practise whenever he was allowed to use the piano, and Sir Keith always responded with positive appraisals of David's talent.

David had written to Sir Keith to tell him of our marriage, and later I had corresponded to let him know of our upcoming trip to England. Eager to meet this very special person, and for David to see his old friend and supporter once again, I wrote and asked if we could visit him and his wife, Lady Falkner – a pianist whom he had met while they were both students at the RCM.

"We are getting older now, but I shall certainly hope to see you whilst you are in London and if possible hear David play", wrote the eighty-six-year-old Sir Keith in reply. While we were in London I rang him, and he invited us for lunch, giving me detailed instructions on how to get to Bungay, Suffolk, where he had retired.

David and I set out fairly early in the morning from the Malvern Hills, and started the long drive which took us right across England. When we finally arrived, Sir Keith and Lady

Falkner came out to greet us. David eagerly jumped out of the car to embrace both of them: he was not agitated, merely glad.

As they led us into their lovely old thatched-roof home, Lady Falkner asked us to call her Christabel. I had seen photographs of Sir Keith in David's scrapbook, and had been struck by his fine, sensitive face. Now, almost twenty years after the photographs had been taken, I knew we were in the presence of a very caring, distinguished gentleman, whose eyes reflected the kindness of his nature.

Christabel was the epitome of graciousness and invited us to sit down for lunch, which David happily proceeded to do. It was still not easy for him to sit at the table with others in those days, and I found it most unusual not to have to plead with him to do so. I knew of the great respect David had for Sir Keith and I could see it was an emotional time for them, as they recollected the various events they had both been a part of, and spoke of many mutual friends.

During lunch, Sir Keith asked us if we had come up from London and, when I told him that we had actually come from near the Welsh border, he was amazed. "You mean you have driven right across England to have lunch with us?", he asked. We would gladly have driven the length of Britain to do so.

Sir Keith was most interested in how David's career was progressing and was happy to know that he was once again establishing himself on the concert platform. He inquired about David's repertoire and then asked him to play.

It would have been impossible to restrain David, and he was soon at the grand piano. Two Liszt works came pouring forth and David sang along. When I tried to indicate to him that he should try and keep quiet, Sir Keith commented that David could sing as much as he liked, which of course impressed David no end. After all, it was "the loveliest singer in England" who had told him this.

Then David launched into the Liszt *Ballade* No. 2. This huge and demanding piece, particularly in the left-hand passages, flowed with majesty and power, and I could see that Christabel and Sir Keith were greatly moved. At the end, Sir Keith sprang to his feet and, with arms held wide open, walked towards David and exclaimed, "Oh David, *that* is what music is all about!" David's face lit up in a radiant smile as he moved to embrace Sir Keith.

We walked around the garden, had afternoon tea and then it was time to return to London. Christabel and Sir Keith walked with us to the car and we said our farewells. As I wound down the window to say a final goodbye, I looked up at Sir Keith and saw tears streaming down his face. "Thank you for bringing him to me", he said quietly.

David had not heard Sir Keith's last words, but as we drove away he kept exclaiming, "It took me all those years! It took me all those years!", until I finally asked him what he was referring to. "What he asked us all in college, of course", replied David. "'What's it all about?' And I had to wait twenty years for the answer. All that time."

Other Lands, Kind Strangers

At the end of July, Peter Feuchtwanger invited David to partici-
pate in his masterclass in Sion, Switzerland. We thought this
was a wonderful idea, as it would give David a chance for wider
communication with his fellow musicians.

My plaster cast came off in London, just days before we
were due to fly to France to collect the hire car and drive to
Switzerland. This was just as well: looking after both the luggage
and David at international airports has always been difficult, but
with one of my arms out of action it was almost impossible.

Airport crowds always used to stress David and he would
become quite agitated. Also, he had this wonderful idea that no

one would ever walk off with any of our cases or bags. If I had to go and deal with any business at the airport before boarding, it was close to a nightmare. As David's mind strayed from the immediate reality of the situation, so too did his body, and the repeated loudspeaker messages about not leaving luggage unattended went unheeded. He would see someone with whom he simply had to shake hands and would wander off to do so. Then, of course, he didn't want anyone near that person to miss out on the Helfgott affection and would continue on with the 'friendship ceremony' until I came to collect him.

Quite apart from trying to stop David from bothering unsuspecting, bewildered travellers, I found it a very unpleasant task to endeavour to make him distrustful of people and explain that some individuals like to steal other individuals' bags, or tamper with them, perhaps attempting to smuggle drugs and thus, in the worst-case scenario, risking our lives.

In his childlike naivety, David simply refused to believe this. "But who would want to do this to us, darling? Why would they do it to me?", he would remonstrate in response to my pleas. And, to a certain extent, he has been proven right over the years. In the hundreds of trips we have taken all over the world, miraculously nothing has ever happened to our luggage when David has gone off wandering.

While my arm was still in plaster, whenever I tried to deal with our cases, David would 'run wild', arousing the suspicion of the customs officials. 'Where the hell has he come from? Is there something afoot here?' was the look on their faces and, at Heathrow, we were pulled aside and questioned in a very unfriendly manner about David's agitation.

I explained David's condition to them as clearly as I could, but they were still a bit doubtful and obviously thought he was on drugs. He was, indeed, but they were prescribed ones, and the amounts were strictly regulated and monitored at all times.

The removal of the plaster cast made our travelling only slightly easier and it was a relief to get David into a car in Paris. At least he was contained, and the luggage was safely stowed in the boot. We started out on our drive to Switzerland on the Friday afternoon before a national holiday and the city's traffic was somewhat chaotic. Still, as we drove around the Arc de Triomphe, my eyes glued to the road as I tried to adjust to driving on what seemed the wrong side – of course, it wasn't the 'wrong' side, it was just 'different' – we had great expectations of a lovely trip through the countryside. Heading down a five-lane boulevard towards the Périphérique, my concentration was broken by the sound of David's hazy and unusually calm voice. "Oh darling, is the car meant to be on fire?", he asked, pointing to the smoke pouring from under the bonnet.

After much tooting and honking from other drivers, we managed to manoeuvre through three lanes of traffic and pull up at the side of the boulevard. Then we had to find a phone and endeavour to explain – my French is nonexistent – where we were. Eventually, a Citroën mechanic arrived, who found that no water had been put in the cooling system of the car.

Some hours later, when we were on the road to Auxerre, I suddenly realised that David had remained calm and patient throughout the whole episode. He had not started whining and begging me to get him away from the stress of the situation.

Neither had he wandered off down Paris streets while my attention was taken up with the mechanic and the car. In fact, he had behaved so well it was almost as if he were not only fully aware of the crisis but also understood how to deal with it. His mind did not 'fog up' the unpleasant reality, and he seemed to have made a conscious decision to stay with it and not run away in either his mind or body.

For the rest of the trip David behaved perfectly, though narrow roads and tunnels caused him some concern as he seemed to feel claustrophobic. Driving through the mountains at the back of Sion towards Crans-Montana, where some Australian friends had generously offered us a house, David became rather nervous, but he relaxed as soon as we arrived at the cosy ski lodge.

Five thousand feet above the smog and noise, the beauty of the Swiss Alps was breathtaking. Each morning, David would set out for a walk through the forest, looking at the birds and squirrels, and head towards a lake for a swim. Though the air was warm, the temperature of the water could hardly have been above zero, and no other swimmers ever joined him.

During the day we went to the masterclass, where there were twenty-five pianists from all over the world. The atmosphere was completely non-competitive – very rare in the piano world – and David could experience a true sense of sharing. For the first time since leaving college in 1970, he was among his peers, and the exchange of ideas and feeling of comradeship were inspiring for him.

Ten days later, on the night of the final concert, David played Liszt and Scriabin, and his music had a completely different quality to it. The phrasing was shaped so that the music seemed to breathe and have an independent life of its own. When Peter Feuchtwanger came out on stage at the end to give a speech, he said that David had taught him much, not only as a pianist but also as a person, and that he felt privileged to have had him in his class. Feuchtwanger was so overcome with emotion that he left the stage in tears.

We met many wonderful people in Sion and made new plans through our contacts with them. A private recital of Liszt works was organised for David to be given in Vienna's Bechstein Sal in September, and Peter Feuchtwanger invited us to another masterclass in Bonn in October. Meanwhile, we were about to head off to Yugoslavia.

An odd choice of destination, perhaps, but, prior to leaving for Europe, Marietta, a good friend of ours in Perth, had told us that if we wanted a holiday between David's lessons we could stay in her house in Medulin, a village near Pula on the Istrian Peninsula. Peter Feuchtwanger's assistant, Marina Horale, just happened to be from Yugoslavia, and, when we mentioned to her that we were about to go to Pula, she said she'd love to join us there in a few days' time.

We arrived in Medulin and then had to do a 'Sherlock Holmes' in order to find the house. Marietta had said to me, "Everyone knows where I live; just ask them." That would have been easy if I spoke Slovenian or Croatian, or they spoke English, but with no common language it was a matter of finding the house through the elimination of possibilities. We walked around the village repeating the word "Marietta", until a woman recognised the name and pointed out the house.

Then we began the search for a piano. With no language and no information about musical venues in Medulin, we set off to Pula, about 45 kilometres away. As we drove along, a song from *Salad Days* kept running through my head: "We're looking for a piano, a piano, just a piano . . ." In our future travels, I was to undertake a great number of such piano-seeking expeditions.

Driving around Pula was like going back to Ancient Roman times, and David was ecstatic as the Roman empire has always been a particular interest of his. There was an amphitheatre that was one of the best-preserved Roman ruins in the world, and was sometimes still used for concerts. We stopped there and David spent a wonderful hour wandering around the arena, feasting on Ancient Roman history.

I found an information bureau where there was a young woman who spoke a little English and she directed us to the Music Academy. When we finally located the building, it seemed deserted. It was August and the academy was not operating. However, the front door was open and we wandered inside. After a few minutes, we found a cleaner in one of the corridors. The woman's cheery face was a welcome sight.

She did not speak any English, and so with many gestures – David's hands flew about in horizontal sweeps, fingers constantly moving – she understood what we were after, and with a great deal of goodwill took us to a practice room and unlocked it for us.

David played for about an hour and, when we came out, she was outside the door, a beaming smile on her face, indicating that she had enjoyed the music. With still more gestures, we arranged to return the next day.

The following morning, the woman was waiting for us on the steps with a look of happy anticipation. She took David by the hand and led him to the same practice room. We were both grateful and slightly amazed at how trustingly she accepted us and the kindness she had shown. When we said farewell and gave her a box of chocolates, she received them with overwhelming thanks, and we both felt warmer for having met her.

Marina arrived two days later and we explored the Istrian Peninsula together. She said she wanted to go for a swim and, not surprisingly, David thought that was a terrific idea. We drove out to the beach and went to sit on the rocks. The Adriatic seemed to stretch out in an infinite shimmer of gold and blue all the way into the light haze on the horizon – a tempting sight for any water lover. Marina pointed across the water and said, "Venice is over there, you know."

We all went in for a dip, and after a while Marina and I came out, leaving David to swim for a little bit longer. We must have become somewhat engrossed in our conversation because, when we looked up at the sea again, David was no longer in sight. After a moment of panic-stricken thoughts, we looked at each other and simultaneously blurted out: "He's swimming to Venice!"

Marina jumped up and ran along the rocks to find somebody who could help us retrieve David. Eventually she found a man with a speedboat, and they set off to catch up with him and bring him back to shore. Once he was safely back, I promised David that on our next visit to Italy I would drive him to Venice.

After Yugoslavia we went back to London, then to Vienna for David's concert and then on to Bonn for another masterclass with Peter Feuchtwanger. This class was organised by Esther Friedman, a friend of Feuchtwanger's, and he had arranged for us to stay with her.

A dynamic and very outgoing woman, Esther was a music teacher at the Bonn Music School in Bad Godesberg, and lived in a large and comfortable home outside Bonn. She immediately embraced David and me as family, and we have been great friends ever since.

Esther was born in Palestine in the late 1930s and her stories of life as a young girl before the establishment of Israel fascinated David. His friendship with Esther gave David his first opportunity in life to discuss his nationality, and Judaism and Zionism in general, in an unbiased and most enlightening way. As he talked with Esther, I was quite surprised to learn that David had a tremendous knowledge of the history of Israel and all its political leaders since the time of establishment, and I resolved that one day we would go and visit that country.

The masterclass was held at the Bad Godesberg Music Academy, and, once again, many pianists had come from different parts of the world to learn from Feuchtwanger and each other. I remember being particularly impressed by a rendition of Schumann's *Carnaval* by a tall, handsome man with dark hair, a moustache and welcoming eyes, who was in his early thirties. He remembers going outside for a cigarette during a break in the lessons, and being kissed, hugged and frantically chattered at by a fellow smoker. Since that day, as he later told me, Nils Ruben's life has never been the same.

It would seem that David's music had reached into Nils' soul and he has marked the experience of hearing David play Liszt at the final-night concert as his musical "Day Zero". An extremely charming and friendly man with an impish sense of humour, Nils is Danish by birth and lives in Copenhagen. We saw a lot of him during the classes and, when it was decided that we would go to Munich for David to play for some of the influential musical people there, Nils decided to come with us. Nils and David just 'clicked', and over the following years our paths would meet again many times, leading to one of the most remarkable nights in David's life.

At the end of October, our time in Europe came to an end. The experiences of the previous five months had made an indelible impression on David. What we had hoped to achieve – contact with fine musicians, people assessing David with an unbiased view and an expansion of his interpretive abilities – had all been achieved. But, in the many great friends we made, we had received more than we had ever hoped for.

A week or so before we departed London for Australia, David and I met Dr Muller at the Rudolph Steiner Lodge, and she offered to give a second opinion about the state of David's lungs. After examining him and looking at more x-rays, she said firmly that if David did not give up smoking completely he would not be around for much longer. At this time, David was down to less than a packet a day, but Dr Muller's words chastened him, and he realised time was running out.

Just before boarding our plane back to Australia at Heathrow, I looked at David, who was still puffing away, and suddenly had an idea. I suggested to him that, since so many friends would be at the airport in Perth to meet us, it might be a good idea if he had given up smoking by the time the plane landed, to give our friends a lovely surprise.

"Yes, darling", he replied. Then he walked over to an ashtray and stubbed out his cigarette. He has never smoked again.

Waterways

When we arrived back in Australia at the end of 1986, several things had changed. Most significantly, Riccardo's had closed down following David's last performance there in May, and Chris had gone off to explore other ventures. Also, the rent for the house in which we were living had increased so much that buying a place of our own seemed like a more viable option.

Thus, in January '87, I rang Mike Parry and asked him if David and I had sufficient funds to put a deposit on a house. He told me that the national tour the previous year had gone well, and that financing would not be a problem.

I quickly scanned the papers and found an advertisement

for a 'development' block which had a decrepit fibro dwelling on it. Having bought and sold many houses in the past, I saw a great opportunity and the property was soon ours. When we finalised the sale and I told the agent we would be moving in straight away, he looked at me in horror and said, "You don't mean you are going to live in it, do you?"

However, the challenge of turning a near-wreck into a cosy home is where I find the most creative satisfaction, and the old carpets were quickly pulled up, the floors polished, the house repainted and some rooms wallpapered. As the block of land was fairly large, we sold half of it and put the money into an invest-ment fund, and, with the help of our good friend Peter Brackley, planted a garden full of palms, ferns, roses and azaleas on the remaining land. For the first time in his life David could have called himself a proud house-owner, but he didn't. It was not until 1994 that it occurred to me that David had had no real awareness of being a wage-earner, and even less understanding of being a property owner.

The Swan River was now virtually at our back door, which was much too tempting for David. Fortunately, the great expanse of water – more than one kilometre wide in places – had fairly light water traffic in that particular section of the river, and I thought it was safe for him to swim, even if he were the only one who dared to do so. But David did have a few lessons to learn in avoiding the occasional rowing scull or sailing boat. He would always swim with his glasses on, holding his head high above the water, observing the "traffic", of which he had become enamoured during our European trip.

"Traffic" was not only cars moving down a street. Crowds

of people moving around, aeroplanes on runways, boats and ferries, birds in flight: all of these were "traffic" to David when he could observe them from a safe place without becoming part of the movement. As we journeyed down European highways, David sat in the enclosed space of our vehicle and observed the movement outside. After doing so for long enough, he realised it was helpful to his concentration. It would seem that the regularity in the pattern and speed of the "traffic" outside had something of a hypnotic effect, and enabled him to sort out the "traffic" of his chaotic and rapid thoughts.

Watching "traffic" became his favourite pastime whenever he was not at the piano. It also became his favourite topic of conversation, and he would natter on about "traffic in Paris" or "traffic in Trafalgar" to anyone who would listen. He would approach complete strangers and launch into monologues about "traffic" the way other people chat about the weather. This, of course, sounded like utter nonsense to most people, even to those who knew him well, and for a long time it was put down to being merely one of David's numerous eccentricities. However, as he continued to talk about "traffic" over the years, he continued to become more coherent in general, until one day he would reveal its real significance.

Meanwhile, swimming in the Swan River, David seemed to have the best of all possible worlds. He was in the water and he could watch the "traffic" passing him both in the river and on the shore. The only thing that could have made the situation better was a floating piano. This seemingly impossible and bizarre idea nearly became reality one day when David was asked to perform at the launch of a new marina near Perth.

The opening was to be televised on an evening program, but the filming had to be done early in the morning. The plan was to place a grand piano on the end of the jetty and do a lot of the filming from a helicopter and the jetty itself. It was agreed that David would play the romantic eighteenth variation from Rakhmaninov's *Rhapsody on a Theme of Paganini*. Before the filming began, I instructed David simply to keep playing the Rakhmaninov over and over until we gave him the sign to stop, as the television crew needed to shoot from many different angles.

It was an extremely hot and windy day, but everyone just got on with the job. David started playing, the crew started filming and everything seemed to be going reasonably well when, suddenly, a particularly strong gust of wind tore the piano lid off its hinges. It went flying through the air, hovered for a moment and then landed with a great splash in the ocean. David continued to play without missing a note, as if nothing had happened. The camera crew were astonished that anyone could have such concentration.

Some surfers pulled the lid to shore, but the crew were devastated when they realised the helicopter was doing a turn at the time and had missed the glory of the lid in flight. Afterwards, when David was asked about how he felt, and what he thought when the incident happened, he seemed slightly baffled. "What's all the fuss about anyway?", he said. "I wasn't scared. I just kept playing 'cause that was the order of the day, that was the *plat du jour* and I just played anyhow. It's just lucky it didn't go towards me and tear me to shreds." David chuckled and then confessed that he actually thought the whole thing had been "tremendous fun". But of course it was – piano, water and even a helicopter in the "traffic"!

A few days after this incident, we received a phone call from a very excited Esther Friedman. She had been in touch with a certain Dr Pol, an influential musical identity in the Bonn region. Esther felt he could be very helpful in arranging recitals for David, and he had offered to have a soirée at his home to present David to other people in the classical music field. Esther hoped that it would be possible for us to fly to Germany to attend this soirée the following month in Cologne.

I rang Mike to discuss whether this sudden trip across the world would be worth our while and, after some consideration, we decided that we should investigate the opportunity. Mike said he would come with us, and use the trip to make a few more contacts in Europe. We booked the tickets, packed all the warm clothes we could find – a strange task given that we were in the middle of Perth's very hot summer – and set off on our second European adventure.

Esther welcomed us into her home with her customary exuberance and elaborated on the proposed plan. It was to be a recital in a private home, followed by a formal dinner for about sixteen people, and it was to be two nights hence.

We arrived in Cologne and all was ready. David was wearing one of his Russian-style shirts – they had become something of a concert uniform for him – and the guests were all awaiting his performance. There was a concert grand Bösendorfer in the large salon, and the dining room was set with elegant china, flowers and candles. I immediately wondered how David would react to such a formal setting for dinner, as he tended to be particularly excited after a performance and not very keen on sitting still.

David came out, bowed to the audience and then started to play some works by Liszt, including the *Ballade* No. 2 in B minor, *La Campanella* and a *Hungarian Rhapsody*. He was in a rather vocal mood that evening. I closed my eyes and began to pray for David to be quiet, trying as hard as I could to send him telepathic messages to please, please, please stop singing, but he showed no evidence of being able to pick up my thoughts.

A short break followed, during which I had a fairly stern talk with him and told him that his singing was completely unacceptable. He went on for the second half and played the *Appassionata* with a lot less vocal accompaniment. Dr Pol seemed impressed and told Mike and me afterwards that it was the best Beethoven he had ever heard. We were filled with great expectations of recitals to follow.

While we were talking to Dr Pol, Liszt's great-granddaughter, who had been present during the concert, approached Esther and said, as Esther would later recount, that she thought David had such a special affinity with Liszt's works that it was possible he could be a reincarnation of her great-grandfather.

However, my concern for David's comfort at the dinner table after the recital was justified. The look on his face told me that he would much rather be back at the piano. In addition, some of the guests were not overly comfortable with his hugs and constant chatter. As the night progressed, I could feel all possibilities of future recitals hopelessly drifting out of reach. And this indeed proved to be the case.

Esther was greatly disappointed with the outcome, as she had worked hard to organise this opportunity for David. However, we were to face many such disappointments and learn how to accept them. In the interim, it became apparent that an even greater effort had to be made to discourage David from singing during performances.

Mike decided that it was best not to worry Esther further when, a day or so later, he walked into her shower – after waiting a considerable time for David to come out of it – took off his clothes, reached for the tap and discovered it was not there. Neither was the rest of the shower unit. It had been detached, reduced to its constituent parts and scattered around the floor, together with orange peel. Water was flowing freely from the wall.

It took Mike more than an hour, but, with the aid of a small pair of scissors and a comb, he managed to successfully reconstruct the shower unit. Esther was never told of the mini-disaster, but she probably thought the manager as eccentric as the pianist, suffering perhaps from a similar cleanliness fetish.

Mike was in for more of David's bathroom catastrophes when we arrived in Salzburg the following week. We were to stay in an old pension in the centre of town. Our room was on the first floor and there was a communal bathroom at the end of a long passage.

Having just driven through heavy snow, we were all cold, tired and hungry. David, however, decided that he would not go to the restaurant downstairs with us, preferring to have some cheese and biscuits in our room. Mike and I left him lying on the floor doing his push-ups and reading.

There were only a few other guests at that time of year, and the whole place was very quiet. After a few glasses of wine and some hearty food, Mike and I felt quite relaxed and decided to head back to our rooms. As we approached the stairs, we noticed that they were suspiciously wet. I felt a tingle of horror and quickly ascended. Lo and behold, there was a steady stream of water winding its way down the corridor and sounds of joyous, slightly out-of-tune singing emanating from the bathroom. I knew the voice well.

I ran into the bathroom and there was David, the plughole of the shower blocked by soap and a face washer, merrily la-de-dahing away as the water ran over the top of the shower base. The taps were immediately turned off and Mike and I grabbed our towels and began an epic mop-up. We were too embarrassed to involve the owners of the pension as we had just negotiated an especially low rate with them. So back and forth we went, mopping and wringing, mopping and wringing. David just ran around laughing, muttering "Oh, sorry, darling. Sorry."

Some years later, Mike commented that, "It was sometimes difficult to join in the general adulation accorded to the maestro, when you had just spent an hour or so cleaning up after the little bugger", and I very much agreed with him. However, after the night in Salzburg, I realised that in future David would need more supervision in bathrooms – not always an easy task for a woman to do for a man – and only once more did we have a major water drama, when David flooded the top floor of a house we were staying in so badly that the water soaked through the floor and started flooding the level below.

All other 'floods' have been significantly less damaging to

our friends' homes, but David developed a new trick instead: forgetting the strength of his fingers, he would periodically turn off the taps so tightly they would fly off their springs. As he obviously has a better feel for the taps at home, it is those in hotel rooms and friends' houses that suffer the most. Recently, after having to repair the taps in a house we were renting for a family holiday, my son recommended to David that, much like performers who take their hairdressers or personal trainers with them wherever they go, David was in need of a personal plumber.

chapter 27

"The Pianist" and "Monster"

We arrived back in Australia just in time for Madame Alice's ninetieth birthday and busied ourselves with preparing a special birthday present for her. After thinking it over, David and I decided that, as what she loved most in life was performing, this would be precisely what we would give her: a recital. We realised that to play for a whole concert on her own might prove to be too demanding, and so organised for her to be a guest artist at one of David's.

When we approached her with this idea, she thought it was marvellous and immediately began to choose her programme. Mike busied himself with the publicity, and the concert – once again at the Octagon Theatre – quickly sold out.

The recital proved to be a very emotional event for everyone present, and Madame Alice received a standing ovation from all her students, friends and admirers after playing a programme of Scarlatti and Liszt. She had played brilliantly and David was amazed at the power of her memory. Overall, our birthday present seemed to have been a glowing success – except for one small hitch.

To end the evening, a special piece had been written by Perth composer Mary Andel, which David had agreed to premiere as an encore. However, he had had little time to work on it and memorise it. As David walked out onto the stage, I glanced at Mary and hoped he would remember it.

David started playing and this very melodic piece was flowing beautifully, when suddenly I realised that he was playing music I had never heard before. I looked at Mary, who had a look of apprehension and slight horror on her face. After what seemed like an eternity, the piece returned to its correct melody and continued to the end.

No one in the audience, it appeared, realised what had happened, and the piece was received well. All Mary wanted to know was how David had managed to extricate himself from a situation she had considered utterly hopeless. David looked rather sheepish and said, "Well, I knew I was in the wrong place, so just went back to the right one."

It was after that concert that Brian Linaker approached us about doing a tour of country towns. At first, David played mainly in the southwest of Western Australia, but then we undertook a tour of the far northwest region, bringing Chopin,

Debussy, Mendelssohn, Schubert, Gershwin and Grieg to the inhabitants of some of the most remote and isolated towns in the world.

The audiences in these tiny towns were very appreciative – after all, not many concert pianists toured their area – and they let David know of their pleasure. Even though pianos were hard to find, we toured Port Hedland, had two recitals in Broome and then went on to Derby, where the nuns from the local convent kindly offered their Yamaha upright.

The Argyle diamond mines township of Kununurra in the Kimberleys then had a population of about 1200, and there was neither a concert venue of any sort nor a piano. One of the local bank managers kindly lent us his own, but, when David and I saw the small upright in the large sports hall, we were rather dismayed.

More than a quarter of the town turned up – I am sure David was the first concert pianist ever to play in Kununurra – and he simply could not disappoint them. Always ready for any challenge, David set out to coax every possible nuance out of the little instrument and communicate his musical message to the audience. In this he succeeded and received one of the warmest standing ovations of his life.

After we left the town, a committee was formed which wrote to us to say they were starting a piano fund to buy a grand piano. Their enthusiasm and hard work showed results, and a year later we flew up to Kununurra for David to give the inaugural recital on a brand-new Yamaha.

These tours of country towns, and a number of television appearances organised by Kirsty Cockburn, resulted in a strange, though rather magical, phenomenon. People began to recognise and talk to David when least expected. A post-office worker in a one-street town, a truck driver at a petrol station on a highway, an old man in a general store in an isolated fishing village and many, many others would see David and immediately start talking to him as if he were a close personal friend. Without exception, they all called him "the pianist" – never "David" – and, in the easy, laconic way that Australians have, they'd say, "Oh! You're the pianist! How are ya, mate? Keep up that piano playing!" And David loved it.

Perhaps it is because when David plays – be it live or televised – he shares so much of his being with the audience that he seems to have no barriers. People who are in any way open to something like that feel a connection with him.

Of course, there were still unfortunate incidents of people occasionally swearing at David, or giving him odd looks, but, whereas before there was nothing in David's experience of strangers to counteract that, now there was affection and warmth, and the few rude remarks were much easier to handle – for me, in particular.

After touring the northwest of Australia, it was time to pack our bags once again for Europe and meet up with Peter Feuchtwanger in Sion for another masterclass. This was again a success and, towards the end of the course, the administrator of the Sion Music School came to ask Feuchtwanger if one of his students would be prepared to accompany the violin students in Ivry Gitlis's class for a few hours. Feuchtwanger was aware of David's fine sight-reading skills and asked him if he would do it. David gladly agreed.

There were about fourteen students in Ivry's class that day. One by one, the students came to play their sonatas and, for their accompaniment, were provided with not only the sound of the piano, but David's voice as well. When the third student had finished playing a Mozart sonata, Ivry stepped to the front of the platform, put his hand on David's shoulder and said, "This man is the personification of music."

Ivry then asked his students to sing while they were playing – a unique experience for them, no doubt. He announced that David should be allowed to sing while playing, because that was the true expression of his musical soul. Though I've never disputed this, afterwards I had to again assure David that audiences, on the whole, prefer more of the piano and less of the vocal. David thought the whole thing rather hilarious, and I saw that this issue of vocal accompaniment would continue to be a challenge.

Prior to heading back to Australia, David and I had a family wedding to attend in Paris. We managed to organise some cheap air tickets, which meant we had to fly out of Gatwick. We had never been to that airport before, and when we arrived I had a very negative reaction to the place.

People were milling around like herds of cattle, their bodies pressed closely together, frantically trying to find their exit gates. All the seats were taken and the restaurants were filled to capacity. It was a very claustrophobic feeling and I made a mental note to pay for better seats in future so we did not have to fly out of this airport again.

David obviously did not enjoy this place, but then I could not imagine anyone who would. I could see fear coming into

his eyes, and his agitation was increasing. His hands were beginning to shake and I was becoming seriously concerned for him.

As we went towards the toilets, we passed a cleaner who
was trying to force a trolley of dirty dishes through the throng.
Just as we walked by, the cleaner, exasperated by his futile
attempts to move even a few paces, sighed and exclaimed, "Oh,
this drives me crazy!" And then we were in hell.

David screamed a piercing cry of agony and threw himself
backwards at me, his arms wildly thrashing about. He looked
absolutely terrified and continued screaming and writhing. I was
taken completely by surprise, and struggled not to let a sense of
panic overtake me. I had never seen David behave like this
before. The crowd seemed to blur and disappear, and then I was
alone with David's torment.

I tried to clasp him in my arms and contain the flailing
arms. I talked. Fast. Everything was fine. Words could not hurt
him. The cleaner meant no harm. I was with him and he was
safe. But David continued to cry and scream, a strange and
devastating sound.

The incident had attracted attention and we were soon
surrounded by police. Fortunately, by this time David had
begun to calm down. A policeman immediately demanded to
know if David was on drugs.

When I explained the situation, the police were quite
understanding, but both David and I were feeling very shaken
and mystified as to the severity of his reaction. Certain words,
like 'mad', 'asylum', 'idiot' and, of course, 'crazy', revived memories of his incarceration and caused David to panic. But nothing
had ever been as frightening and painful as this.

After the police left, a kindly older woman who had witnessed the whole incident asked if she could be of any help. I told her that David was now all right and thanked her for her thoughtfulness. It was very reassuring and soothing to look into the kind face of a stranger and know of her concern and willingness to help.

Everything seemed fine for the next week or so and David was much like his usual self when we returned to Australia. However, he soon started becoming a bit more restless during the day and at night his sleeping pattern was more disturbed. With each day, I felt it was harder to dismiss David's condition as just an extreme mood swing.

One evening we went to the Brackleys' for dinner and David was slightly more agitated than usual. After the meal, when everyone moved to the lounge room, he seemed strangely ill at ease and was very fidgety. Peter Brackley sat down on the couch next to David and picked up the family cat, Minker. As he patted and stroked the cat, Peter started playfully chanting: "Minker is a stinker. Minker a stinker."

Suddenly, David's whole demeanour changed. He jumped up, became extremely agitated and started jabbering faster and more incoherently than ever before. Then he flung himself backwards onto the couch with such great force that he tipped it over. His arms flew about, his head jerked around and there was a terrified look on his face.

I swooped down on him, trying to hold him tightly and physically contain this apparent seizure. It was an extremely frightening experience and none of us really knew what to do, or why it was happening. After a few moments – which to us felt like aeons – David regained his composure.

Barbara, Peter and I were overcome with helplessness, and Peter was desperately sorry that his innocent words about the cat seemed to be responsible for the attack. In some ways, it was similar to the one at Gatwick, but "stinker" seemed to be a really harmless word. So why did it cause such an eruption?

When we went home, David revealed that Peter Brackley's words suddenly reminded him of being, as he put it, "very *shmutzig* at *l'école*". In other words, hearing the cat being called a "stinker" took David back to the time when he was a five-year-old losing control of his bowels in school and feeling mortified and frightened as he ran and hid from his classmates and their jeers.

This, I knew, could not possibly be the whole truth of the matter, as David had spoken about that time in his life many times before, and had never reacted in this way to the memory. Why, then, was it so distressful now?

During the night, David became very sad and was overcome with fear and hatred of himself. He just kept repeating that he had turned into a "monster", and seemed to be terrified of never being able to return to his real self. I watched the man I loved rattle the cage of his tortured emotions and my heart filled with anguish.

The next morning, I received a call from Barbara's mother, Rix Weaver. An utterly remarkable woman, Rix was the first Australian to study at the Jung Institute in Switzerland and had actually met Jung. Upon her return to Australia she established the Jung Society and, though in her eighties, was still a practising Jungian analyst. She lived in the same house as her daughter, and knew David well. When she had arrived home the previous night, and had been told about the incident, she immediately offered to help. Thus, every day for the next two weeks, Rix talked with David about his "monster".

She had asked me to buy David a large scribbling pad and, each day when he went to see her, he drew the "monster". At first, his scribbles were wild and hysterical. Swirling, jagged and irregular, they were surprisingly obvious in representing the torment of his mind. As the sessions progressed, however, the lines became more symmetrical, depicting far less agitation. After two weeks, when David drew fairly plain and clear circles, Rix asked him to draw a fence around them. Thus contained, that "monster" never returned.

After the last session, Rix had a long talk with me and revealed that, while we were in Europe, David had taken himself off his medication. The disaster at Gatwick was the first indication of this. Life, apparently, had become so wonderful for David, and he was feeling so content, that he had simply decided he no longer needed any "medicaments". However, as he feared that neither I nor any doctor would agree with this assessment, and rightly so, he had disposed of the medicine surreptitiously.

I was astonished. Ever since our first night together, when he had desperately searched for his medication, I had understood David to be particularly dependent on it and always willing to take it. We had been together for three years and never once had I ever had to remind him to take it, much less monitor whether he actually did so. Now, I realised, I would no longer be able to trust David to act responsibly in this matter.

Rix said that it was absolutely essential for David to be on medication at all times, and also to have occasional sessions with a psychiatrist. However, as she felt she was too old to take David on as a long-term patient, she offered to make some inquiries and find somebody who would be suitable. As it happened, she found someone who was just perfect.

Wynning the Past

Dynamic, warm and incredibly erudite, Dr Susan Wynn immediately won David's affection with her wicked sense of humour and feminine energy. In Dr Wynn, David and his whimsical word games, jam-packed with alliteration, mercurial metaphors and literary allusions – tactics which he usually deployed to keep strangers at bay from the true state of his thoughts – had found a worthy opponent.

David would try all his verbal tricks on his new doctor but fail to distract her from the issue at hand, as she would often snooker him into laughter and then lead him to admitting the truth. Dr Wynn was always quite blunt with David, supporting her honesty with wit and humour, which he greatly appreciated. "Coming to see you", he has told her, "is like having a fiesta!"

In order to really concentrate and discuss things on a serious level, David has always needed to sit very close to his interlocutors, often hugging them or leaning his head against theirs, and he made no exceptions for Dr Wynn. During their sessions, he would sit as close to her as she would allow him, and constantly try to touch her. From the very first session, Dr Wynn began to explain to David the notion of personal space. This, she and I believed, was a crucial lesson for him to learn if he were to cope more comfortably with others in society. The process is ongoing.

On the very first day, Dr Wynn explained to David that she was not keen on the idea of him touching her legs above a certain point, which she calls "the Plimsoll line". This became a game in itself. Occasionally, David's hand would start creeping higher and higher, and, feigning innocence, he would cheekily ask, "Is that above the Plimsoll line?"

"You know bloody well it is", she'd say. "How would you feel if I whacked those lovely little fingers of yours with the heel of my shoe?"

In reply, a chastened David would pull his hand away and mutter, "Well, it was worth a try."

Unusual behaviour for a psychiatrist perhaps, but David presented as one seriously unusual patient. If there were no guide books for living with David, then there were no routine methods for 'treating' him, either, as his condition did not meet any known medical criteria. One thing was certain: some medication calmed him down and prevented the seizure-type incidents.

To begin with, he was immediately put back on Serenace, but as he was no longer a young man in danger of the drug's common side effects of muscle spasms and tightening, he no longer needed Cogentin to counteract them. The period of careful dosage-adjustment began again, and new drugs were tried.

Lithium proved to be the least effective. Though David became much quieter and calmer on it, he was also rather 'flat', on one occasion even stopping in the middle of a piece during a concert – something he had never done before and has never done since. Eventually we settled on a mixture of Serenace and Tegretol, the dosage adjusted to suit the circumstances and David's apparent mood. For example, during travel, which rather unsettles him, the dosage is slightly increased.

Some of the main symptoms of David's condition are his near-permanent state of elation and slight manic tendencies. In simple terms, most of the time he is sick with happiness and excitement. A chemical imbalance in his brain speeds up his thought processes, hence the rapid speech; makes him incredibly alert, hence the ESP-like qualities of being able to see, hear and feel more than would seem possible; and makes him easily distractible, although his concentration at the piano is almost superhuman.

Dr Wynn was supportive of the notion that, whatever the type or dose of medication David might take, it should calm him somewhat and protect him from the torment of his thoughts without wiping out his personality or numbing him.

Determining the correct medication, however, was the easy part. Solving David's almost tangible pain about his father, and

reconciling him with the demons of his past, was far more complicated. Mainly, Dr Wynn would work through whatever David
brought to her for their session, and, from the start, the process
had the advantage of David's genuine desire for a reconciliation
with his father. Dealing with one little thing at a time, they
would discuss Peter and David's childhood whenever David
wished. With Dr Wynn's guidance, some emphasis would always
be placed on positive things and, ultimately, she would move
on to frequent reminders that it was all in the past and no longer
happening.

In some ways the latter was easier, as Peter Helfgott had
died in 1975 and all the events associated with him were definitely no longer happening. Holding 'peace talks' with a ghost,
however, was much harder. There also seemed no single point
in the past, no single event, to which David could reach back
and make the foundation for forgiveness. And forgiving Peter
was the only way for David to break out of the torture chamber
that was his past.

Though the early years of his life contained some lighter
moments, these had been significantly dimmed by the events that
followed. Peter's banishment of David was not a positive memory,
and little, it seemed, could be found in the years after David came
home from London and before Peter died.

The return from London itself contained a painful
memory. David was so unsure of Peter's reaction that he did
not even go home after he arrived on Australian soil. Instead,
he caught a cab to the home of the long-suffering Mrs Luber-
Smith, who had to pay the cab driver – David was yet again

destitute – and give David clothes and accommodation for the night.

The following day, he must have gathered sufficient courage – with much reassurance from some of his supporters in the Jewish community, no doubt – and was driven by a rabbi to the family home.

However, if the son was courageous, the father was not. Having received a phone call about David's imminent arrival, Peter left the house and vanished into the streets of Perth, in the hope that he would not have to come face to face with his shattered dream. "He was scared, scared, scared. Running scared, running scared", remembered David.

"For hours and hours he just went walking the streets", David recalled one night in our early months together, while sitting in our car in the driveway of the Lathlain house. "I just talked to Louise all afternoon. Poor Louise. Louise kept me alive." David chuckled with profound sadness at the memory of that afternoon, overwhelmed with pity and understanding for the difficult situation his eleven-year-old sister had found herself in at the time.

"But then he came in!" David brightened up somewhat at the recollection. Seeing his father, it would seem, was much less frightening and painful than realising that he was not welcome in his father's house or heart. "He came in and said, 'Hi, David! No problem. No problem at all', and he gave me some Farex and he gave me some water and milk." Strange memory, this, of reassurance and comfort food – Farex being a baby cereal and a favourite of Peter's.

Peter would have found his son in a very bad state:

incoherent, scatter-brained and unable to stand up straight or walk without constantly stumbling. Just how much anguish Peter experienced upon seeing David after the four-year interregnum was never really apparent to David, but, at that time of his life, very little of reality was.

Within ten days, David was admitted to the psychiatric wing of Charles Gairdner Hospital with the help of a psychiatrist recommended by Madame Alice, and this doctor treated him there. "Barmy-on-the-army", brother Les, would come and visit David, and the two would play table tennis – that is, whenever David was awake. Most of the time when Les came, he was told that David was asleep and would remain asleep for quite a while.

Deep-sleep therapy? Perhaps, but nothing is really known about David's treatment in any of the hospitals he stayed in during the '70s. When Dr Wynn made inquiries, she found only irrelevant, uninformative notes. She was told that some things had been lost or mislaid during a move, or that a nurse had misfiled them. Whatever the truth is, David's treatment and medication during his years of incarceration will forever remain an unsolved mystery.

Peter Helfgott came to visit David during his first week in hospital as well. He had a long chat with David's doctor, and asked the doctor whether there was anything physically wrong with his son, and, if so, was that the reason for David's inability to walk properly. After being told that there was nothing physically wrong with David, Peter never came to see him in the hospital again.

However, it would seem that the doctor told Peter a few other things about David's condition, indicating that it was Peter and his actions which were primarily responsible for his son's problems. Shocked that David would reveal to a stranger some of the dark and extremely personal family incidents, Peter went home in a rage. There seemed little he could do to show his son just how furious he was, as David was 'out of it' and in the hospital. But he did have a suitcase of his son's private possessions – forwarded by a London friend shortly after David had returned – and among these things Peter found a little bundle of KSP's letters.

"Father burnt them all, set them on fire!", David recalled, always extremely saddened by the memory. "It was done very surreptitiously, it was done very brilliantly. It was out of spite, 'cause I said something about the father and dad wanted to punish me for that, by burning the letters. I don't think dad liked those letters anyway, 'cause they were all so affectionate to me and dad got a bit jealous I'm afraid. He knew those letters were very valuable and very intimate and they were full of love. Ah, what a *shamus!*"

Of course, David was not to know of his great loss till he came out of hospital some months later. When he did find out, though filled with grief, he could also see some irony in the situation. "The funny thing was that KSP wanted her letters to be burnt, anyway", David explained. Indeed, KSP had asked all her friends and relatives to destroy her letters and any unfinished manuscripts after her death. "But I was determined not to burn them, to disobey," David would say quite firmly, "'cause they were very intimate. They were expressing love to me. And I reckon I should be proud. I thought those letters should be saved for posterity. I thought they were very nice letters and I thought they should survive. And it's funny how dad made her wish come true, 'cause she always tried to make his wish come true by telling me to be grateful to him. So, just like that, dad brought her wish to fruition!"

Bewildered by Peter's perverse act, David hardly saw his father or any other members of his family over the next three years, during which he attempted to rebuild his life, married Clara, and eventually became even more unwell.

After being discharged from a sixteen-month stay at Graylands Hospital in June 1975, David was again homeless, and, by now, a severely debilitated man. "I was unwell when I went into hospital, but I was *really* sick by the time I came out" is one of David's favourite dark little quips. Having nowhere else to go, he asked his family if he could come home. Those of his siblings who were still living there refused, as David was obviously incredibly difficult to handle and they had enough problems of their own without him. They also knew that, due to a failing heart, Peter's health had deteriorated. He was now a feeble seventy-two-year-old who simply did not have the physical strength to look after David.

And yet, Peter decided to come to his son's rescue. "The family wasn't very co-operative", remembered David. "All muddled up. We've all been through heaven and hell. The family fought courageously, but dad took me in anyhow. Dad fought the big battle of Stalingrad and Leningrad with them to get me into the family. Dad was looking after me, so I'm gonna be eternally grateful."

The "big battle", it seemed, was fought and won for nought, as David soon left home again and moved into a motel with Vera, a patient whom he had met at Graylands. And it was only after that relationship failed that he came home for good.

To keep his son occupied, Peter handed him a violin and told him to play the famous Chaikovsky Violin Concerto. At the age of twenty-eight, David began to learn a new instrument. "It was quite fun most of the time", he recalled. "I persevered and I did get to play the Chaik, and I thought I was playing quite well. But after dad died, I stopped playing the violin, I stopped trying."

David's last few months of living at home – he was re-admitted to hospital in March 1976, never returning again to live in the Helfgott family house – were quite timely, as these were also the last few months of Peter's life. He died on 29 December 1975.

Peter's death seemed to have very little effect on David. He was too 'fogged up' to comprehend or feel much of anything. It did, however, leave him without any concrete resolution of the conflict with his father, and the massive resentment he felt for the man who had caused him so much pain, and, as David always believed, caused his illness.

During Peter's life nothing, it seemed, was said or even hinted at between father and son to alleviate David's anguish about the 'America incident', the "punishment" of the "hate night", the banishment, or the burning of KSP's letters. The more David talked to me and Dr Wynn, the more we tried, in our different ways, to talk to him of the love that Peter must have felt for him. We clung on to every tiny account of affection or kindness, and encouraged David to concentrate on those memories. We also encouraged David's search for the reasons behind his father's actions, and to keep concentrating on these positives.

David's natural frame of mind is not a morbid one by any means, as much of the chanting he does when he talks to himself is filled with positive affirmations. "Gotta be positive" had gradually appeared in David's monologue over the years since I'd met him. Several hundred times a day (no, this is not an exaggeration) David would tell himself to banish the encroaching quicksand of negative thoughts, fears and anxieties.

To aid this, he would also say to himself, "Must be aware, gotta be aware, foggily aware", and try to focus on the reality surrounding him, and, indeed, become aware of it before his thoughts pulled him back into the "fog". For David, awareness of reality is crucial not just because it is 'reality', but because it also often leads to the happy feeling of gratitude.

"Gotta be grateful", he mutters over and over, reminding himself to be grateful for a sunny day, for the blue of the sea, for the food on his plate, for the flowers in the garden, for the piano he plays, for the friends who hug him and tell him they love him, for the audiences who come to hear him – joyously grateful for all the little things that most of us forget to be grateful for; joyously grateful for every moment during which one is alive and not in pain. And, David's reasoning seems to follow, if there is so much in life to be "aware" of and be "grateful" for, then why not be wholly "positive" about things?

David's naturally optimistic predisposition, then, had to serve as the foundation for the healing process. And with constant reminders that he was living in the present, where everything was fine, we would build on that.

As the years went by, the "*dommage*" was relegated to the past, and one day David simply had to admit that "All the damage *has* been done. The past is the past, what's done is done. But we can do something about it, though. We can just be aware of the now. We can cheer up! We can sort of *jolly-holly* our way, can't we?"

Having firmly established himself in the present, David found it was quite safe to look back into the past, even to the 'America incident', and say, "Father made a huge mistake, but he did it out of love, I'd say." This became an affirmation for a while. Whenever he spoke of Stern and Breckler and Peter's final decision, he would end by saying to himself: "I reckon the father really loved you, David, really loved you, and he just wanted the best for you."

Reassurance was also derived from statements in which David would refocus his relationship with Peter and objectify it: "Father wanted the best for *all* us family. Perhaps father really loved us." And, as David became stronger, he began to qualify these types of statements with: "He just loved us in a wrong way or too much, much too much, or perhaps it was a wrong sort of love he was giving out. He loved a bit extremely, and it was a *shamus* really."

However, before the feeling of *shamus* had a chance to overwhelm him, David would quickly add, "Never mind, never mind, too bad. Still, poor father apparently did his best, just like all the fathers do, and probably never meant to be so cruel. I reckon father couldn't help it, father just couldn't help himself."

David continued along this line of thought for a couple of

years, until one day, when talking to a young friend who had also been through a difficult time with her father, David calmly recommended: "You shouldn't have a 'father' thing. Just break out of it! Just break free!"

Having heard David for years call his father a "tyrant", a "dictator", a "two-faced Janus" and a multitude of other damning names, the friend was taken by surprise and David felt the need to explain. "You know," he said, "in this world it's not all black and white. It's every hue, different hues, isn't it? It takes all types, all types, and you have to be much more accepting in this world. See, it's not so black and white, 'cause I was probably a bit mean to my father too, and so everyone has to be forgiven now. All has to be forgiven. There is no point hanging on to these grudges."

Whether or not David had been "a bit mean" to Peter was rather beside the point, as forgiveness through any means was the goal. And the goal was achieved via an extraordinarily simple and logical train of thought. At some stage during his conversations with me and Dr Wynn, it occurred to David that, if Peter's holding "grudges" against the "rich Jews" was the starting point of everything that went wrong in his son's life, then holding grudges was definitely a bad idea. This was not a new concept for David, as he had always disapproved of Peter's "grudges". What was new, however, was the simple question: why emulate something you disapprove of?

Though David still talked often of his troubling memories, they began to have a significantly different slant. Even the stories of Peter's childhood and relationship with his father, Djadja, were reinterpreted. When someone asked David if he thought his problems with Peter could possibly stem from Peter's problems with Djadja, he cocked his head to the side and, choosing not to dignify this rather simplistic pop-psychology notion with an answer, slyly asked, "Does it repeat itself? Does it sort of repeat itself?" He paused and then rather haughtily came out with: "Yes, well, I think you can break out of it. You don't have to be in this vicious-Aloysius sort of thing. You can improve on the father."

"I must improve on the father!" became one of David's regular mantras, until one day he even added, "And father can learn from me now." After David decided to dispose of the "grudge", no painful memory about Peter was ever recounted without a "but we must forgive now, forget and forgive". Besides, forgiveness seemed to make the memory so much easier to bear.

Though it took more than a decade, and sometimes David merely paid lip service to all these noble notions, overall he began to like his father, and then even to love him. After all that had happened, as David might well say, "Imagine that!" And it was only then, when David's attitude towards Peter had become understanding, forgiving and loving, that his mind tossed up the incident for which he had been searching through the annals of his memory all along.

As with many of our discussions, it began with a mutter. "Dad couldn't see the forest for the trees and he made a mistake, made a mistake with me", I heard David say to himself as we drove along a country road one day.

"What was that, possum?"

"A huge mistake", replied David, and then revealed the incredible: "And father acknowledged that huge mistake and that was the only time in his life that father ever acknowledged making a mistake. Because the father was too proud."

After all these years, this new little addition to the saga, albeit a rather significant one, came as a huge shock. "When did he acknowledge it?"

"Well, when I came home from London in the after-years, dad said to me, 'I made the biggest mistake of all my life with you' or something like that. And it was very heart-rendering and poignant. Because, you see, the father felt very guilty about all those things about me, really."

"He apologised to you?"

"More or less, more or less."

"What exactly did he say?"

"Very sorry. Dad was sitting up on the hospital bed and it was very very sad, and he had his eyes closed, just sitting there and thinking about me."

"He came to see you in hospital?"

"No. Dad was in hospital, 'cause he had pleurisy. Dad had that old ticker, you know, and I came to visit him and he was just thinking about me and I think dad was really sorry about all that damage and everything."

"And what did he say? 'Oh David, I'm sorry'?"

"He didn't actually articulate it in that sort of way. Father never actually said 'I'm sorry.' He just looked as if he was sorry, all very contrite and sad. We were just talking about something completely different, altogether."

"So how did you know he was sorry?"

"I just read his mind somehow, and he was saying he was sorry. 'Cause father once told me that you can read minds, that there is a sort of telepathy or something. He was just very quiet, very quiet. He had his eyes closed, sleepy, but I know he was thinking about me. Poor father. 'Cause, you know, he was a pincushion, every half an hour they would stick a needle in his arm. He was an absolute pincushion and he never complained. And he lost all his *dentifies* and he lost all his hair, 'cause that's what happens when you get old. Stripped pine, stripped pine. Lost everything . . ."

"You read his mind and you knew he was sorry?"

"Yes. He was very sorry when he sees me damaged and realised that he'd damaged me. Father's very sorry about it."

"How did it make you feel when you knew he was sorry?"

"Well, I felt very grateful, I felt better myself. Of course, he was helpless, he was helpless. My father was a bit foolish. He said funny things sometimes . . . I like to remember the father in the ideal situations when they're poignant and remorseful and nice and gentle. A nice way to remember the father, a loving way."

David was quiet for a moment, looking out the window of the car at the rapidly retreating "traffic" of gum trees. He sighed, "'Course, you know, the father was very complex."

To the
Never Never

Before David and I went to Europe for more masterclasses and recitals in 1989, I did a lot of astrological research on the state of the economy in Australia and concluded that it would be wise to sell our house. The planetary transits were showing that the property market would fall quite significantly while we were away.

As we had been thinking of relocating to the eastern States of Australia anyway, for the sake of David's career, we put the house on the market and sold it very quickly. When we returned from overseas, the market had indeed gone down and the agent who had handled the sale told me how lucky we were as the house's value had dropped by about $30,000. Luck, of course, had little to do with it.

Though we now had enough money to start looking for a property on the east coast, we were not quite sure exactly where we wanted to live. In the interim, we rented an apartment with spectacular views of the city and the Swan River, which was now across the road from our front door.

If I had thought about it carefully, I would never have rented this apartment. The building was situated on something of a peninsula on a bend of the river, so we had water surround-ing us on three sides. The location was also right near where one of the main bridges crossed a major section of the waterway used by most of the big ferries on their way to Rottnest Island.

All of this was great for David, but it proved to be a terrible frustration for me. He still loved to swim, of course, but, with his improved health and ever-increasing confidence, he began to wander off and 'go walkabout', often disappearing for hours. It was then that we both became well acquainted with the local police.

When we were living in our previous house, I had become quite used to David going off to swim in the river, and, as he had always returned safely, felt he was quite capable of looking after himself. Also, I would never even think of locking him up at home, nor could I mind him every minute of the day.

In our new apartment, David would look out the window, see the great expanse of water beckoning him, and reason that there was no need to stay just near home. Feeling brave and strong, he would set out for a jog, run a few kilometres along the river, take off his clothes and dive in. He would then swim for a long time and often forget where he had entered the water. Much too impractical even to think about looking for his clothes, he would jog all the way home in his bathers, and then I'd be forced to go on a usually fruitless clothes search.

After a month or so of this behaviour, David had lost numerous pairs of trousers, five pairs of shoes, about ten pullovers and countless towels and T-shirts. This, however, was a minor inconvenience compared to the one he caused the ferry captains, who had to spend their time trying to dodge David's bobbing, bespectacled head as he swam back and forth under the bridge. I had no idea that David was causing so much trouble until the police brought him home one day and pleaded with me to persuade him not to swim in the path of the ferries.

David agreed, but then decided to go to the widest part of the river and swim right across it, from South Perth to the University at Nedlands. When he got out of the water on the other side and began to gabble at people about "traffic in Trafalgar", many were naturally concerned. The police were called and, though David knew exactly where he was and how to get home, he was not entirely successful at explaining this to either the police or the crowd that had gathered around him by that time. Dr Wynn had to be called and, over the following weeks, she became quite used to picking up the phone and hearing a constable or sergeant on the other end of the line saying, "We have a David Helfgott here."

My family and friends had nicknamed David "the Pink Panther", because of the quiet, stealthy way he has of moving about whenever he is trying to 'nick off' with forbidden quantities of sugar or coffee, and because of all those times when he is under everyone's feet one minute and has vanished the next. David's Swan River adventures culminated in one memorable night when he performed just such a 'vanishing'.

That night, Dr Wynn, Dr Wynn's husband, a pianist friend of ours, Cara Kelson, and her husband all came for dinner. It is significant that, apart from myself, there were four people in the room who were very familiar with David's sneaky little ways, and yet he still managed to disappear.

When we became aware of this, we went to the river – I had no doubt that he was swimming – and the search commenced. But, as it was dark, all our efforts proved futile. Rather dejected and tired, we returned to the apartment in the hope that David would soon turn up of his own accord.

After a considerable time had passed, there was a knock on the door. When I opened it, I saw my husband standing there stark naked, wet and shivering, with two policewomen, guns on hips, on either side of him. Apparently, David had again decided to swim in the path of the ferries – extremely dangerous at nighttime – and on this occasion did not bother to wear his bathers. Dr Wynn shook her head and, laughing at the pathetically funny sight of her infamous patient, said, "Oh boy, David, you're really in deep shit this time!" The policewomen did not contradict her, and gave David a very stern dressing-down.

All these incidents made me aware of David's need for a place where he could run free and wild without bothering other people. I knew then that, wherever we settled on the east coast, the place would have to accommodate these new demands of his healing process.

As David's awareness of the world expanded, and the 'fog' was no longer his main problem, he began to attempt to focus and organise his thoughts. In addition to his little affirmations about awareness, gratitude and positive thinking, he began to tell himself to concentrate. "Concentrate, concentrate, gotta concentrate, gotta keep to the point", he would repeat to himself hundreds of times a day, and still does.

Looking at "traffic" was helping his concentration. Doing a great deal of physical exercise exhausted him sufficiently for his mind to be calm as well, and made him feel stronger and physically healthier. However, he then found a new tool to aid his focusing abilities: the "*imago*".

Imagos were images, such as pictures or photographs, which David would carry with him at all times. Whenever he felt his thoughts were about to go haywire, he would stare at an *imago* and focus on it until his mind was no longer in danger of rambling. The first *imago* was the back of a Sustain cereal packet, which had pictures of sportspeople on it. All of David's *imagos* from then on were somehow associated with strength and fitness. He even carried an empty Milo tin with him. Why Milo? Because, as David informed me, Milo was a famous wrestler who lived in the sixth century BC, and had numerous victories at the Olympic games – trust David to immediately make the connection between a chocolate drink and ancient history!

Each *imago* would last a surprisingly long time, and would become rather grotty and tattered, until David would eventually lose it and replace it with another one. No one suggested to David that he have these pictures; he just decided this was the best way to train his mind, and, while doing so, constantly encourage himself to train his body. All he needed now were peaceful surroundings and complete freedom of movement.

In retrospect, it was rather fortuitous that, at about this time, our journalist friend Kirsty Cockburn invited us to come and stay at a property she and George Negus had bought near Bellingen on the north coast of New South Wales. David had two recitals scheduled in Newcastle and, as there was a week's break between them, we decided this was a perfect opportunity for a drive up the coast.

There was a flood in Bellingen at the time, but our destination lay some 13 kilometres away, up into the gum-scented hills, then down into what the locals for more than a hundred years have called the "Promised Land" valley. Mountains of lush, subtropical greenery rose to the sky on all sides of the valley. Ancient gums, white cedars and silky oaks dotted the hills and rows of furry casuarinas swayed along the banks of the crystalline Never Never Creek, which wound its way down from the mountains, through the valley and towards the Bellinger River. This was paradise and it was 'Peter Pan' – the boy who wouldn't or, in the case of the person sitting next to me in the car, couldn't grow up – who had finally led me here.

Built on the banks of the Never Never Creek, Kirsty and George's house is a fascinating structure of corrugated iron and wood. Supported on stilts, it nestles in the trees and merges with the landscape, with some of its walls designed to open out fully so that the house can be completely at one with nature.

Our visit with George and Kirsty was an unforgettable experience and we came back on many occasions during the year to stay with them in their magical 'treehouse'. Kirsty even bought a piano. Though she had always wanted to have one and learn how to play, its purchase was no doubt hastened by David's frequent presence in her home.

During one of our visits, in 1990, David went for a jog down the road and saw an auction board on a block of land just past Kirsty and George's house. He came back and said, "Darlinka, it's all been planned. There is a sign that says 'This land is for sale' and you must buy that land. I just have this *intuitive* that you should buy this land."

I was surprised at the seriousness of David's request – he had never before asked me to buy him anything except cigarettes, chewing gum, manuscript books and Coke – and was delighted that he was so sure of what he wanted, and could state it so firmly and clearly.

After the auction five days later, the land was ours and our house was built and finished by July 1991. It is not a very big house, but it was designed specifically for our needs. The main room can accommodate more than seventy people and has a small dais on which we placed David's Yamaha grand. The floor-to-ceiling windows look out to the mountains on all sides and the all-round bull-nosed verandah provides cool shade on scorching summer days. An outside shower with tungsten-tough plumbing has been especially installed for David, so that he can take as many showers as he likes without causing minor flooding of the house.

A small creek, fed by mountain springs, meanders through the trees at the front of our property and then meets the artificial lagoon, before flowing on to join its big cousin, the Never Never. This creek provides us with an endless supply of water for the house and garden, but fresh rainwater is collected in tanks for drinking.

As soon as we moved in I busied myself with digging and planting, and the garden of natives, fruit trees and flowers soon began to flourish. Anything planted in the especially warm and moist climate of the Promised Land simply thrives. Roses, azaleas, jasmine, gardenias and lavender surround the immediate vicinity of the house, while fresh herbs and vegetables grow in an abundance too plentiful for our consumption.

Even the occasional drought has never hampered the overall development of our garden or the luscious greenery of the valley. In times of drought, the locals look up to the sky and wait to see black cockatoos – exotic parrots which descend into the valley from the rainforest of the mountains above – whose screechy croak is an omen of forthcoming rain. And then the rains come, and stay for days until the usually serene Never Never runs in foaming rapids and floods the bridges, submerging the paddocks in water.

Apart from the cattle and horses which wander around the surrounding properties, dreamily chewing the grass, there is a rich native wildlife in the valley. Sunrise is filled with the joyous shrill of a myriad of birds: from cackling kookaburras to flocks of large white cockatoos, to tiny butterfly-like honeyeaters which flit inside large flowers and feed on the nectar. Wild ducks waddle around and dip into the lagoon. Elvis, our golden pheasant, can usually be seen dashing from one corner of the property to another. Large goannas crawl out of the shrubbery by the side of the road for a sun-bath, as do some local snakes, which have to be carefully avoided when one is driving. Local dogs bark the night-time away at the wild rabbits, possums and wallabies who stray from their hiding places in the bush.

David and I adore our home in the Promised Land. When a woman who was coming to visit rang up one day to inquire about our address, I was out in the garden and David, atypically, picked up the phone. "Where do you live, dear?" she asked. "In Heaven", he replied.

Heaven

David never refers to his home as anything but "Heaven", and, when a city-dwelling friend once asked him what he liked most about it, David grinned and launched into a rave: "I feel secure there, I feel aware, I feel free and very very satisfied! I wake up *joyeux*. I wake up and break out of bed, and run around and swim in the 'cathedral' and look at the *catillas* and the *canards* and I have my piano and I can do what I like all day! It's wonderful, all perfectly set up and planned just for me, and I'm very privileged and I'm very grateful."

The Promised Land provided David with safe, peaceful surroundings in which he could finally feel totally free. In the first years of our life there, he would often wake up at sunrise, make himself several "*monstaroonies*" or "*fixes*" – very strong cups of tea – and then disappear into the hills.

David would leave the house wearing clothes, carrying a manuscript book for *composedlies*, a pen and an *imago*. He would return completely naked, usually without the manuscript book and pen, having left it all somewhere in the bush, but most often still clutching his *imago*. As there was little chance of David running into other people while he roamed the hills, there was really no need for him to wear clothes, so I never forced him to do so.

Always barefoot, he would run along the road or cut through the paddocks and then go swimming in his favourite parts of the Never Never or the little creek on our property. He developed a preference for a particularly shallow part of the creek, and for months he only swam there, coming home caked in mud. I was happy when this phase ended with David's discovery of the "cathedral", this being his special name for the deeper part of our lagoon where the branches of the trees on the bank arch over into the water, forming something of a canopied dome under which he swims.

With all the poisonous snakes, spiders, leeches and other nasties lurking in every crevice and corner of the bush, many people have been amazed that, no matter where he strays, nothing ever happens to David. Though some have been badly bitten both on land and in water, David seems to have worked out a special relationship with the local creatures, and they never touch him. Visitors wishing to wander about the uninhabited parts of the valley just follow David, absolutely convinced that, as long as they stay near him, they will not be in danger, and he always reaffirms their faith in him.

David and I were also 'adopted' by Lizzie, a blue heeler who is said to have once belonged to novelist Peter Carey when he lived in the valley, and, before Lizzie became too old to keep up with David, she used to follow him around and guard him.

After a couple of years, David's new environment began to manifest a miraculous healing power which I had never even dreamt of. Genuine peace started to take over David's mind and soul. For the first time since I had met him, he would spend long periods in quiet contemplation. At sunrise and sunset – his favourite times of the day, which he calls "*morningtide*" and "eventide" – he would walk to the boundary line of our property and stand there very still, communing with nature.

"What do you think about when you stand there looking at the mountains?", I asked him one day.

"Well," he sighed, "it's a sense of freedom, it's a sense of wonderfulness, it's a sense of creativity. I think of the great music I'm gonna write here one day, when I settle. Yes, and I'm gonna play some great piano, and I'm going to be much more loving, much more caring and much more different altogether, and I'm going to be much more aware. I'm going to get an awareness of the world – it's the only cure. And I have to accept too, I have to accept the help, and I have to have lots of chutzpah and lots of courage . . . Be completely different, completely different, you know?"

I did know. David had already made such incredible progress and still, every day, he was following his intention of becoming "completely different" and transforming in front of my eyes. His need to 'go walkabout' gradually waned, and he would spend many more hours at the piano, interrupted only by short, frequent swims in the "cathedral". Over the years, David's stoop had been slowly disappearing and, in the Promised Land, he straightened out completely. With his shoulders firmly held back, he stands and walks tall and proud.

David loves saying that he is particularly privileged, and I often have to agree with him. In all our travels around the world I have not heard of any other international pianist who gives recitals at home. David, on the other hand, has played nearly thirty recitals in "Heaven" since 1991.

The performances usually start at 5 pm. David plays for approximately seventy minutes and then the guests wander out into the garden for a stroll and a champagne supper. During this interval, David has a chance to go for a swim – definitely not something too many concert pianists are able to do halfway through a concert – and emerges from the water to don a superb black robe dotted with notes and the word "RELAX" inscribed on the hem in large red letters. The robe, a wonderful present from Kirsty, usually attracts considerable attention.

After the interval, everyone returns to the house for the 'request' part of the evening and the guests have often commented to me how special they feel to be able to listen to David in his own home, and how they love the interactive part of the performance. These recitals are always completely booked out well in advance.

In 1994 we found it necessary to build a separate studio in the garden. An office was needed for the administration of David's ever-growing career, and I could no longer manage it from an area in the house about the size of a shower recess. One day, when the studio – which David calls "*italia*" – was nearly finished, David and I were standing in the garden examining it. David looked slightly puzzled and said, "The *italia* must be very costly." I assured him it was. He looked even more puzzled and asked where all the money had come from. "From your performances", I replied.

David was pensive for a moment, then said, "What about the house?" I explained to him that the money had come from his many performances and from my working as his manager, and that the bank also had a slice of it.

"Is it mine then?", he asked, and it was then that I realised that, though he had owned a house in Perth and had lived in "Heaven" for almost four years, he had only now understood that he, David Helfgott, was actually capable of owning property.

I assured him that the house, the land and the studio were most certainly his. David wiggled his shoulders back and, puffing out his chest, a beaming smile on his face, said, "Well then, I think I'll go for a walk around *my* property." And off he went, head held high, with an even-paced, confident stride, carefully exploring every single nook and cranny of our five acres as if he had never seen any of it before.

After that day, David's contributions around the house changed dramatically. This hitherto disorganised creature took over the making of the beds, the vacuuming, the sweeping of paths, the pegging-out of the washing and a multitude of other household chores. What was even more spectacular was that he completed them all with an immense sense of satisfaction.

Also, the new-found home pride gave David the courage to answer the phone. Previously, he had left all responsibility for communication with the outside world to me and our answering machine, rarely picking up the phone when it rang, and even more rarely actually initiating a phone call. It seemed he could not believe that anybody would ever want to call him, or want to hear from him.

Now he was glad that someone was ringing *him* at *his* home, and he developed a very particular phone manner. When the phone rang, he dashed to answer it – even if I was nearby – and invariably greeted the caller with a warm " 'Allo, 'allo, 'allo . . .", then continued to natter nonstop about anything that came into his mind, usually confusing the poor caller about the purpose of their call. At the close of a conversation with his loved ones, he would also invariably say, "Love you to bits and pieces."

After a year or so, my family all learnt that, in order to end David's stream-of-consciousness monologues on the phone, all they had to say to him was, "Love you to bits and pieces", to which he would then reply, "Love you to pieces and bits", and hang up.

It was also around this time that David began to say very often that things had been "planned", "set up" or "computerised", and that there was no need to worry about anything. He would point at the traffic when driving down the highway and say, "Look, there's a pattern in that traffic there, it's all been planned, there's a meaning there." He would say the same of a flock of birds in flight. He would point at a calf suckling a cow and ask, "Are they computerised, Darlinka?", and when I'd laugh and tell him, "That's nonsense", he'd shake his head and quite firmly say, "I think they're computerised; computerised and controlled. We all are, everything is."

For any small problems or mishaps, major dramas or confusing anxieties, David always seemed to have an answer: "Don't worry, it's all been set up. It'll all be all right."

The more we talked of his "computer", and the way it controlled everything in the world, I began to realise that David's belief was not as eccentric as it first seemed to be. If billions of people are capable of believing that everything in life has a reason and a meaning because of an entity they call "God", then why was it strange for David to think that there was an order and a pattern installed in the world by something he called a "computer"?

Then, as David continued to talk about the patterns in "traffic", I began to see that, quite apart from it being a device to enable David to focus his thoughts, "traffic" was also a metaphor for anything that happens to us in life which seems to have no reason or meaning.

When one stands by the side of a road and watches the cars pass by, one usually has no idea just where any of them have come from or where they are going, but the passengers in each car usually do. They have left some place with a destination in mind, and a reason for that destination, and, just because their journey has no particular meaning to the observer, it doesn't necessarily mean their journey has no meaning at all.

"Yes! Yes!", David exclaimed when I put this theory to him. "It's just like in life! Everything happens and you don't know why it happens, but it just follows a plan. The computer

looks after everything, and everyone's here 'cause of a plan, and
if you just follow that plan then you defuse fear and get a rhythm
and a reason and a purpose. 'Cause, I mean, how else do you
manage to stay alive? And yet everyone seems to, and everyone
is in a very fragile condition, and we're all only flesh and blood,
and that's why, I reckon, everyone should be grateful."

I realised then that, in the process of healing himself, David
was not only gaining confidence, courage and strength, but that
his ever-increasing awareness of the world had brought with it
pure and absolute faith.

When night falls in the Promised Land, and the moon
slowly rises over the mountains, it is another awe-inspiring
moment for David. He will rush into the house calling, "Darlinka, Darlinka, you must come and see! Now!" And we will
walk out into the garden and stare at the infinity of stars and
the Southern Cross and he will say, "Can we see the world as
a wonderful world and just have fun? I reckon we can. We can
choose to have the world as a wonderful world and look at the
world as brightly sparkled and just enjoy all this awesomeness!"

The Globetrotters

Though there is no doubt that David loves his home in the Promised Land, many people who know him well have been rather puzzled by his absolute refusal to claim it as his favourite place on earth. Without exception, whenever David is asked about it he firmly replies, "Wherever I am at the moment is my favourite place and I reckon I should just make the most of it, make the most of the here and now." And he means it, too.

Whether it takes David an hour or a day to settle into a new environment, when he finally does so he immediately tries to focus on everything that is wonderful about it – and, for David, finding wonders in the world is easy. Then he feels truly grateful for the opportunity to experience it all, whatever it may be – after all, this is a man who rejoices at a traffic jam.

This is just as well, because since 1986 David and I have travelled around Australia and the rest of the world a great deal. Just prior to meeting David I had my numerology done and was told that, over the next couple of years, I would pack my suitcase and never fully unpack it for the rest of my life. Being a triple Sagittarian, I gladly accepted that idea and, in the past ten years, have not spent more than eight weeks without having to pack.

Not all our journeys have been connected to music, though. In 1988, an opportunity arose for us to visit Israel. For a number of reasons, I believed it was very important for David to see Israel at least once. When I met him he was struggling with the concept of being Jewish – quite understandable, considering his upbringing. Though David's knowledge of Jewish history was encyclopaedic, he had a great number of complex and confused emotions about the Jews, preferring to tell people he was "Hebrew", because, as he explained to me, it sounded more "melodious" to him. I felt that having some direct experience of the rich culture and history of his people might clarify some issues for him.

Also, David's elder sister, Margaret, had been living in Israel since the mid '70s and, though she had come to visit us briefly in London in 1986, David had had very little contact with her during the past twenty years and had not met her husband, Alan, or the rest of her family in Israel. Margaret often wrote inviting us to come and see her, and finally David and I had a chance to do so.

Jerusalem proved to be a historical feast for David, and he was constantly feeling "Terrific!" Perhaps because he knew so much about the place, and had constructed so many notions about what it was like, everything was a surprise to him, being quite different, apparently, from how he had always imagined it.

When we arrived at Margaret's home in Beersheba, we were warmly received and, for old times' sake, brother and sister launched into a transcription of Dvořák's *New World* Symphony – a duet they had often played for Peter as children.

The next day, Margaret and Alan drove with us to Masada and, as we passed Jacob's Well going on to the Negev Desert, David and I felt as if we were time-travelling into the Biblical era. David was eager to see the ruins of Masada and spent most of the journey telling me about the heroic stand the Jews had taken there and their ultimate destruction.

After walking through the ruins of what had once been houses, halls and meeting places, we stood on the plateau and looked down at the Dead Sea, the salt floating on it like puffs of meringue. We clambered down the mountain and went for a swim. David thought it was funny and strange to lie on top of the warm, salty water, gazing up the sky. "It's not very good exercise is it?", he said, as he rushed off to the showers to wash off the salt.

A few days later Margaret drove us to Tel Aviv, where we went to visit the Jewish War Memorial, Yad Vashem. As David and I walked through the museum, which graphically tells the story of the Holocaust with photographs, recorded talks and film, David was quite shocked by the stark simplicity with which the horror was depicted. This horror grew as we walked from room to room and, when we came to a table with a pile of children's shoes on it, the tragedy of it all overwhelmed us. Racked with tears and unable to speak, I let David – who was only slightly more composed than me – lead me out of the building.

Apart from those of David's relatives who had arrived in Australia before the war, and Uncle Johnny and his mother, Bronia, who miraculously got out of the concentration camps alive, the rest of David's family on both Rachel's and Peter's side was destroyed. Perhaps it was not so surprising, then, that David, who had grown up with this horror so close to him, was not as shattered by what we saw as I was.

We stayed in the garden of the museum, trying to collect ourselves, before going into the final room, where candles on the floor marked the position of each of the concentration camps. I felt an immense sense of gratitude for having been born in Australia, and for never having suffered any loss through war.

The tour of Europe which followed our visit to Israel included a special Australian Bicentenary recital in the Australian Embassy in Vienna. It was such a success that we went back to Europe on tour the next year – but with the bonus of another masterclass with Peter Feuchtwanger. We were pleasantly surprised to find that our Danish friend, Nils Ruben, was attending it as well.

After the masterclass David had a few recitals to do in Germany, but nothing was scheduled beyond that. Nils recommended that we should come to visit him in Denmark, where he would arrange a private recital for David. We had never been to Scandinavia and Nils' offer was irresistible. Our love affair with Denmark was about to commence.

When we arrived in Copenhagen Nils took us to the home of his parents, Dr and Vera Ruben. They live in a grand old home on a cliff overlooking the Sound. We were to stay in a cottage at the bottom of their garden, which was right on the seashore – and, yes, David did go swimming there, in any weather.

Nils' wife, Charlotte, and his parents welcomed us as if we were family, and each day David would go to Nils' house and practise in the music room. Nils' influence on David's playing was evident during the ten days we spent with him. I could see that Nils and David seemed to have formed a special understanding and, when I asked David about it, he said, "Nils is so gentle, such a good musician. He doesn't actually teach me, but he coaches me, he inspires me and uplifts me." This was precisely the type of musical interaction which David had been longing for in Australia and which, for a long time, was so difficult to secure for him there.

As promised, Nils had arranged a recital for about forty people in his home. Among the audience was Theresa Waskowska, a leading music critic. She was so impressed by the performance that she asked to do an interview with David the next day and we gladly agreed.

During the interview, poor Ms Waskowska did not quite know what to make of David, as he was not in a particularly co-operative mood. He kept trying to unbutton his shirt and was becoming rather restless, eventually jumping up from his chair and going to lie on the floor, where he proceeded to do several hundred of his strange little 'push-ups'. At the end of the interview, Ms Waskowska asked Nils about his plans in regard to David's future concerts in Denmark.

Her question came as a bit of a surprise, because Nils and I had never discussed this. Crossing his fingers behind his back, Nils smiled and quite confidently told Ms Waskowska that David was returning the following year to do a concert tour of Denmark.

I held my breath, but, after Ms Waskowska left, I gave Nils a kiss to congratulate him on his new job as David Helfgott's personal manager in Denmark. Fortunately, David's behaviour did not prevent Ms Waskowska from writing a very comprehensive feature article about him, and thus introducing him to the people of Denmark.

The first major recital Nils organised was the following year, 1990, in the famous Louisiana Museum north of Copenhagen. The museum hall was packed and, as usual, David lay on the floor of the dressing room before the concert doing his 'push-ups', wearing only his pants.

"Now, you remember what you are playing tonight, dear?", I asked.

"I have no idea, darling. I have absolutely no idea", the star of the evening muttered foggily.

This little exchange was a running joke between David and me, but Nils, who was not yet familiar with our private humour, nervously paced the room. I suppose he had some serious grounds for concern. In the two days leading up to the recital, Nils had heard David practise for untold hours, but not one note from the concert programme had been played.

"Okay, David, it is time to start", Nils said. David jumped up from the floor and, in less than a second, disappeared through the door on his way to the podium – still half-naked.

"David!", I called out. "Come back! Quickly now, put on your shirt and go directly to the piano. Don't shake hands with the audience and don't kiss anybody!"

At this point, Nils sank into the nearest chair, just about ready to start tearing his hair out. I had to reassure him that everything would be all right – as, indeed, it was. In fact, it was quite spectacular.

The recital included many seldom-heard virtuoso items, such as Gottschalk's *Pasquinade, Souvenirs d'Andalousie* and *Grande Scherzo*, and de Falla's *Ritual Fire Dance*. The audience went wild: calling out "Bravo!" and stamping their feet, they demanded no less than five encores. Nils could now relax, and this he did when David played his next concerts in Holstebro and Århus.

After Denmark, we began our first trip to Eastern Germany by visiting Leipzig and the famous Blüthner piano factory, where we met Mr Blüthner himself. David was particularly fascinated as, at that time, he had an 1877 Blüthner, which we planned to restore.

We then moved to Chemnitz, where David had a concert and swam in a very beautiful Bauhaus-style pool. David likes to swim wherever he is on the planet, and it has taken a lot of detective work to find out where all the swimming pools are. Now, I feel I could just about write the Michelin guide to the swimming pools of Europe. In Hamburg, for example, there is a huge, impressive pool, but it is a bit overwhelming; Bonn's is smaller and friendlier; Copenhagen's has a lovely design and great intimacy; while central London's is very crowded. What they all have in common is the helpfulness and friendliness of the staff. I do not know the reason for this, but every single pool attendant we have ever encountered has been caring and gentle with David.

After we returned to Australia, David offered to do a fund-raising recital for disabled children. The venue was owned by a leading Japanese businessman, Mr Handa, who also writes music and composes under the name Seizan Fukami.

Some months later, we met with Mr Handa and he told us he wished to write a *Rhapsody for Piano and Orchestra* for David. He invited us to come to Tokyo in September 1991 to perform it at the Sony Music Hall.

In August, two weeks before we were due to leave, the score finally arrived. It turned out to be a most interesting work, with Japanese and Western themes intermingling, and containing a number of large romantic passages that David revelled in. As time was short, and the work was large and quite complicated, David hardly left the piano in the days leading up to the trip.

Even though our plane arrived in Tokyo at 6.30 am, ten of Mr Handa's staff turned up to greet us at the airport. They were extremely courteous and kind, and we were driven to the beautiful Imperial Hotel.

A music room was made available for David to practise in. The room, much to his delight, overlooked the railway and a freeway – so much "traffic"! – and the indoor swimming pool enabled him to swim whenever he wished.

For the next week, David busied himself with rehearsals.

While the Japanese are generally a somewhat reserved people, when David was with the musicians there were no barriers. Even if he did rather mystify them with his original personality, his music, as always, spoke for him.

Quite by chance, George Negus was on his way back from filming a documentary in Russia, and faxed us to say he could be in Tokyo for David's concert. There are few things in life that give David greater happiness than someone travelling a long distance to hear him play, but little did George know how much time he would be giving.

Narita Airport is a considerable distance out of Tokyo, and the traffic is horrendous. George was collected by one of Mr Handa's cars and brought to the Sony Music Hall. The trip took hours and George arrived just in time to hear the concert. Then he had to get straight back in the car and start the excruciatingly slow trip to the airport. He just made the plane, but later told us it was all worth it. The audience of 2500 loved it as well.

In the days that followed, apart from being taken to wonderful restaurants and shown various aspects of Tokyo life, David recorded a tape of smaller pieces by Mr Handa and a CD of the *Rhapsody*. It was a magical two weeks, and we felt a great sadness when we had to leave, farewelled at the airport by ten more of Mr Handa's most gracious staff.

Our globetrotting continued and, in early 1993, Charles Blair, a friend with great entrepreneurial spirit, arranged for David to perform a concerto in St Petersburg. As soon as David heard about this, he immediately began to fantasise about performing his 'Rak 3'. Unfortunately, as the orchestra available for the proposed concert had less than fifty musicians, and the 'Rak' requires about ninety, David's fantasy had to remain just that.

Charles suggested that David could play any number of other concertos and was particularly keen on the Schumann A minor. David, however, had always felt a great sadness whenever Schumann was mentioned. Though David had played the *Fantasie* and other Schumann pieces in his youth, after his breakdown he became extremely sensitive about Schumann's tragic life, and empathised deeply with the composer's suffering in the asylum where Schumann saw out the end of his days. After considerable discussion, however, David agreed to do the Schumann because it had been written during a less troubled period of the composer's life.

Once the decision was made, David had only one month to learn the work. In the meantime, Charles wrote to Albania offering David's services to perform either the Schumann or the Rakhmaninov Second. This was somewhat of a compromise: Charles really wanted to accommodate David's desire to play Rakhmaninov on this tour, even if it wasn't to be in Russia, but he felt the Second would be handled better by the Albanian orchestra than the huge Third.

Suddenly, David was offered an extensive tour of Denmark, just prior to Russia and Albania. The schedule then looked very full, and the idea of David preparing the Rakhmaninov Second – which he had not performed since 1984 – as well as the Schumann did not seem wise. As Charles had not heard back from Albania as to which concerto they wanted, he wrote to confirm that David would do the Schumann.

The Danish tour was a great success and then, with fond memories of our previous visit, we were off to St Petersburg. We were met at the airport by Helen Ivchenko, who worked for a Russian cultural body and was a friend of Charles's.

We were eager to walk around the city and, after Helen had given us a few tips about buses and trains, we set off. What confronted us was a very different city from the one we had seen only seven years earlier. Roads and buildings had badly deteriorated, what had been a well-cared-for place under communism was now falling into disrepair, and the overall atmosphere seemed far less prosperous.

David enjoyed working with the orchestra on the Schumann, but, as many State subsidies were no longer available and musicians were finding it difficult to get any work, it somehow did not seem to be appropriate for David to be there. However, he was not paid for his performance, and the Bellingen Arts Society in Australia subsidised the orchestra with US$200 – quite a sum by Russian standards.

The performance was given in the historic hall at the Rimsky-Korsakov Conservatorium, opposite the Marinsky Theatre. At the end, people came up and put flowers on the stage: single roses, tulips and carnations. This was particularly touching when one realised the sacrifices these people must have made in order to buy the flowers, just so they could demonstrate their love and respect for the artist and the music.

Helen had also arranged for a small recital in Rimsky-Korsakov's home, which was now a museum. One felt that the composer had just gone out for a walk, as the house contained all his books, pictures, and even papers and pens. As David sat down at Rimsky-Korsakov's piano, he saw the magnetic and fiery eyes of Mussorgsky looking down at him from a portrait above the instrument. David immediately began to play *Pictures at an Exhibition*. He was overcome with joy and there were tears in his eyes. When he finished, he said, "Oh, Darlinka! Never in my life did I even dream that I should be so privileged ... Life is such a mystery, such a wonderful plan, set up so uniquely!"

But more overwhelming experiences were ahead for David, as after Russia we flew to Weimar, where Roland Binz, David's German manager at the time, had arranged for him to play to the Music Committee of Weimar in the Liszt House.

As we approached the building, David could hardly contain his excitement about playing the composer's own piano. The Music Committee greeted us warmly, but, as they did not speak any English, it was fortunate that Roland was with us and could interpret.

David ran to the piano as soon as we entered the house. It was an historic Bechstein, which had been handmade for Liszt by Mr Bechstein himself. The powerful, surging left-hand passage at the opening of the B minor *Ballade* completely filled the salon, and from that moment the audience was all David's. *La Campanella, Un Sospiro* and a *Rhapsody* followed. Some members of the Music Committee were tearful, others seemed in awe, and David was glowing.

Afterwards, we were taken around Liszt's house, which still contained some of his personal belongings, and one could sense something of the essence of the great man himself. As we stood very quietly in the corner of one of the rooms, David said, "That was the most spiritual and moving musical experience of my life." It is the only time I've ever heard David use the word "spiritual".

Some years later, when David was asked how he had felt playing Liszt's works and touching the same keys as the composer had when he was writing them, David could only recall the least spiritual aspect of that event. "I really enjoyed that time", he said. "I thought it was great fun, 'cause every time I started to sing Gillian would kick me with her toe, and it made me smile and it brought out a good spirit in me and I played even better then!"

This was true. The recital in Liszt's house was one of the many occasions when I had had to perform my 'muffling' duties.

After Weimar, David gave a recital in Dresden and then we drove to Rome, where Clelia March, the Cultural Officer of the Australian Embassy, quickly dealt with our visas for Albania and arranged our accommodation in Tiranë.

I had a strange intuition that something was not quite right, and asked Clelia if she would just confirm with Tiranë that everything was organised for David's performance of the Schumann three days later. When she rang the TV and Radio Orchestra Manager, she was told David was doing the Rakhmaninov Second.

Horrors! Where had the misunderstanding occurred?

This did not really matter, however, as Clelia soon discovered that the Albanians wanted Rakhmaninov and nothing but. David did not even have the score of the concerto with him and we were about to drive south for a recital in Gallipoli before taking a boat from Otranto to Albania. Even if we did have the score, David would not have any time to practise until two days before the performance. Fortunately, at least the first half of the problem was quickly solved when Clelia located a copy of the score in one of the music shops in Rome and, when we finally arrived in Tiranë, all we had to do was find a piano.

The first rehearsal was the following morning at the television station, and the performance was to be in the large Opera House two nights hence. The conductor, Ferdinand Deda, was a delightful man and spoke a little English, which was most reassuring. The orchestra was rather hampered by the quality of their musical instruments, but the musicians were very enthusiastic. The rehearsal went quite well and the conductor was thrilled with David's interpretation. Back at the hotel, David spent the evening studying the score.

The following day's rehearsal was proceeding perfectly until I mentioned that David would require a page turner for the performance. Though the conductor had no problem with this request, the director of the television station – a very commanding figure – immediately rushed over to tell us that it was impossible for David to use music as the performance was being televised.

I told him about the mix-up with the concertos, but he was adamant. He also said that David's playing was too restrained for Rakhmaninov. I had to explain to him that this was only a rehearsal and that there was no need for David to give it all he had at this time because he had to conserve his energy for the real thing on the following evening, when he would most certainly fill the Opera House with his sound.

We requested that David be able to stay after the rehearsal and practise further, as there was no piano at the hotel. When we were finally granted clearance from the security people, David was allowed two hours at the piano for some concentrated work on his own. After we returned to our hotel, David studied the music until midnight.

The following day there was to be a final rehearsal at 6 pm prior to the performance in the Opera House, but, as no one turned up except for David and one violinist, the rehearsal didn't eventuate. At 7.30, the lights dimmed in the crowded hall and David sat at the piano without his music. I must admit I was terrified.

But I need not have worried. After a slightly shaky start, the piano and orchestra soon meshed, the performance gained confidence and great passion, and the famous lyrical passages were sensitively and beautifully rendered. At the conclusion of the dramatic third movement, many of the audience were in tears. The conductor embraced David, who then wanted to kiss all the orchestra, but was fortunately confined to kissing the front row of the strings.

After all the difficulties, the Albanians were deeply touched, not only by the performance, but by the fact that David had come all the way from Australia to play for them. It was one of the proudest moments in my life with David. His professionalism, charm and warmth dispelled all the tensions.

Peter Helfgott once told his son that he would one day end up "dead in the gutter". David also recalls that, when he came back from London, Peter said, "You thought you were so smart. You thought you would go from one concert hall to another. Well, you weren't so smart after all, because you'll only ever be going from one hospital to another, instead."

Peter Helfgott had rather underestimated his son.

Taree

After another exciting tour of Denmark in 1992, David wanted to stop over in Perth for a few days and share his triumphs with Dr Wynn, before heading home for some much-needed and well-deserved rest. During his talk with Dr Wynn, David told her with pride of all his recent adventures, and that session was a particularly happy one.

As we no longer had a home of our own in Perth, we stayed with Barbara Brackley's daughter, Rikki, and her husband, Nic Kebbell, who had also become very special friends of ours. With incredible generosity, they had bought a two-storey house with a separate flat on the ground floor, which they decreed was for our use any time we came to Perth. I even purchased a Yamaha Clavinova for this little flat, and whenever David and I are in Perth we stay there, and feel completely at home.

The day after David's session with Dr Wynn was forecast to be a 'scorcher' and Nic, Rikki, David and I decided that an early-morning swim was the best way to start the day. We packed the car with towels and sun lotion, and headed down from the hills to Fremantle, arriving at the beach at about 7.30 am. The sea looked irresistible and David was first in, the three of us following him in a leisurely way.

The crowd was growing by the minute, as was the temperature. After paddling about for a while, we came out of the water and Nic suddenly looked back to the sea and said, "Where's David?"

We carefully inspected the other swimmers, but David's peculiar swimming stoke was not evident. Then we examined the people walking or running along the water's edge, but David was not among them, either. We decided to walk around the beach and have a harder look. But there was no sign of him.

It was now 9 am and I wondered if he had swum past us or forgotten our spot. Rikki was concerned that David might have swum out too far and that something might have happened to him, but I knew he was always safe in the water. On the east coast of Australia he had once swum to Shark Island and back, three times in a row, and nothing had happened to him – that is, until the terrified locals had called the police and, for his own safety, David had been fished out and brought home.

There was nothing to do now but walk to the next beach

around the point and see if he had run or swum there, and had not realised it was a different beach from the one he had started out at. However, he was not there and the time was racing by. We returned to the original beach, got into the car and sped off to the next bay.

I had never been there before, and was somewhat surprised to discover it was a nudist beach. I felt terribly uncomfortable having to inspect rather intently all the nude men and women to see if David was talking to any of them. I guess they thought I was very odd, and I started to have some uncharitable thoughts about my husband.

By 3.30 pm we had still not found him, and went to the police station. I knew David was safe – I have always felt he is indestructible – but I just wished I knew where he was. The police took pages of details and then rang their patrol cars to check whether any of them had seen David. One car said they had seen him earlier in the day near the port of Fremantle.

Back into the car we went and another futile search ensued. As we were all supposed to go to the Brackleys' that evening, we rang Barbara in the vain hope ... But no, she had no news for us and, really, why should she have? Her home was some 25 kilometres away. It was now about 42°C, David had no money, he was wearing only his bathers, and I could only hope he had not lost his new contact lenses in the water.

Around 6.30 pm, we started to head down Stirling Highway towards Perth. We called Barbara once more and, surprise, surprise, she said David had been found safe, and a friend was bringing him over to her place.

We arrived at the Brackleys' with very mixed feelings.

Though I was genuinely glad and relieved to see David, at that moment I also wanted to trade him in on a new model, and cheaply. Nic and Rikki did not look at all amused. After a long interrogation, we managed to piece together the story of how David had spent his day.

It had all begun when he had come out of the water and started to jog in the wrong direction, arriving at the next bay. Then, feeling disorientated, he had walked along the road, not the beach, back to Fremantle port. This is where we had missed him.

After aimlessly wandering around for a while, telling himself to "concentrate" and be "positive", David had had more swims and walked up and down the beaches that we had, by that time, already checked.

By mid-afternoon he had decided that, as there was no other way of meeting up with us, he would jog to Barbara's – not fully realising the distance that would involve, of course. By the time he was heading into Perth, he was nearly collapsing from severe dehydration and exhaustion.

It was then that he saw, as if in a dream, the shimmering apparition of our old friend Frances Hebb pull to the side of the highway in her car and beckon him to her. Not even knowing that we were in Perth, Frances was just as astonished to see David – wearing only his bathers and running in that horrific heat in the middle of nowhere – as he was to see her familiar hand proffering him a bottle of cold Coca-Cola. "I was very impressed and I was very grateful when this fantastic car came up and pulled over", said David, still slightly in awe of that vision. "And I said I was glad and very very grateful for this whole, full bottle of Coke, especially opened, especially for me!"

When David explained to Frances his intended destination, she immediately told him to get in the car, drove him to her apartment and phoned Barbara. Meanwhile, David drank anything cold and wet he could find in Frances's fridge, and, when satisfied, went to the piano and proceeded to play as if nothing had happened.

I went over and gave him a hug. "You know, Darlinka, I've had a terrible day", he muttered. "Welcome to the club" was all I could muster. Sensing we all needed some reassurance, David smiled and said, "No worries! It's all been planned. Someone will always look after me, someone's gotta do the job! It's a miracle! It's a miracle that I'm alive at all, but the computer always seems to decide who's gonna look after me!" Oh, if only we could all have David's unquestioning faith.

A few days later, we flew to Sydney and picked up our car for the 600 kilometre drive up the coast to Bellingen. As we drove out of Sydney, David seemed rather excited. I thought it might have been due to his recent adventure in Perth, and thus did not pay his behaviour the attention that, on reflection, I should have.

We drove for about four hours and then I felt a short break was needed before facing the remaining three hours of the journey. I pulled over by a service station and convenience store. David was in the passenger seat beside me, merrily scribbling down a *composedly*. I told him I would rest for a bit, closed my eyes and immediately drifted off to sleep.

An awareness of something terrible awoke me. I opened my eyes and saw a panic-stricken David running towards the car screaming, followed by a burly man who was clearly pursuing him. I called out to David to quickly get in the car and, as I tried to drive off, I heard the man shouting at me that David had assaulted his wife and he was ringing the police.

David was absolutely beside himself, and just kept repeating, over and over, "I didn't touch her! I only wanted a Coke! I didn't touch her!" I tried to pacify him, but I knew it was essential to put some space between the man and David. Shouting had always severely upset him and he was very frightened. I knew, without the slightest doubt, that David could never harm a human being, an animal or even an insect. I had never seen any evidence of anything except utter gentleness in him.

Though David was no longer hugging complete strangers, he still liked to reach out his hand to them for a shake, and Dr Wynn and I had explained to him on numerous occasions that people could misinterpret his reaching out to them as being invasive of their space. It seemed that this was precisely what had happened with the woman in the shop, from the few disconnected phrases David mumbled when he began to calm down a little.

As we drove off towards Taree, I knew that if there were a real problem the police would soon come and speak with us. And, indeed, as we approached the town a police car came up the highway and indicated for us to pull to the side. The policeman said he needed to question us as a complaint had been made.

We were taken to the police station and David's agitation, which had decreased somewhat in the car, began to escalate to an alarming state. He looked terrified and was becoming hysterical. He kept crying out that he had not hurt anyone, and the officer had to lead him away and lock him up in a cell.

To see David in agony and frightened, pacing up and down the cell, shaking and staring at me through the bars with a trapped and bewildered look on his face, was almost more than I could bear. I have never known such a sense of desolation and helplessness.

David did not seem to have any understanding of why he was locked up and the terror within him made him more incoherent than ever. I was not even allowed to go into the cell and hold him, and the pain was excruciating.

An officer led me back into the office and gave me a cup of tea. I could see the police were getting no joy out of David's anguish. I decided that some extra medication might be helpful and, when the senior officer arrived to talk to me, I gave him David's tablets. He asked me about David's medical history and I gave him a brief outline. I told him David took his medication regularly, had been on the same dosage for the past four years and had obtained a very good balance. I then gave him Dr Wynn's phone number.

The officer went to have a talk with David in the cell and, when he returned, he told me David had confessed to throwing his medication down the sink for the past few days.

I then realised that, after the heady success of the tour in Europe, David had probably been feeling much too content with life and thought he could cope without any 'help'. Even though I put the tablets into his hand every night and watched him put them into his mouth, I did not always stay around to see him actually swallow, lulled into a sense of trust by his complete co-operation over the preceding four years. Now, David's manic phase must have manifested again, and his hyperactive excitement and gesture to the woman at the service station had obviously frightened her. But David was adamant he had not touched her.

The officer told me he had two options. One was to send David down to the psychiatric hospital in Newcastle – about two hours south – where he would be detained for observation for a few days. This, I told the officer, was not an option, as I knew it would cause David enormous grief and panic. Even the thought of an ordinary hospital frightened him; the fact that this was a psychiatric one would be devastating.

The second option was that David could be admitted to the town's hospital, under observation, and that I would be allowed to stay in the room with him. This was a new experiment by the mental health people; they felt it was better to have a loved one in the room with a patient than for anyone to be incarcerated on their own. My sense of relief and gratitude to the officer was overwhelming. He told me he could see that David was not well and he had no pleasure in locking him up.

We were then taken to the hospital and seated in the outpatient area. Dr Wynn was called and then the local psychiatrist, Dr Richmond, came to speak to David. He was very gentle with him and David started to calm down.

After that, David was admitted to the security room, which had bars on the windows. A reclining chair was brought in for me. Dr Richmond sedated David, and I sat on the bed and held him in my arms. I looked at his gentle face as he slept. His pain had been great, but the manic phase was now gone and a certain peace was returning to him. The door was closed for the night after the nursing sister on duty outside the door had made sure we were comfortable. As I settled down, the outline of the bars on the window was a haunting reminder of the cell and what might have been.

In the morning, David was still sedated and Dr Richmond came to see him again. He said we needed to stay for a few days until he was sure David was stable again. He told me I could move out of the room for a walk, but I did not want to leave David. He slept nearly all day and, when he woke up late in the afternoon, he seemed to be back to his infectious and lovable self. The nurses responded to him with great warmth, and, with Dr Richmond's permission, David asked if he could play to some of the patients the next morning.

The day dawned with lovely sunshine flooding the hospital room, and the bars did not seem so threatening any more. The police officer came to the hospital and told me he had explained the whole situation to the couple at the service station and they had agreed not to pursue the matter any further. Dr Richmond came in again and said he was satisfied that David was now stable and that he was free to leave later in the day. In the meantime, David prepared for his informal recital.

The piano was in the recreation room and some of the patients, nursing staff and doctors came to share David's music. He played with much feeling and joy, the music flowing through the barren room, and I could see his sense of self returning. The patients and staff relished this surprise bonus, and their cheers and applause helped guide his soul out of the labyrinth he had just passed through.

As I drove away from the hospital with David calmly sitting at my side, I resolved never, ever again to trust him with his medication, even if that meant I had to run my finger around his mouth to make sure he was not hiding the tablets under his tongue.

Not very romantic, I know. But what greater love can a woman have . . .

Shine

6 April 1995

Dear David and Gillian,

I am writing just to share a memory and to say how wonderful it was to read that you are to make a movie.

I remember David when we both attended Forest High School in Lord Street, Highgate. It was an 'industrial' type of boys school, so music or the arts was a <u>rare</u> thing. However, there were two musicians in the school: David and me.

David was, of course, David. This skinny, energetic, <u>happy</u>

kid who played <u>amazing</u> piano with such energy and joy. I had learned the trumpet in a brass band in the country and moved to Perth, and had begun playing in a leading senior band here whilst taking lessons from the conductor, who was also principal trumpet with the WASO.

Anyway, for a small recital at school assembly we organised for David to 'accompany' me on some corny old popular pieces such as *Caravan* and one or two others, as well as David playing some Liszt or whatever.

To practise together we went up the road to my aunty's place. My mother, my aunty and I have all been "fans" of David's ever since, and have been touched and made joyful by his story and by his re-emergence.

The year after David and I played together, I had progressed into Year 11 at Perth Modern School, but during that year my Dad took his own life, and, without counselling of any sort whatsoever, I remained in a form of shock for thirty years. I changed, did rough things, chose the wrong career, married in haste, gave away my music in favour of my career, etc. It all still looked fairly 'normal' to most people and successful, too – but it wasn't the real me.

After a crisis five years ago, I began the big 'clean-out' and reclaimed myself. I had kept playing music, but in a sort of dull, plodding way, so I still had the touch, but now it is alive and bright and I am playing the high 1st trumpet parts in a seventeen-piece big swing band, as well as doing many other creative things. Re-married to someone who loves me to bits, and back in touch with life, feelings, reality, God, joy – the whole thing.

So you can see how one story of a life regained can be so important to retaining hope in another life or perhaps in the lost lives of tens of thousands of people you may never have met. Do your story for them so they can hang on to hope, and for us so that we can share the joy at the end.

Warmest regards

P____

I did share the joy at the end of this most unexpected letter, from someone I had never met. In fact, I wept, grateful to David's old school friend for sharing his story, and helping David and I retain hope.

When the letter arrived, the film *Shine* was already being made. The story of the film's coming to fruition was in itself one of steadfast hope, stoic faith and determination. For director Scott Hicks, it had been nine very long years from the day he had first approached me with the idea of the film at David's concert in Adelaide.

After talking to me, Scott wrote a proposal outlining his ideas and sent it to us when we were in Yugoslavia. I felt great trust in Scott's sincerity and began to discuss the idea with David. He wanted Scott to tell his story and thought that re-living his past all over again would be quite therapeutic – for others as well as himself. He was also quite excited by the idea of having to play for the soundtrack.

As both of my children work in the film industry, I had no illusions about film-project dreams coming true. Nevertheless, I had great confidence in Scott Hicks's ideas and abilities, and, after David and I had given our approval, Scott and writer John MacGregor began their research. Little did any of us know just how long the journey we were starting out on would be.

After three years of research in both Australia and England, and endless interviews with David's family, his friends, his colleagues, David himself and me, the script began to take shape. In 1990 writer Jan Sardi joined the project, and *Shine* in its present form was born.

Throughout the whole writing process, Scott, Jan and John kept in close contact with us, and I remember having one particularly funny phone conversation with Jan during which we discussed 'Gillian' as some entirely objective character. The conversation felt somewhat unnatural to me, as objectivity is not always my greatest quality.

David and I were given the script in 1992 and we then had the most peculiar experience of sitting down, reading about our lives and discovering just how profoundly we identified with the characters of 'David' and 'Gillian'. Of course, there were some very painful moments for David, but he just told himself, "Gotta have courage", and turned the page. He cried and shared his pain with me, but I could sense that reading about his own life in this rather distancing way was also a partial healing for him.

When Geoffrey Rush, the actor Scott wanted for the part of the adult 'David', came to visit us in the Promised Land, I immediately sensed that he was the perfect choice. I knew then that David's character would be safe with Geoffrey, and never doubted that he would succeed in capturing the unique essence of my mercurial husband.

It was now six years since Scott had first decided to film David's story, and, no matter what other projects he had worked on during this time, he had never once lost sight of his goal. In the next few years, his dedication was to be tested even further, when his commitment to Geoffrey Rush became a battleground for finance.

Scott took the screenplay to Hollywood, but, though the screenplay was well received, the Americans refused to fund the project unless a well-known Hollywood 'star' was cast. Scott held firm to his ideals and his vision – no Geoffrey, no film – and turned away a fistful of dollars. When he phoned me with the disappointing news, I cried – I, too, was now beginning to feel the length of the journey – but my respect for Scott's single-minded dedication deepened.

Again Scott went to work on other film projects, but he persevered with the search for finance. Finally, at the beginning of 1995, after all our hopes had risen and fallen several times, the financing came together through producer Jane Scott. Shooting of the film commenced in London in March 1995.

So as not to unsettle and distract the cast and crew with the presence of 'the real people', I only came to see the filming of one scene: David's comeback concert. This moment was particularly precious to me. David's sisters, Suzie and Louise, and I hid in the crowd of extras and, as the filming started, I was overcome with memories of David's dramatic journey to that point in his life.

Meanwhile, David's hopes of being involved in the film's soundtrack were realised and he was busy rehearsing and recording with composer David Hirschfelder.

When the film was completed, I could not help but feel anxious about David's reaction. Both Scott Hicks and I were keenly aware of David's vulnerabilities, and it was decided that it would be best for him to first see the film at a private screening, in case he might need to take a break from it or leave the room.

Jane, Scott and I sat on a couch, while Scott's wife, Kerry, sat on the floor with her arms around David, who was leaning back against my legs. The film commenced and, when David's delighted chuckle filled the room at the sight of his ten-year-old 'self' chasing the piano across the stage, Scott and I began to relax. David then laughed and cried his way through the film, his eyes never once leaving the screen. Three-quarters of the way through the film, David suddenly exclaimed, "This is a wonderful movie!"

There were tears in Scott's eyes and I, of course, was a hopeless mess. I was not prepared for the huge emotional impact the film made on me.

During the nine years it took to get the film made, a special bond developed between David and Scott. While Scott lived through those years thinking about David and all of his traumas and triumphs, David felt an enormous gratitude to the man who had decided to honour him and his life in this way. Even during the times when the project seemed to be on hold, Scott always kept in touch.

When an opportunity arose for David to perform at the Royal College of Music in 1994, Scott, who by that stage had done much research there, was extremely sorry he could not be with David on the day. And though he was in the middle of a film shoot on the other side of the globe, he sent David a huge bouquet of flowers, with a note apologising for not being able to make it and wishing David the best. David was very touched.

A quarter of a century had passed since the night of David's great 'Rak' performance on the hallowed stage of the RCM. In some ways, it was pleasantly ironic that David's first recital there since his re-emergence was for a charitable purpose. It had been organised by Vanessa Denison-Pender for the Tait Memorial Trust, which supports Australian performing artists and musicians studying and working in England. The boy for whom the only chance of overseas study had lain with just such charitable organisations was now a man, able to give something back.

The recital of Mendelssohn, Beethoven and Liszt was attended, among others, by Australian High Commissioner Neal Blewett and several of our Australian friends who were in London at the time. David was enormously pleased to be performing at the RCM again and glowed with joy throughout the entire night.

Back in Australia, during a New Year's Eve party, one of our friends asked David what it had felt like to play on that stage after all those years. Partly joking and playing the devil's advocate, the friend asked, "So, David, when you were playing, were you thinking, 'Ah ha! Now I'm back and I'm gonna show you all what I can really do!'?"

"Show you all!?" David repeated the question, quite incredulous at the concept. Then he frowned and, shaking his head, endeavoured to explain: "No, it can be a disaster if you say, 'I'm gonna show you.' You should play in the spirit of giving, caring and sharing. You shouldn't play in the spirit of 'I'm gonna show you.' Of course you have to be a show-off, you have to be an exhibitionist and have lots of chutzpah, but that's different. I just pick out someone in the audience and I play to them."

Now it was my turn to be surprised, as David had never told me of this little trick before. "Do you pick someone at every performance?", I asked.

"Well, usually, I very surreptitiously look around the audience, you know, I just peep around for images. It just has to be a nice, positive image and I play the whole concert to them."

"Are these people mostly men or mostly women?", I asked.

"Well it varies, it can be either. It can be a man or a lady. That's 'cause I'm omnivorous", chuckled David and, with a sly grin, added, "One has to be more flexible, you know."

"And are they usually young or old?"

"Well, sort of medium rare. I just pick someone who reminds me of someone. It can be anybody. That night in London it was Neal and Uncle Ralph."

I could not help but laugh at the quirky little ways in which David's mind worked. "Neal" was the Australian High Commissioner and "Uncle Ralph" could only attend the recital in the form of his famous portrait on the wall of the hall – unless, of course, David saw Vaughan Williams' ghost in the audience.

As the clock struck midnight in the Promised Land, and we all raised our glasses to welcome in the New Year, David and I were filled with a sense of great expectation, but nothing could have prepared us for the tremendous highs that were in store for us.

Not only would *Shine* be made, but, after more recitals in Germany and London, we would return to Denmark for the event that David had been dreaming of for more than twenty-five years. He was once again going to perform his beloved 'Rak 3' with an orchestra, and, thanks to Nils' efforts, this time it was also going to be recorded.

David joyously immersed himself in practice for the event, and, in order to do some final polishing, played the work for the Russian Rakhmaninov expert, Mikhail Solovej, in Melbourne. By the time we arrived in Copenhagen, David was raring to go.

Two rehearsals were scheduled with the Copenhagen Philharmonic Orchestra and the conductor, Milan Horvat. During the first, David asked for a faster pace and the concerto gained a passionate, breathless momentum. Everything was ready for the second rehearsal, which was to be just before the 'try-out' recital in Holbeck the following day.

Though the day dawned fine, the weather soon began to change and, when Nils came to pick us up for the one-and-a-half-hour drive to Holbeck, he told us that he had just heard a forecast of a snowstorm.

We set off in high spirits, but after about twenty minutes the snowstorm hit. Neither David nor I had ever seen anything like it before, and he was as delighted as a child. However, my enthusiasm at the sight of the horizontally swirling white drifts was dampened by the fact that we were now driving at 15 kilometres per hour. The traffic was bumper-to-bumper and progress was painfully slow. David couldn't have been more thrilled, of course; he kept pointing out the window, exclaiming, "Look! Oh, look at all that traffic!"

Looking at traffic was all we could do and, by about 7 pm, when we were still nowhere near the hall, we knew that there would be no second rehearsal. Nils and I then began to worry about whether the conductor or the orchestra, who were travelling separately, would even be there on time for the start of the actual concert.

When we finally arrived at the hall, we were greatly relieved to see the orchestra unpacking, but there was no sign of the conductor. A few minutes before the lights were about to dim, Milan Horvat walked in looking very tired and frayed. He was an elderly man, and said that, though he could do the Rakhmaninov justice, he would not have enough strength to then conduct Chaikovsky's Fifth Symphony which was programmed for the second half.

Only half a programme for the audience, who like us had battled the snow to get to the concert, was simply not acceptable, and I was asked if David would be able to play a solo recital in the second half. This placed me in a terrible dilemma.

I knew that the great 'Rak 3' was one of the most arduous pieces to perform. Playing through all of its three movements has been likened to shovelling ten tons of coal. I was also aware of the fact that this was only supposed to be a 'try-out' and, after getting through the ordeal in Holbeck, David would need to retain his energy for the following night's main recital at the Tivoli Concert Hall in Copenhagen.

Time was running out and a decision had to be made. I went up to David, who, as always, was doing his 'push-ups' on the floor, completely unconcerned with all the drama – why would he be, when everything in his world is "planned" and "computerised"? – and asked him if he would mind giving a solo recital after the interval.

He smiled: "Oh, Darlinka, can I really? What a great treat! I'm lucky, I'm lucky. I'm privileged. Can I play the *Dante*? Yes, I want to play the *Dante* and some more Rak, and ..." There was no stopping him. To play for an audience anywhere, anytime, was a great "privilege" and thoughts of exhaustion could not have been further from his mind.

The concert started ten minutes late and, considering there had been no rehearsal or sound-balancing in the hall, it was a creditable performance. David was not satisfied, but his big opportunity was still to come.

The orchestra and conductor packed up and went back to Copenhagen. The piano was all David's, and the audience was soon his also. He played Chopin and Rakhmaninov, ending the night with Liszt's *Dante* Sonata, just as he wished.

The next morning, David awoke completely unaffected by either his mammoth task of the preceding night or the long drive back through the snow which had followed it. It seemed that all the adventure merely heightened his eagerness for the Tivoli performance.

David swam his way through the day in a heated swimming pool – not even he was brave enough to dive into the Sound in this weather – and by the evening was perfectly focused, calm and ready. Nils and I only wished we knew

David's secret, as our nervous tension increased with each passing hour.

The orchestra was on stage and, as soon as David went on, Nils and I moved into a private box to get a direct view. My heart was pounding so loudly I was sure Nils could hear it. I got up and went to pace up and down the passage until the opening of the first movement filled the hall with its restrained grandeur. David's words about these first bars echoed in my head: "It is like the river, like the river or the sea. It just flows. Nothing could be simpler. It's the hardest piece in the world, but it's actually simple. That is the secret, Darlinka, yes, that is the secret."

I could hear the "river" and the "sea" this time and it *was* simple. He made it sound so; he made it sound effortless. I returned to my seat and spent the next forty minutes in awe. At the end, Nils and I jumped to our feet, along with 2000 others, and cheered.

Afterwards, as we walked outside into the softly falling snow, David was unusually serene. "You know, Darlinka," he said very quietly, "father is proud. I was aware of him out there in the audience, and he says he was listening and he is happy for me and proud. And I enjoyed it very much. I had a great time."

I could not reply. There were snowflakes in my lashes and, as I blinked, tears rolled down my face. Pulling me closer to him, David gently pressed his cheek to mine, and continued to mutter, almost whispering: "See, somehow father's aware of everything. He is aware of how I'm doing and he is pleased. He was there at the concert just in a way, in a subtle way, in a sort of mysterious way, in the spirit, in the residue."

David hugged me tightly and sighed: "So, I reckon that's how we all have to be, really. The past doesn't matter all that much, it just accepts the present. There are all these extremes in life, but I reckon I should be grateful and I needn't have ever worried 'cause it was all planned perfectly."

David's Dictionary

These are just some of the special words David uses liberally; most appear in this book. Some are French, or based on French words, others come from Italian, Russian, Polish or Yiddish, while others appear to be entirely of his own making.

agitato	agitated
l'arbre	tree
articulata	articulate
l'assiette	plate
bibliothèque	library
boîte à joujou	box
bubby	baby, child
camion	truck
canards	ducks
candillas	candles
catillas	cattle
chai	tea
chaise-longue	chair
composedly	musical or word composition

compri	compromise
confiance	confidence
contraire	contrary, opposite
cost-the-world	very important or expensive
costly	very important or expensive
couteau	knife
demitasse	cup
dentifies	teeth
difficile	difficult
discabilish	disciplined
dogola	dog
l'école	school
ensemble	together
finickety	fussy
fixes	cups of coffee or tea made just for him
gâteau	cake
gluclous	happy
goblets	spectacles, drinking glasses
greedos	greedy
hors-d'oeuvre	order, command
imago	image
intuitive	intuition
italia	studio

jolly-holly	make merry, cheerful
joyeux	joyous
kochka	cat
kronos	watch
le lit	bed
le livre	book
marmena	mother
matinata	morning
miroir	mirror
monstaroonies	cups of very strong tea
montagnias	mountains
morningtide	sunrise
les oreilles	ears
parce que	because
parentally	using the rights of a parent
plentchuous	much, many, a lot, plenty
posturepedic	posture
potchnagoola	kiss or kiss me
press	pressure
prodigies	a prodigy
prodiguy	prodigious
rados	radio, heater

scarydiest	most scared
shamus	shame
shmoks	socks
shmutzig	dirt, dirty
terrazza	terrace
toccare	toccata
traffic	cars, ordered movement
tullies	towels
vino	wine
wishywashy	dirty laundry
woolly	jumper, pullover
les yeux	eyes
yump	jump

acknowledgements

Gillian Helfgott

I would like to thank Charles Blair for suggesting in 1988 that this story should be written; Scott Hicks for encouraging me to do it; Mike Parry for his vivid recollections and humour; Nils Ruben for his wonderful tales, love and loyalty; Cara Kelson for her constant support and sweet memories; Brian Warren for his generous comments; Adrienne Mahoney for her reminiscences of Riccardo's; Robbie Spence for her transcription work and her delightful company; and Peter and Jill Nance for their love, support and warm hospitality.

Also, I would like to thank Carolyn Sawarde for her encouragement throughout the whole project, and indeed at all times; Nic and Rikki Kebbell for their guidance and support, and for sharing their treehouse and their cats; Suzie Helfgott for family photographs, unfailing common sense and friendship; Austin Prichard-Levy for his wise council, practical help and persistently cheerful voice on the phone; and my sister, Diana Oldmeadow, for her unconditional and unswerving love.

Most thanks go to my son, Scott Murray, who guided me on this journey; Alissa Tanskaya, who worked on the project with much care, skill and patience; and my husband, David, who has so honestly and willingly shared his pain and joy.

Alissa Tanskaya

First and foremost I would like to thank Gillian Helfgott for offering me the opportunity to work on this amazing story.

Also, many thanks to Fran Lebowitz at Writers House Inc. and Austin Prichard-Levy for taking care of the 'business' and letting me get on with the 'art'; Bob Sessions at Penguin for his courage, honesty and strength, and Katie Purvis for her editorial diligence; Helen Gul and Jack Braun for their steadfast encouragement and support; Nic Kebbell for knowing well ahead of time that everything was going to be all right; Elisabeth Brimer for her sensibility, sensitivity and kindness; Peter Horton at the Royal College of Music library for the facts; and Dr Susan Wynn for the facts, wit and humour.

My overwhelming gratitude is reserved for my best friend, Scott Murray, for making sure I slept, ate and breathed while this book was being written; for encouraging, bullying and cajoling me to keep going; and for being vigilant with every single word.

Last, but not least, I would like to thank David Helfgott for allowing me to drag him away from his piano for weeks of interviewing, for his patience with my naive questions, and for constantly reminding me that for the tape-recorder to work the little red light should be on. Also, my everlasting thanks to David for teaching me how to "concentrate" and be "aware", "grateful" and "positive".

Index

Now hear David Helfgott playing Rachmaninov

Having read *Love You to Bits and Pieces*, you may like to hear David Helfgott playing Rachmaninov on a new CD, issued by RCA, a label that also features other great pianists, such as Rubinstein and Horowitz.

Rachmaninov: The Last Great Romantic is now available from RCA, and includes a remarkable performance of Rachmaninov's Third Piano Concerto ('Rak 3', as David calls it) – the work which so many people will associate with David Helfgott after reading this book and seeing the movie, *Shine*.